MOGREB-EL-ACKSA

When R.B. Cunninghame Graham set off for the city of Taroudant in 1897, the southern Moroccan province of the Sus was forbidden territory for the European. These were the years of the imperialist scramble for Africa. A vociferous opponent of imperialism, Cunninghame Graham nevertheless shared the period's sense of adventure. His love of Spain and South America fuelled his curiosity about Spain's Moorish past. Because of the deep suspicion of Christians by the local populace and the fear of the authorities about imperialist adventurers, Cunninghame Graham disguised himself as a Turkish doctor, and set out for Taroudant. Within sight of the city, however, he was arrested and detained by the Caid of Kintafi for a fortnight. *Mogreb-El-Acksa* is his account of the adventure.

The book was instantly acclaimed by his contemporaries. His friend Joseph Conrad praised its 'skill, pathos, humour, wit, indignation'. Wilfred Scawen Blunt 'put it next to Doughty's as a true portrait of Arab ways, and far before anything that Burton did'. Bernard Shaw based his play, *Captain Brassbound's Conversion* on *Mogreb-El-Acksa* which he described as 'an excellent book of philosophic travel and vivid adventure'. Fellow Scottish writer, Hugh Macdairmid reckoned it 'one of the best books of travel ever written'. Wyndham Lewis, in his own Moroccan book, *Filibusters in Barbary* (1932), drew heavily on *Mogreb-El-Acksa* and prophesied that it would be 'read again some day'.

Robert Bontine Cunninghame Graham was born in 1852, the son of a Scottish laird and descended from Robert II. He spent much of his early life in South America where ranch life and the work of a cattle drover gave him a lifelong passion for horses. In 1886 he became Liberal MP for North-West Lanarkshire, adopting a radical position on many issues, before espousing the cause of Scottish nationalism. He died in 1936 in Buenos Aires. Joseph Conrad, himself one of English literature's more adventurous and reflective characters, once wrote to Cunninghame Graham: 'When I think of you I feel as tho' I had lived all my life in a dark hole without ever seeing or knowing anything...'

Philip Healy has lectured in Japan at the University of Tokushima and at Keio University, Tokyo. He has also written the introduction to the Century reprint of Cunninghame Graham's *A Vanished Arcadia*. He now lives and works in London where he is also a part-time Tutor-Counsellor with the Open University.

Jean Cunninghame Graham, Lady Polwarth, is R.B. Cunninghame Graham's great niece, and she is currently working on a new biography of him.

MOGREB-EL-ACKSA

R.B. Cunninghame Graham

Introduction by Philip Healy

Foreword by Jean Cunninghame Graham

CENTURY
LONDON MELBOURNE AUCKLAND JOHANNESBURG

First published by Heinemann in 1898
Introduction © Philip Healy 1988
Foreword © Jean Cunninghame Graham 1988

This edition first published in 1988 by Century,
an imprint of Century Hutchinson Ltd,
Brookmount House, 62–65 Chandos Place, London WC2N 4NW

Century Hutchinson Australia Pty Ltd,
PO Box 496, 16–22 Church Street, Hawthorn, Melbourne,
Victoria 3122, Australia

Century Hutchinson Group New Zealand Limited,
PO Box 40-086, Glenfield, Auckland 10, New Zealand

Century Hutchinson South Africa (Pty) Ltd,
PO Box 337, Bergvlei, 2012 South Africa

British Library Cataloguing in Publication Data

Cunninghame Graham, R.B. (Robert Bontine),
  1852–1936
  Mogreb-el-Acksa.
  1. Morocco. Taroudant. Description & travel
  1897, Biographies
  I. Title
  916.4'6

  ISBN 0-7126-2422-8

Printed and bound in Great Britain by
Richard Clay (The Chaucer Press) Ltd, Bungay, Suffolk.

CONTENTS

FOREWORD

My great-uncle, Robert Bontine Cunninghame Graham, was an exciting person to have in the family. I remember him well: his dignified posture was that of the Scottish aristocrat, or the Spanish hidalgo, for he was both. His flare of white hair was brushed back. His well-modulated voice could speak fluent Spanish, or turn to the Scottish idiom, at the drop of a hat. He was courteous to children, dogs, horses, and even to most grown-ups. He died when I was eight years old, my birthday being four days before his own. He was in his eighty-fourth year and could still ride his Argentine horse like a gaucho, or an Arab tribesman. The horse was called 'Chajá' after the Argentine bird which calls its own name on the pampas—the South American pampas that, in the 1870s, had been Uncle Robert's apprenticeship for life.

After his death in 1936, when my father and mother took me to live in his house, Ardoch, on the River Clyde, close to Dumbarton Rock, I too was allowed to ride the ageing Chajá over the tidal sands below our house; a gentle, well-trained horse, just right for an old man or a young child, but always ready for a good controlled gallop over the sands which would have earned him the Arabs' descriptive term 'wind-drinker'.

My first impression of Uncle Robert's house was that it was like Aladdin's cave, filled with exotic objects that titillated the imagination of a child. There were raw-hide ropes, lazos, and bolas from his youth in South America; there was a Mexican saddle and the silver horse-gear used by his wife, Gabrielle, and himself in the early 1880s, during their two years in Texas and Mexico. But most exciting of all, to me, were the brilliant colours of the striped

Moroccan rugs and the embroidered saddle-bags Uncle Robert had used on his expedition into the Atlas Mountains.

It was in 1897 that he had set out, disguised as 'Sheikh Mohammed El Fasi', for the city of Taroudant, in the province of the Sus, which was still forbidden territory to Christians. This was to be Uncle Robert's final great adventure, before the 'man of action' became the 'artist', as Edward Garnett kept urging him to be since he had discovered Graham's latent literary talent. This was to be his glorious escape, after six frustrating years, from 1886–92, as the *enfant terrible* of the House of Commons.

Joseph Conrad, one of Robert's closest friends, was the first to describe *Mogreb-el-Acksa* as a 'philosophical work'. The book made an immediate impression on him, as we know from the letter he wrote to Robert, on receiving a copy:

> The book arrived by the evening post. I dropped everything, paper-knife in hand, and rushed at it.
>
> A man staying here has been reading it over my shoulder. We have been shouting, slapping our legs, leaping up, stamping about. The individuality of the book is amazing—I do not know how really to express the kind of intellectual exultation your book has awakened in me, and I will not stay to try—I am in too much of a hurry to get back to the book. My applause, slaps on the back, salaams, benedictions, cheers. Take what you like best of these, what you think most expressive. Or take them all. I can't be too demonstrative.
>
> Ever yours with yells — Conrad.

The 'man staying here' turned out to be none other than H.G. Wells. Max Beerbohm wrote to say that he had just finished reading the book and that he firmly demanded another. Arnold Bennett scribbled a note which said, succinctly, 'You do me good. Thank you.' Galsworthy told Robert, 'Your philosophy is one of the most valued things walking, or rather riding about amongst us nowadays.'

Those who have come to admire Cunninghame Graham's writing

in our own times are apt to think that all his adventures happened in South America, and that his politics were uniquely connected with Scottish Nationalism. This is to ignore the huge canvas on which his life was painted, to narrow his 'life and works' into too constricted a mould. Robert came from a long line of Whigs, and from a cosmopolitan family who had always travelled. Whether his politics were influenced by his travels, or the other way round, it is hard to tell. He was certainly an idealist, but a practical idealist for the most part. As a child he was brought up near Glasgow where the Industrial Revolution was gathering momentum. (His childhood home, Finlaystone, was not far from Govan, where a future political colleague, Keir Hardie, was being raised among the shipyards.) The conditions of the working people obviously influenced Robert's decision to set off in search of 'El Dorado'—to find a place somewhere in the world where 'man's inhumanity to man' was unknown.

To Uncle Robert the British Empire and its builders were like a red rag to a bull. He could never see the point of imposing the British way of life, or its religion, on races and tribes in foreign countries, who managed their affairs perfectly well without the interference of the Queen Empress. Robert was convinced that there was, in turn, plenty to be learnt from these people, if travellers would only keep their ears and eyes open, and behave courteously when they went abroad. In this frame of mind, Robert Bontine Cunninghame Graham set out to find his 'holy grail' in the city of Taroudant, in the heart of the Atlas Mountains, a place where no Christian had ever set foot.

A year later he published 'the history of a failure to accomplish what I tried'. In the preface to *Mogreb-el-Acksa* he explained that he had, instead, brought together in his book, 'a sack of cobwebs, a pack of gossamers, a bale of thistledown, dragonflies' wings; of Oriental gossip, of old-world recollections, and of lore of horses' colours.' He was looking for a paradise which had been described to him as, 'a land of vines, of orange gardens, olive yards, plantations of pomegranates, Roman remains, and rich mines'. At this point, he could not resist adding, with the irony that was such a hallmark of his writing, 'a land, therefore, doomed to languish without pauperism, prostitution, and the modern vices which man brought with him into the old-world'.

There is a surprising timelessness in his writing when he tells of his Syrian interpreter's early life in the Lebanon, amongst the 'undying enmity between the Turk, the Druse, the Maronite, and the Old Catholics, leaving on my mind the feeling that the Lebanon for a residence must be as undesirable as was Scotland when they burnt witches, and when the narrow-minded clergy made the land a hell.' We suddenly realize that he may have been talking about 'then', but he is also talking about 'now'. This is only one instance of many familiar passages which will surprise and entertain his readers; quite apart from the telling of a first-rate adventure story, a story that might equally well have been made for Richard Hannay or James Bond.

Mogreb-el-Acksa was published in 1898, but thanks to Century Hutchinson, it is now to be made available again in their excellent Century Travellers series; and there will be a new generation of readers who will, like G.K. Chesterton, be able to say, 'Cunninghame Graham's greatest achievement was the adventure of being Cunninghame Graham'.

Jean Cunninghame Graham

INTRODUCTION

When it was published in 1898, *Mogreb-el-Acksa* ('The Far West') was Cunninghame Graham's first full-length book. He was forty-six years old, and the book was rich with the experience not only of his Moroccan journey but also of a lifetime of travel and event. *Mogreb-el-Acksa* met with instant acclaim. For his friend, Joseph Conrad, it was 'the book of travel of the century'. He praised its 'skill, pathos, humour, wit, indignation'. Another of his well-travelled friends, Wilfred Scawen Blunt, wrote to him: 'I put it next to Doughty's as a true portrait of Arab ways, and far before anything that Burton did'. For W.H. Hudson, the book was 'one that one reads and does not forget', although what he described as the 'you-be-downness' of Cunninghame Graham's tone was not always to his liking.

Later writers were to continue to hold *Mogreb-el-Acksa* in high regard. Wyndham Lewis devoted a chapter of *Filibusters in Barbary* (1932) to a portrait of Major Spilsbury, 'lifted (with apologies) out of the brilliant and lively pages of Mr. Graham's book'. He feels sure that *Mogreb-el-Acksa* 'will be read again some day—it is one of the daintiest dishes of the "Nineties"'. In his centenary study of Cunninghame Graham, Hugh MacDiarmid was to surpass even Conrad's praise for *Mogreb-el-Acksa*: 'one of the best books of travel ever written'. MacDiarmid found it 'perhaps his best and most enduring book'.

The greatest accolade, however, that the book was to receive came in its appropriation by Bernard Shaw as source material for his play *Captain Brassbound's Conversion* (1899). Shaw's note to the play is generous to a fault:

I claim as a notable merit in the authorship of this play that I have been intelligent enough to steal its scenery, its surroundings, its atmosphere, its geography, its knowledge of the east, its fascinating Caids and Krooboys and Sheikhs and mud castles from an excellent book of philosophic travel and vivid adventure entitled Mogreb-el-Acksa (Morocco the Most Holy) [sic] by Cunninghame Graham.

On reading *Mogreb-el-Acksa*, Shaw wrote to Cunninghame Graham with a five-page list of detailed questions about Morocco, the answers to which he incorporated in his stage directions.

The one thing Shaw did not borrow from the book was Cunninghame Graham himself. He had decided against making him the hero of his play because he feared that 'so incredible a personage' would have destroyed its verisimilitude. Cunninghame Graham was definitely larger than life. Instead, Shaw drew on the detail provided by Cunninghame Graham for a parable of his own of the ways in which justice is swayed by class interest in modern society. His recourse to the dramatic device of equating justice at the hands of a Moroccan sheikh and an English judge was, no doubt, prompted by Cunninghame Graham's own cultural even-handedness.

Cunninghame Graham told his biographer, A.F. Tschiffely, that practically everything he had written was really autobiographical, and *Mogreb-el-Acksa* is no exception. The attentive reader will learn that Cunninghame Graham (1852-1936) had a deep love of Scotland and Spain, including an impressive knowledge of Spanish proverbs; that he had travelled widely, particularly in South America, Mexico and Texas; that he was a great horseman; that he had a cynical familiarity with parliamentary procedure; and that he had served a sentence in Pentonville.

An intriguing mixture of Scotch laird and Spanish hidalgo, Cunninghame Graham had sailed to South America as a young man to seek adventure, which he found in plenty as a gaucho and cattle-driver. Later, from 1886 to 1892, he was Liberal MP for North-

West Lanarkshire. His spell in Pentonville was as a result of his part in the 'Bloody Sunday' demonstration in Trafalgar Square in 1887. In the 'eighties and 'nineties, he was heavily involved in Labour politics, but became disillusioned, not with the causes, but with the cant of his fellow politicians. He devoted his political energies for the rest of his life to Scottish Nationalism. He wrote extensively, mostly studies of Latin American history and short stories or 'sketches', which were usually based on his own experiences around the world.

The attempted trek across the Atlas to the southern province of Sus, which is retold in *Mogreb-el-Acksa*, was not Cunninghame Graham's first journey to Morocco, but his previous visits had always been to the north, to Tangier and the Riff. His fascination with the country arose from his interest in Spain, the land of his maternal grandmother. His reading of Spanish and Latin American history had convinced him that the only way to understand the Spanish thoroughly was to cross the Straits of Gibraltar and become acquainted with the Moors, who had left their deep impress on Spanish culture.

In setting out for the city of Taroudant, Cunninghame Graham was deliberately flouting the Sultan's prohibition on European travel to the south of the country. What therefore were Cunninghame Graham's motives for undertaking the journey? And what were the Sultan's reasons for the ban?

Cunninghame Graham wished to visit Taroudant out of simple curiosity, mixed no doubt with a certain wilfullness—traits typical of the man. Although Taroudant was known to sixteenth- and seventeenth-century European travellers, only a handful of Europeans had visited the city since, and little was known of it. Taroudant was therefore an ideal objective for the contemporary traveller looking for adventure. There was the additional thrill of danger in that 'infidels' would be at considerable risk from the zealous Muslims of the remote region. As he donned his disguise, Cunninghame Graham would certainly have had the example of Sir Richard Burton in mind, who had ventured, in Arab disguise of course, into the holy city of Mecca earlier in the century. The Sus was a troubled region, not wholly under the Sultan's control. The British authorities had advised Cunninghame Graham against travelling in the area.

Nothing daunted, Cunninghame Graham left Tangier on 1 October 1897 with two companions: his interpreter, Hassan Suleiman Lutaif, a Syrian Christian and a gentleman, and Haj Mohammed es Swani, a Moor of the Riff who had twice made the pilgrimage to Mecca. The latter had often accompanied Cunninghame Graham on his travels in Morocco; *Mogreb-el-Acksa* is dedicated to him. At Mogador, Cunninghame Graham employed as their guide to the Sus, Mohammed el Hosein, a Berber muleteer, and rumoured to be a slave-dealer. With him came Ali and his mule.

European travellers in Morocco had ensured their safety by adopting a disguise. When Charles de Foucauld had explored the country in 1883, he had done so under the disguise of a Jewish rabbi. Cunninghame Graham's plan was to impersonate a Turkish doctor, and to that end he even equipped himself with some elementary medicines. But when he had put on his robes, he looked so like a Sherif from Fez that it was decided to say nothing of his identity and to trust that the two layers of disguise would be sufficient to deter even the most inquisitive.

Having left Mogador on the twelfth, the party had reached the last ridge of the mountain pass before the descent into the Sus on 20 October. Taroudant was only a few hours' journey away, but they were never to reach their goal. They were arrested by the Caid of Kintafi's men and taken back to his kasbah.

Caid Si Taieb ben Si Ahmed El Hassan El Kintafi was one of the three most powerful caids, or governors, of the Atlas. His fellow caids were El M'touggi and El Glaoui. Their story, but in particular that of El Glaoui and his brother, is told in Gavin Maxwell's enthralling book, *Lords of the Atlas* (1966). Cunninghame Graham and his companions were held under guard by El Kintafi for twelve days before being sent back to Mogador via Marrakesh.

The reason for the Sultan's prohibition on European travel in the

Sus—and thus for their arrest—was bound up with the murky commercial and imperialist machinations of the Great Powers. The local manifestation of this unwanted interest was the Globe Venture Syndicate, with its agent, Major Spilsbury. The Syndicate hoped to win important trading concessions in the Sus and the Sahara by selling arms to the disaffected chiefs of the region. The Syndicate believed it could rely on British protection, and since that would almost certainly have to be invoked at some time, given the disturbances in the Sus, the manoeuvre was tantamount to annexation. Understandably, the Sultan was determined to defend his patrimony. With an ironic turn of history, however, the land of the Moors, once an infamous haven of pirates, had now itself fallen victim to a band of latter-day pirates, the filibusters and free-booters of imperialist Europe. (Although 'filibuster' was then understood in its older piratical sense, Cunninghame Graham would have savoured its later parliamentary usage, and found the development fitting.)

Morocco in 1897 was particularly vulnerable. Her Sultan, Abdul Aziz, had come to the throne in 1894 at the age of fourteen. He was still a minor, and under the thumb of the self-serving Grand Vizier, Ab Ahmed. The Sultan was not to gain a free hand in governing his country until the latter's death in 1901. Although Abdul Aziz wanted to see reforms, it was by then too late. Moreover, he had succumbed to all the toys and gadgetry which unscrupulous Western salesmen had offered him, often at exorbitant prices. His palaces were littered with bicycles, gramophones, typewriters, clockwork toys and musical stuffed birds. He had even brought a hansom cab and a state coach, although there were no roads in Morocco at the time.

How much longer could Morocco retain its independence? France had occupied Algeria since 1828 and was looking to safeguard her colony's western flank. The British needed at all costs to keep the Straits of Gibraltar free for shipping. Spain felt that she had interests in the area. And Germany was determined not to be left out in the scramble for Africa. In fact, the Kaiser's dramatic arrival in

Tangier in 1905 prompted the Conference of Algeciras the following year, which brought Morocco's loss of independence a stage nearer. There were a few more international crises, and various incidents in Marrakesh, Casablanca and elsewhere, involving violence to foreign nationals, before France persuaded Morocco in 1912 to sign the treaty which made her a French protectorate. Morocco was to remain as such until 1956.

Mogreb-el-Acksa provides a vivid eyewitness account of the state of Morocco in the crucial period before she finally lost her autonomy. Stylistically, Cunninghame Graham's writing certainly lacks elegance; his syntax is often ungainly. Its strength, however, lies in its vigour and engagement. Most European writers on the East expatiate at length on the racial characteristics of the native populations. Morocco, in particular, with its indigenous Berbers, and its subsequent influx of Arabs and Negroes, not to mention its Jewish community, lends itself to such disquisitions. Cunninghame Graham is no exception when it comes to this theme. But the tone of out-and-out superiority which is so common in nineteenth-century European travel writing is held severely in check in his work. What strikes us most about Cunninghame Graham is not his judgements on Moorish decadence and cruelty, but his sympathetic attempt to understand the local culture on its own terms. He does this most effectively by translating a Moroccan incident or trait into an English setting. The Moors see some of their towns in foreign hands 'and like the fact as much as we should like the Russians in the Isle of Wight'. The Caid of Kintafi's Chamberlain and other officers 'perjured themselves as cheerfully, and with as much delight in perjury for the mere sake of perjury, as any minister answering a question from the front bench of the grandmother of all parliaments'.

It is this appreciation both of human nature and its different cultural and moral manifestations which informs Cunninghame Graham's anti-imperialist stance. Europeans have no proprietary claim on other countries because of some 'higher' morality which they enjoy. He is the first to acknowledge the cruelty of Moorish society: he sees the Caid of Kintafi's prisoners lowered into their well every night. But he questions whether the Caid's 'tyranny' is different in kind—he accepts that it might be in degree—from that of 'the manufacturer in the manufacturing towns of England, who lives upon the toil of several thousand workmen'. Cunninghame Graham can even find a good word to say about the barbaric treatment of prisoners in Morocco: they were not 'cut off in sentiment' from their fellow men, unlike their European counterparts in 'model' prisons.

While his sympathies lay firmly with Moroccan independence, he was not unconscious of the political circumstances of the age. In his review of the likely apportionment of the Moroccan spoils by the European powers, he even suggests to his British readers that 'it might perhaps be still advisable to seize the south'. It is, however, significant that of the three Moors with whom he converses on his return journey to Mogador, the first two call for British intervention, while the last, Sherif Mulai Othmar, makes an impassioned defence of Moroccan independence. Independence has the last word.

His attitude to Major Spilsbury is also instructive. He is a type, together with Dr Jameson, of British imperialism. While the latter is blatant in his advances, and fêted by the British army, Major Spilsbury is more subtle, and all the more insidious for that. Yet, despite his 'feelings of disgust at the peddling syndicate', Cunninghame Graham cannot suppress his 'admiration for the man who was going quietly to risk his life in such a wretched cause'. Cunninghame Graham knew an adventure when he saw one, and to that extent he was a man of his times. But at least he had the honesty to admit his 'mingled feelings', and that was his protection against the cant of the day.

Underlying his anti-imperialism and socialism was a strong, romantic distaste for the industrial civilization of the nineteenth century—'our shoddy paradise'. Its monuments were the Crystal Palace and the gasometers at Battersea. What could it offer the Moors but bicycles and Gatling guns, and all the other trash which

was already piling up in the Sultan's palaces? Cunninghame
Graham yearned for the 'Arcadia grafted on feudalism or feudalism
steeped in Arcadia' that he saw around him in Morocco. But he
feared that its days were numbered as the European Powers
prepared to pounce. His socialism drew its distinctive quality from
this yearning for a vanished arcadia. The note it sounds is more
often that of a Chestertonian romanticism than of a Shavian
rationalism. It is poignantly heard at the end of *Mogreb-el-Acksa*
when Cunninghame Graham tries to catch the rhythm of the
Berber shepherd's song, but fails because his ears still echo 'with
the roar of cabs' and the 'whir of machinery'. Despite that, as the
boy sings, 'the noise of trams and omnibuses' fades away; 'the
smoky towns' grow fainter; 'the rush, the hurry, and the incredible
nothingness of modern life' sink out of sight, and he sees again, in
his mind's eye, the valley of the N'fiss and the life of the Caid of
Kintafi's giant kasbah.

Philip Healy
December 1987

PREFACE

SIRS, the Holy Scriptures which, as we know, were written for our learning, seem to imply that some of us are fools.

This may be so, and when I moralise, wrapped in the frequent contemplation of my travels, upon lost opportunities, lack of discernment, and on the general folly incident to all mankind, but which each man deems centred in himself, I think so too. But still a traveller in this travelling world, going perhaps to nowhere, or to some place that he would rather never visit, cannot but find his most congenial public amongst wayfaring men. Therefore to you who, like myself, have crossed, or even now are crossing, desert or pampa in the night; riding towards Capella, if in the southern hemisphere (Sohail in Africa), keeping the wind a little blowing on your right cheek, dismounting now and then to smoke and rest the horses, then camping on some river, sleeping fitfully and rising oft to view your horses feeding so quietly under the southern stars; or you, who in the liner, ocean tramp, or even "windjammer" are going somewhere for no special reason, I now address myself.

Writers, I take it, firstly write to please themselves, if not, 'tis ten to one their writing pleases nobody. Following my postulate I have set down that which pleased me upon my pilgrimage, hoping that it may please at least some two or three who, like myself, have wandered. Therefore in this, my modest book of travels, I have tried to write after the fashion that men speak over the fire at night, their pipes alight, hands on their rifles, boots turned towards the blaze, ears strained to catch the rustle of a leaf, and with the tin tea mug stopped on its journey to the mouth when horses snort; I mean I strove to write down that which I saw without periphrasis, sans flag-wagging, and with no megrim in my head of having been possessed by some great moral purpose, without which few travellers nowadays presume to leave their homes.

I fear I have no theory of empires, destiny of the Anglo-Saxon race, spread of the Christian faith, of trade extension, or of hinterlands; no nostrum, by means of which I hope to turn Arabs to Christians, reconcile Allah and Jahve, remove the ancient lack of comprehension between East and West, mix oil and vinegar, or fix the rainbow always in the sky so that the colour-blind may scan it at their leisure through the medium of a piece of neutral-tinted

glass; and generally I fear I write of things without a
scrap of interest to right-thinking men: of humours,
sayings, proverbs, traits of character; little of eating,
drinking, or night alarms of vermin, as travellers
will; but, on the contrary, of lonely rides, desolate
camping places, of ruined buildings seen in peculiar lights, of simple folk who pray to Allah
seven times a day, and act as if they never prayed at
all; in fact of things which to a traveller, his
travels o'er, still conjure up the best part of all
travel—its melancholy. So I apologise for lack of
analysis, neglect to dive into the supposititious
motives which influence but ill-attested acts, and
mostly for myself for having come before the public
with the history of a failure to accomplish what I
tried; and having brought together a sack of cobwebs,
a pack of gossamers, a bale of thistle-down, dragonflies' wings, of Oriental gossip as to byegone facts, of
old-world recollections, of new-world practices half
understood; lore about horses' colours, of tales of men
who never bother much to think, but chiefly act, carving their lives out, where still space is left in which to
carve, and acting thus so inconsiderately whilst there
still remain so many stones unbroken, social problems
to be solved, and the unpuncturable pneumatic tyre
not yet found out.

Touching my traveller's privilege I propose to use it
sparingly, but at the same time not to blurt out the brutal
truth too trippingly, for truth, I take it, suffers by too

much comprehension, in the same manner as the Mass
has suffered even by its transmutation into Elizabethan
English. Religion, once made understandable of all,
loses its authenticity, and soon degenerates into the
arid dialectics of the self-righteous Nonconformist.
What so consoling to a religious man, as in a building
(with the entry free), to join in singing praises to an
unknown God, in an uncomprehended tongue? And
so perhaps the truth,* declare it quite unblushingly,
and it may become as little interesting as is an ill-
concocted lie.

It may be, that my poor unphilosophic recollections
of a failure, may interest some, who, like myself, have
failed, but still may like to hear that even in a failure
you can see strange things, meet as strange types, and
be impressed as much with wild and simple folk, as
any traveller who thundered through the land, Bible
and gun in hand, making himself no spiced conscience,
but putting into practice the best traditions of our
race, confident that the one way to win a " nigger's "
heart " is to speak English to him," and doing so even
at the rifle's mouth.

But if they do not interest, then I fall back again
upon my wanderers, and hope that in my slight impressions, they may find something they recognise, something that they have felt before upon the journey that
they make across the Pampa of their lives, making it as

* And Jesus said "truth is from Heaven;" Pilate answered, "therefore truth is not on earth." Gospel of Nicodemus, chap. iii., verses 12
and 13.

they do in general on horses hipshot, lean and saddle-galled, asking their way from those they meet, who answer them as wise as they, " Ride on to the lone tree on the horizon, then bear a little to the right, and if you keep the line, you cannot miss the houses, for the barking of the dogs will guide you, if it falls dark."

And then comes evening, and the travellers still kicking at their horses' sides, straining their eyes, keep pushing forward, stumbling and objurgating on the trail.

R. B. CUNNINGHAME GRAHAM.

MAP OF SOUTHERN PORTION

OF

MOROCCO

SHEWING AUTHOR'S

ITINERARY.

ROUTE·----►

MOGREB-EL-ACKSA

CHAPTER I.

SOUTH-SOUTH-WEST, a little westerly with a cloudy sky, and with long rollers setting into the harbour of Tangier, and the date October 1st in the last year of supposititious grace. The old white town, built round the bay with the Kasbah upon its hill, and the mosque tower just shining darkly against the electric light, for Tangier passed from darkness to electric light, no gas or oil lamps intervening, gave the effect as of a gleaming horse-shoe in the dark. Outside the harbour, moored twice as far away as the French ironclad, swung the *Rabat* at anchor, for the captain, a Catalan of the true Reus breed, was bound to supplement his lack of seamanship with extra caution, and towards her we made our way late in the evening in a boat manned by four strong-backed Jews, and seated silently, for it was the first stage of a journey concerning which each of our friends had added his wisest word of disencouragement. Nothing so spurs a man upon a journey as the cautions of his friends, " dangerous," " impossible," " when you get there nothing worth seeing," and the like, all show you plainly that the thing is worth the venture, for you know the world is ever proud to greet the conqueror

with praise and flowers, but he has to conquer first.
And if he fails, the cautious kindly friend wags his
wise head and shakes his moralising finger, thinks
you a fool, says so behind your back, but cannot
moralise away experience, that chiefest recompense
of every traveller. So in the boat besides myself sat
Hassan Suleiman Lutaif, a Syrian gentleman, who
acted as interpreter, and Haj Mohammed es Swani,
a Moor of the Riff pirate breed, short, strong, black-
bearded, turned-up moustache, and speaking Spanish
after the Arab fashion, that is without the particles,
and substitution of the gerund for every portion of
the verb. El Haj and I were old acquaintances,
having made several journeys in Morocco, and being
well accustomed to each other's ways and idiosyn-
crasies upon the road.

Our bourne was Tarudant, a city in the province of
the Sus, but rarely visited by Europeans, and of
which no definite account exists by any traveller of
repute. Only some hundred and fifty miles from
Mogador, it yet continues almost untouched, the only
Moorish city to which an air of mystery clings, and
it remains the only place beyond the Atlas to the
south in which the Sultan has a vestige of authority.*

Outside its walls the tribesmen live the old Arab
life, all going armed, constantly fighting, each man's
hand against his neighbour, and, therefore, in a
measure, raised against himself. And yet a land of
vines, of orange gardens, olive yards, plantations of
pomegranates, Roman remains, rich mines; but cursed
"with too much powder," as the Arabs say, and
therefore doomed, up to the present day, to languish

* Since writing this it has been shown that he has more authority in the
Sus than was thought, as witness the landing of the Globe Venture
Company's filibusters, which was promptly checked.

without pauperism, prostitution, and the modern vices which, in more favoured lands, have long replaced the old world vices which man brought with him into the old-world. Even my friends were all agreed that to reach Tarudant in European clothes was quite impossible. Thus a disguise became imperative. After a long discussion I determined to impersonate a Turkish doctor travelling with his " taleb " *—that is, scribe—to see the world and write his travels in a book. God, the great doctor, but under Him His earthly vicegerents, practicants, practitioners, with or without diploma, throughout the east, enjoy considerable respect ; they kill, they cure, and still God has the praise. No one asks where they studied, and if faith in his powers helps a doctor in his trade, the east of all lands should be most congenial to all those who live by lancet, purge, and human faith. My stock of medicines was of the most homeric type, quinine and mercury, some Seidlitz powders, eye wash for ophthalmia, almost, in fact, as simple as that of the old Scotch doctor who doctored with what he styled the two simples, that is, laudanum and calomel.

The multitudinous dialects of Arabic, the constant travelling, either upon the pilgrimage or for the love of travel, which seems inherent in the Arab, render it possible for a European occasionally to pass unrecognised, even although his stock of Arabic is as exiguous as was my own. Behold us, then, approaching the *Rabat*, a steamer of the Linea Trans-Atlantica Española, bound for Mogador, some five days'

---

* " Taleb " literally means a learned man, but in Morocco it is applied to everyone who can read and write, in fact, as the Spaniards say, " sabe de pluma " ; my " taleb " did not fall under the latter head, being a learned man, and a gentleman.

journey below Tangier, the point at which I intended
to put on Moorish clothes, buy mules and horses,
engage a guide, and set out for Tarudant, the city
where La Caba, Count Julian's daughter (she whose
beauty tempted Don Rodrigo, and to avenge whose
honour her father sold Spain to the Moors), lies
buried, though how she came to die there is to historians unknown. On board the ship no light, no
look-out, and the accommodation ladder triced up for
the night, stewards asleep, and the long narrow
vessel dipping her nose into the rollers, rolling and
heaving in the dark, whilst we in Spanish, English,
Arabic, and Portuguese rang all the changes upon
ship ahoy. At last a sulky, sleepy quartermaster
deigned to let down the ladder, and we scrambled
upon deck.

Next morning found us off Arzila, the Julia Con-
stantia Zilis of the Romans, a small walled town lost
among orange gardens, and girt by walls built by the
Portuguese. Over the gateway the half-obliterated
arms of Portugal can still be seen, but mouldering to
decay, as is the country that they represent. Close to
the walls rises the tomb of the Saint of Arzila; the white
dome springs from a dense thicket of palmetto, dwarf
rhododendron, berbenis, and aromatic shrubs, a tiny
stream bordered by oleanders (bitter as is an oleander
is a proverb in the land) runs past it; above the dome
and red-tiled roof two palms keep watch, and whisper
in the wind the secrets palm trees know, and tell
each other of the East, and of the various changes,
Arab and Berber, Moor and Portuguese, they have
seen during the course of their slow growth and long
extended days. Columbus visited the place; the
battle of Trafalgar was fought a few leagues off,
and an old shepherd, still living where he was born,

above the lighthouse on Cape Spartel, remembers to have seen it as a boy when he lay out upon the hills tending his goats.

Inside the town decay and ruin, heaps of garbage, a palace falling here, a hovel there. A town almost entirely given up to Jews, who carry on their business fleecing the Moors, and still complaining when at last the cent. per cented victim turns and rends. The best-known citizen is Mr. Ben Chiton, an Israelite of the best type, old, and white bearded, and with round, beady eyes like an old rat, Consul of seven nations, with all the seven flag-staffs on his hospitable roof. Dressed in the Jewish gown girt round the waist, wearing his slippers over white cotton stockings, and the black cup badge of the servitude of all his race throughout Morocco. His house is neat and clean, almost beyond the power of endurance, " Rahel " and " Mordejai " labouring incessantly with broom and whitewash brush, and he himself talking incessantly in the Toledan* dialect and thick Jewish accent, of politics, of kings, ambassadors, and as to whether England and France will go to war over the question of the Niger and the like, whilst all the time he presses brandy on you in a lordly glass holding about a pint, which you must swallow no matter what the hour, the while he calls upon the God of Isaac to bear him witness that the house is yours, and shows you, with just pride, the chair on which he says the Prince of Wales once sat, although historians do not seem to chronicle his passage through the town. An Israelite

---

* The Toledan dialect is the old Spanish of the Jews, who were expelled from Spain. They speak the Spanish of the sixteenth century, using the X instead of J, and with other peculiarities. They inhabit the towns of Tetuan, Tangier, Alcazar, Arzila, Larache, and Rabat, and are the highest caste Jews of Morocco. The Jews of the interior speak Arabic, come from the East, and are in general of a lower type.

of Israelites, a worthy Jew, come of the tribe of Judah,
as he says, one to whose house all travellers are
welcome; loved by his family with veneration, as the
heads of Jewish houses are; long may he prosper,
and may his roof grow broad as a phylactery, and
become strong enough to bear the flag-staffs of all
the nations upon earth, and his house long remain to
show the curious what most probably a Jewish house
in Spain was like before the Catholic Kings, in their
consuming thirst for unity, expelled the Jews, sweeping
at one fell blow commerce and usury out of their
sacred land, and setting up a faith so uniform that to
be saved by it was so easy that one wonders any one
was lost.   A few hours' steaming brings us to Larache
(El Areish), once a great stronghold of the Moorish
pirates who infested the narrow straits, and who at
times ran as far north as Plymouth, westward to
Naples, and made the coasts of France, Spain, Italy
and Portugal their especial hunting grounds.

Three of their galleys still lie rotting in the Luccos,
and at low tide their ribs can still be seen projecting
from the sand. The city, painted red, white, and blue,
and the whole scale of tints from brown to Naples yellow
stands on a hill, and is to-day the haunt of Consuls of
all nations, who have replaced the pirates of the
times gone by. Consuls of France and Spain, of
Portugal, of Montenegro, Muscat, Costa Rica, Brazil,
United States, their flag-staffs rear aloft from almost
every house-top, and their great flags, large in proportion to the smallness of the state they represent,
flap in the breeze; the caps of liberty, the rising
suns, and other trade-marks of the various states
seeming to wink and to encourage one another in the
attempt to be the first to show the glories of the
commercial system to the benighted Moors.   All

round the town the walls and ramparts run, built by the Portuguese during the period when they possessed the place. At the west side a ditch remains, now turned into a garden, and in it artichokes, egg-plants, and pimentos grow, and the green stuffs of various kinds for which the Moors are famous, so much so that in the times they lived in Spain, it was a current saying of a good farmer "that he grows as many egg-plants in his garden as a Morisco gardener."* Just at the corner of the ditch the walls run into as sharp an angle as the bows of a torpedo boat, and on the ramparts usually is seen a colony of storks, who build their nests amongst the mouldering gabions, ravelines, and counter-scarps, and sit and chatter on the brass guns and carronades, with curling snakes around the touch-holes, and with inscription setting forth their date, the place of casting, and the legend "Viva Portugal!" their gunners gone, their carriages long mouldered into dust, and the storks left to sit and mock the pomps and circumstance of foolish war.

From the town sallied out (in 1578) the army under Don Sebastian, who met his fate fighting the infidel at Alcazar el Kebir, near a long bridge over a marshy stream known as El-Ma Khassan. The battle still is called amongst the Moors "The Three Kings' Fight," for besides Don Sebastian fell two Moorish kings. With Don Sebastian there fell the flower of the nobility of Portugul, and by his death the crown passed quickly to Phillip II. (the Prudent) of Spain, who knew far better than to embark in expeditions into Africa. The battle was memorable, for Abdel-Malik, King of Fez, died of exhaustion on the field, and Don Sebastian, rather than survive disgrace,

* Coge mas berengenas que un hortelano Morisco.

plunged, as did Argentine at Bannockburn, into the thickest of the fight, and fell or disappeared, for though his faithful servant, Resende, claimed to have seen his body, so much doubt existed of his death that the strange sect known as Sebastianists arose in Portugal. Their tenet was that Don Sebastian was still alive, but kept in durance by the Moors, and in remote and old-world villages believers linger even to the present day. I myself saw a sort of pterodactyle, years ago in Portugal, a strange old man dressed in black clothes, and wrapped, in heat and cold alike, in a thick cloak. The people of the village called him mad, but, looking at the thing impartially, madness and faith are the same thing, the only difference being as to the mountain which the believer wishes to remove.

Lela Mamouna, the female saint who guards Larache from pestilence and famine, sudden death, and the few simple ailments which Arabs suffer from, has her white crenelated sanctuary on a hill which overlooks the sea, and to her tomb women who wish for children to carry on the misery of life, repair, and pray or chatter with each other, and no doubt the saint is just as tolerant of scandal as are the wise old men who sun their stomachs at the windows of a club.

But at this cursed port, Larache, of the Beni-Aros, after a signal had been made by a man mounted on a mule, who held one end of a row of flags, the other being made fast to a post, a great annoyance fell upon the blameless captain of the good ship *Rabat*. The bar at El Areish is three times out of four impassable when steamers call, as here the river Luccos* meets the tide, and such a surf gets up

* Luccos is the El Kuos of the Arabs, and the Luxos of the Romans.

that as the people have no surf boats, communication from a vessel to the shore is always dangerous,
and not infrequently impossible. This, to an ordinary
steamer, means either delay or loss of cargo, generally the latter, for when the bar is bad it often takes
three or four days to become passable, and as the
anchorage is most precarious a south-east gale causes
great danger to a vessel lying in the open roads. On
this occasion, though the sea was like a sheet of
ice, smooth, shining, and the bar just marked by a
thin line of foam, to the astonishment of the uniniti-
ated passengers the fury of the captain knew no
bounds, the officers turned sulky, and the one man on
board who seemed unmoved was the unlucky priest,
who shipped to please the owners of the line, or to
appease the folly of the nation, or for " empeño,"* or
for some other reason at present not made known,
passed all his time in fishing when in port, or when at
sea in studying counterpoint, and playing on a piano
which was tuned about the time Queen Isabella was
expelled from Spain.

A narrow, nine-knot crank and Clyde-built steamer
was the *Rabat*, full five-and-twenty years of age,
boilers too small, but engines sound, and the whole
vessel kept as clean as holystone and paint could
clean, brass work all shining, and herself ever a-
rolling like a swing-boat at a fair, sailed out of
Barcelona, owned by the Spanish Trans-Atlantic
Company (Chairman : the Marquis of Comillas), and
subsidised by the Spanish Government to carry mails
down the Morocco coast in order that the majesty
of Spain might fill the eyes and strike the imagination
of the Moorish dogs, and show them that the Spaniards

---

* " Empeño" means " a job."   The phrase is well understood throughout the Spains, and the practice much indulged in.

were on a level with the other nations, such as
" Inglis," "Frances," "el Bortokez" (Portuguese),
"el Brus" (the Germans, that is, Prussians), and the
Austrians, called by the Moors "el Nimperial."

Captain from Reus, taciturn, and shaved each
Sunday when the priest said mass, for it is decent
for a man to stand before his God with a clean chin,
at other times a stubble on his face on which a man
might strike a match, so that the match had not
been made in Spain. Four officers: an Andalusian,
two Catalans, and a Basque; two engineers, and the
aforementioned priest, together with a crew of eighteen men and half a dozen stewards, served to get
the craft, whose utmost measurement could not be
above twelve hundred tons, across the sea.

The Pope had granted plenary indulgence in the
following terms: "for looking to the circumstances, the
weather, etc., I deign to grant full dispensation according to the ecclesiastic law, from fasting and from abstin-
ence (from meat) to all those who by reason, either
of their profession or as passengers, find themselves
on board the vessels of this Company, and that for
three years' time, excepting (if it can be done without
too great an inconvenience) on Good Friday and on
the Virgils of the Apostles, Saint Peter and Saint
Paul, also on Christmas Day and any other day which
may be opportune . . . . on which three days I
also dispense from sin the passengers and crew if any
difficulty unforeseen by me makes their compliance
an impossibility." Given "en Vaticano" and through
the Bishop of Madrid and Alcala under whose ægis
it appears that Spanish ships all sail armed with
this plenary indulgence; manned with the priest and
men and duly subsidised, it could not be expected that
the *Rabat* cared much for passengers, still less for

cargo; so when the lumbering "barcazas" approached the ship, curses loud, guttural, and deep were heard on every side. The unwilling sailors, mostly Valencians and Catalans, stood by to work the donkey engine; but their fears were vain, for it appeared that all the cargo was but four bales of "Zatar" (Marjoram) for the Habana and a few thousand melons for the Sultan's camp. The bales of "Zatar" soon were dumped into the hold, but five long hours were wasted passing the melons up from hand to hand; in counting them, recounting them, in storming, and the whole time a noise like Babel going on, shouting of Moors, cursing of Spaniards, and the confusion ten times intensified because no man could speak a word the other understood. The *Rabat* having been only five years upon the coast, no one on board could speak a word of Arabic. Why should they, did they not speak "Christian," and are Spaniards and sailors to be supposed to burrow in grammars as if they were schoolboys or mere Englishmen. A miserable Jew, fearfully sea-sick, balancing upon the gunwale of a boat, in a mixed jargon of Arabic and Portuguese kept tale after a fashion of the melons, and at last the vessel put to sea amid the curses of the passengers, and having earned the name amongst the Arabs of "Abu Batigh," the Father of the Melons. Amongst the Arabs almost every man is Father of something or some quality, and lucky he who does not find himself styled, Father of the "ginger beard," or of "bad breath," or any other personal or moral failing, peculiarity, or notable defect.

Once more we urge our nine-knot course, and now find time to observe our fellow-passengers. In the cabin a German lady and her daughters are enduring agonies of sea-sickness, on the way to join her

husband at Rabat.* The husband, known as the
"mojandis," that is, engineer to the Sultan, proves,
when we meet him, to be a cheery polyglot blas--
phemer, charged with the erection of some forts at the
entrance to the harbour of Rabat. For a wonder the
bar of the river Bu-Regeh proves passable, and the
German lady and her husband can land, which is, it
seems, a piece of luck, for the bar is known as the
most dangerous of all the coast. Rabat, perhaps the
most picturesquely situated of any city in Morocco,
stands on a hill underneath which the river runs, and
the spray from the bar is drifted occasionally into the
houses like a shower of snow. Here is the richest
colony of the Spanish Jews, and here the best
Morisco† families took refuge after the expulsion of
the Moors from Spain. The town is estimated to
contain some 20,000 inhabitants, and it is one of the
four official capitals‡; the Sultan has a palace with
enormous gardens on the outskirts of the town. Just
opposite is built Salee, called by the Moors "Salá,"
famous for having given its name to the most enter-
prising of the pirates of the coast in days gone by.
To-day it is a little white mouldering place, baked in
the fierce sun, or swept by south-west gales, according
to the season and the time of year. The inhabitants
are still renowned for their fanaticism, and the traveller
who passes through the place is seldom able to dis-

* The Germans are slowly but surely driving us out of the coast trade in
Morocco. It may well be said of them that they are conquering the world
with the trombone and the ophicleide, as the Romans did with the pick and
shovel. Where these "bummel bands" once get a footing, their empire
and all that, is sure to follow

† The Moriscos went to Tetuan, Fez, and Rabat, and in consequence the
upper classes of all these cities are fairer in colour and more enlightened
in mind than those of any other city of Morocco.

‡ The others are Fez, Marakesh, and Mequinez. The system of an
ambulatory capital also obtained formerly in Bolivia.

mount, but traverses the place trying to look as dignified as possible amid a shower of curses, a sporadic curse or two, and some saliva if he ventures within range of mouth. Many a poor Christian has worked his life out in the construction of the walls, and the superior whiteness of the inhabitants would seem to show that some of the Christian dogs have left their blood amongst the people of the place. Men still alive can tell of what a scourge the pirates were, and I myself once knew a venerable lady who in her youth had the distinction of having been taken by a Salee rover; an honour in itself to be compared alone to that enjoyed by ladies who are styled peeresses in their own right. Robinson Crusoe, I think, once landed at the place, and the voyages of imaginary travellers make a place more authentic than the visit of the unsubstantial personages of real life. A little up the river is the deserted city of Schellah, and on the way to it, upon a promontory jutting into the stream, is built the half-finished tower of Hassan, an enormous structure much like the Giralda at Seville, and by tradition said to be built by the same architect who built that tower, and also built the tower of the Kutubich, which, at Morocco city, serves as a landmark in the great plain around. The Giralda and the Kutubich spring from the level of the street, but the Hassan tower excels them both in site, standing as it does upon a cliff, and "looming lofty"* as one passes in a boat beneath. Schellah contains the tombs of the Sultans of the Beni Merini dynasty. El Mansur (the victorious) sleeps underneath a carved stone tomb, over which date palms

---

* Once looking at a steamer coming up London docks in a thick fog, I said to an aged shell-back standing near, " She looks very large somehow," and received the answer, " Well, she do loom lofty in the mist."

rustle, and by which a little stream sings a perpetual dirge. The tomb is held so sacred that till but lately neither Christians nor Jews could visit it. Even to-day the incursions of the fierce Zimouri, a Berber tribe, render a visit at times precarious. The walls of the town enclose a space of about a mile circumference; sheep, goats and camels feed inside them, and a foot-path leads from one deserted gate-house to the other, a shepherd boy or two play on their reeds, and though the sun beats fiercely on the open space, it looks forlorn and melancholy, and even the green lizards peering from the walls look about timidly, as if they feared to see a ghost. On gates and walls, on ruined tombs and palaces, the lichens grow red after the fashion of hot countries, and the fine stone-work, resembling the stucco work of the Alhambra, remains as keen in edge and execution as when the last stroke of the chisel turned it out. Outside the town are olive yards and orange gardens, and one comes upon the long-deserted place with the same feelings as a traveller sees Palenque burst on him out of the forests of Yucatan, or as in Paraguay after a weary following of dark forest trails, the spires of some old Jesuit Mission suddenly appear in a green clearing, as at Jesus or Trinidad, San Cosme Los Apostoles, or any other of the ruined " capillas," where the bell-bird calls amongst the trees, and the inhabitants take off their hats at sunset and sink upon their knees, bearing in their minds the teaching of the Jesuits, whom Charles III. expelled from Spain and from the Indies, to show his liberalism.

Our most important passenger was Don Jose Miravent, the Spanish Consul at Mogador, returning to his post after a holiday; a formal Spaniard of the old school, pompous and kind, able to bombast out a

platitude with the air of a philosopher communicating
what he supposes truth. At dinner he would square
his elbows, and, throwing back his head, inform the
world "the Kings of Portugal are now at Caldas"; or
if asked about the war in Cuba, say: " War, sir, there
is none; true some negroes in the Manigua* are giving
trouble to our troops, but General Blanco is about to
go, and all will soon be over; it is really nothing
(no es na), peace will, please God, soon reign upon
that lovely land." At night he would sit talking to his
cook, a Spanish woman (the widow of an English
soldier), whom he was taking back to Mogador; but
though he talked, and she replied for hours most
volubly, not for a moment were good manners set
aside, nor did the cook presume in any way, and
throughout the conversation talked better than most
ladies; but the "tertulia" over, straight became a
cook again, brought him his tea, calling him "Amo"
(master) "Don Jose," and he quite affably listened
to her opinions and ideas of things, which seemed at
least as valuable as were his own. A Jewish merchant dressed in the height of Cadiz fashion, and
known as "Tagir"† Isaac, occupied much the same
sort of social state on board as does a Eurasian in
Calcutta or Bombay. Tall, thin and up-to-date, he
had divested himself almost entirely of the guttural
Toledan accent, but the sign of his "election" still
remained about his hair, which tended to come off in
patches like an old hair trunk, and at the ends showed
knotty, as if he suffered from the disease to which so
many of his compatriots in Morocco are subject, and

---

* Manigua is the Cuban name for a tropical forest.

† Tagir means a merchant and is a highly honourable title in Mohammedan countries where the feudal system never made trade be looked
down upon. "Caballer," *i.e.* Caballero, is a more modern and, so to
speak, gentleman-like appellation.

which makes each separate hair stand out as if it were alive.*

But, as is often seen even in more ambitious vessels than the *Rabat*, the passengers of greatest interest were in the steerage. Not that there was a regular steerage as in ocean-going ships, but still, some thirty people went as deck passengers, and amongst them was to be seen a perfect microcosm of the eastern world. Firstly a miserable, pale-faced Frenchman, dressed in a dirty "duster" coat, bed-ticking "pants," black velvet waistcoat, and blue velvet slippers, with foxes' heads embroidered on them in yellow beads, his beard trimmed to a point, in what is termed (I think) Elizabethan fashion, and thin white hands, more disagreeable in appearance than if they had been soiled by all the meanest work on earth. His "taifa"† (that is band) consisted of one Spanish girl and two half-French half-Spanish women, whom he referred to as his "company," and whom he said were to enact "cuadros vivos," that is "living pictures," in the various ports. They, less polite than he, called him "el Alcahuete," which word I leave in Spanish, merely premising (as North Britons say) that it is taken from the Arabic "el Cahueit," and that the celebrated "Celestina"‡ was perhaps in modern times the finest specimen of the profession in any literature. So whilst our captain read "Jack el Ripero" (it cost him two pesetas when new in Cadiz), I take a glance

* Perhaps a kind of Plica Polonica, or perhaps the "scald" of the Middle Ages, as when Chaucer says to his scribe who did not correct his proofs, "Under they long lockes mayst thou have the scald."

† Taifa is the Arabic word for a company or following. It is generally applied contemptuously, as in the phrase "Reyezuelos de Taifas," used by the Spaniards during the time the Moors were in Spain to designate the Kings of Almeria, Ocsonoba, Huesca, and other small Principalities.

‡ "Celestina, Tragi, Comedia de Calisto y Melibea por Rodrigo de Cota."

at the inferior races, who were well represented in the steerage of the ship.

Firstly, I came across a *confrère* in the healing art who hailed from Tunis, a fattish Arab dressed in Algerian trousers, short zouave jacket, red fez, pink and white sash, and watch chain of two carat silver with an imitation seal of glass, brown thread stockings and cheap sand shoes after the pattern to be seen at Margate. "Tabib numero Wahed," that is an A 1 doctor, so he says, has studied in Stamboul, where he remained nine years studying and diligently noting down all that he learnt. But, curiously enough, all that he now remembers of the Turkish language is the word "Mashallah," which he displayed to my bewilderment, until Lutaif, who spoke good Turkish, turned on a flood of pertinent remarks, to which the doctor answered in vile Tunisian Arabic, not having understood a word. Though not a linguist, still a competent practitioner, trepanning people's heads with ease, and putting in pieces of gourd instead of silver as being lighter, and if the patient died, or by the force of constitution lived through his treatment, the praise was God's, Allah the great Tabib (doctor), although he sends his delegates to practice on mankind, just in the same way that in the east each man commits his work to some one else to do. At least he said so, and I agree, but fail to see the use of substituting gourd for silver, seeing the vast majority of heads are gourds from birth. Quinine he had, and blistering fluid, with calomel and other simples, and when the Christian quinine ran out, he made more for himself out of the ashes of an oleander stick mixed with burnt scales of fish and dead men's bones, and found his preparation, which he styled "El quina beladia" (native-made quinine), even more efficacious than the drug from over sea. Also he used the seven herbs, known as the "confirmed herbs," for tertian fevers, with notable success. A cheerful, not too superstitious son of Æsculapius, taking himself as seriously as if he had had a large brass plate upon his door in Harley Street, and welcomed by his surviving patients in Rabat on our arrival with great enthusiasm.* His wife, a shrouded figure lost in white veils and fleecy shawls, had the dejected air that doctors' wives often appear to labour under, even in countries where they can rule their husbands openly.

A group of high-class Arabs sat by themselves upon the decks, waited upon by a tall tribesman faced like a camel, and with the handle of his pistol and curved dagger outlined beneath his clothes. This group, composed of sherifs† from Algeria, all high-caste men, dignified, slow, and soft of speech, deliberate in movement, their clothes as white as snow, nails dyed with henna, each with a heavy rosary in his hand, their business somewhat mysterious, but bound to see the Sultan in his camp. Throughout Algeria the sherifs are not allowed to receive contributions from the people openly, but it is said in private they receive them all the same. Of all the population they are the least contented with French rule, as since the conquest naturally they have fallen somewhat from the position they once occupied, and cannot go about receiving presents for the pains they have taken to preserve their lineage, as they do in Morocco, making themselves a travelling offertory.

* This may serve to illustrate the retrograde condition of medicine in Mohammedan countries. Who would welcome the return of a doctor in a European country ?

† A sherif is a more or less authentic descendant of the Prophet. They occupy a semi-religious semi-political position, and are as numerous as the " ancestors came over with the Conqueror " people in England.

All of them wished to know of the late war between the Sultan of Turkey and the " Emperor of the Greeks." They seemed to think the latter was a descendant of the *Paleologi*, and asked if it were true the Sultan had killed all the Greeks except fifteen, and if these latter had not fled to "Windres" (London) to seek protection from the Great Queen and to advise her to make preparations against the " Jehad "* to come. With them they carried sundry hide bags of gold with which they said they wished to purchase permission from the Sultan of Morocco to export grain, as the harvest in Algeria had not been good owing to locusts, and the lack of rain. Of course this may have been the object of their visit, but since the Greco-Turkish war all the Mohammedan world is on the stir, and men are travelling about from place to place disseminating news, and all the talk is on the victories of the Turks, and on the rising of the tribes in India; in fact, a feeling seems to be abroad that the Christian power is on the wane, and that their own religion once again may triumph and prevail.

At Casa Blanca—called by the Arabs Dar el Baida, that is, the White House—the sherifs go ashore, and I last saw them seated on their bags, outside the waterport, their backs against the ramparts of the town, their eyes apparently fixed upon nothing, though seeing everything, telling their beads and waiting patiently, enduring sun and flies until their servant should return and tell them of a lodging fit for persons of their quality. Of all the towns on the Morocco coast Dar el Baida has the most business, the country at the back of it is fertile and grows much wheat, the tribes are fairly prosperous, and the best

---

* Jehad—religious war—generally applied to a war entered into from self-interest, as that of America against Spain.

horses of the country come from the districts known as Abda and Ducala, a few leagues from the place.

Consuls abound, of course, so do hyenas—that is, outside the town—but both are harmless and furnish little sport, except the Consul of America, my good friend Captain Cobb. He, if my memory fails me not, piled up his brig some thirty years ago upon the beach in the vicinity, liked the climate, became a Consul, naturally, and to this day has never returned to his sorrowing family in Portland, Maine.

In thirty years tradition says he has not learned a word of Arabic with the exception of the word "Balak" (look out), which he pronounces "Balaaker," and yet holds conversations by the hour in Arabic, and both the patients seem contented with their lot. All the attractions to be met with in the town do not detain me; what takes my fancy most is to see tribesmen from the country, armed to the teeth, and balancing a gun full six feet long upon their saddles, sit on their horses bargaining at shops in the same fashion I have seen the Gauchos at a camp-town in South America, their horses nodding their heads and looking half asleep, their owners seated with one leg passed round the pommel of the saddle, and passing hours seated as comfortably as in a chair.

Back to the steamer in a boat, and at the waterport we pass a group of Jews washing themselves, in preparation for a feast. Lutarf ranks as a wit for saying that the Jews will defile the sea, for any wit is small enough to bait a Jew with; and the Arabs, though they will say the same things of a Christian behind his back, all laugh consumedly when a Christian takes their side against a Jew.

On board the uneasy ship, tossed like a buck-jumper in the Atlantic swell, we find more Oriental

items ready to hand. The first a tall, thin, cuckoldy-
looking Arab knave, dressed in a suit of slop-made
European clothes, his trousers half-a-foot too short,
his boots unblackened, and himself closely watched by
two Franciscan Friars.* It appeared he was a convert. Now, in Morocco a convert is a most rare and
curious animal, and he is usually not a great credit to
his capturers. On this occasion, it appears, the convert had been dallying with the Protestants, had
given them hopes, had led them on, and at the last,
perhaps because he found the North-British water† of
their baptism too cold for him, or perchance because
the Friars gave a dollar more, had fallen away to
Rome. However, there he was, a veritable " brand,"
a sheep, who had come into one of the folds, leaving
the other seven million nine hundred and ninety-
nine thousand and ninety-nine still straying about
Morocco, steeped in the errors of Mohammedanism.
His captors were a gentlemanlike, extremely handsome, quiet Castilian, who to speak silver (hablar en
plata) seemed a little diffident about his prize, and
went about after the fashion of a boy in Texas who
has caught a skunk. The other guardian had no
doubts, a sturdy Catalonian lay-brother, who pointed
to the "brand" with pride, and told us, with a phrase

* For the last two hundred years the Franciscans have had missions in
the coast towns of Morocco. They, at present, confine their labours to the
Spanish population. The vineyard is stony. Formerly they worked
amongst the captives. Your captive generally is inclined to listen to a friar
or to any one else who will talk to him. The late Prefect of the Franciscans in Tangier, Father Lerchundi, was a most erudite man, having
composed many treatises on the Arabic language, which he knew perfectly.
At his funeral, Jews, Christians, Moors, and other mutually described
infidels, turned out in great numbers, and for a brief space the "Odium
Theologicum" was laid aside, and the cross, the crescent, and the other
symbols of the three jarring faiths went up the main street of Tangier in
seeming amity.

† The Protestant missionaries in Morocco are almost all Scotchmen.

verging upon an oath, that he was glad the Protestants had had their noses well put out of joint.
The victim was a merry sort of knave, who chewed
tobacco, spoke almost every language in the world,
had travelled, and informed me, when I asked him
where he was going, that the "Frayliehs" (Friars)
were taking him to Cadiz "to have the water put
upon his head." He seemed an old hand at the
business, and recognised my follower, Swani, as an
old friend, and they retired to talk things over, with
the result that, e'er night fell, the "convert" was in
a most unseemly state and singing Spanish songs
in which Dolores, Mercedillas, and other "Chicas"
figured largely, and were addressed in terms sufficient
to upset a convent of Franciscan Friars. Peace to his
baptism, and may the Protestants,* when their turn
comes to mark a sheep, secure as fine a specimen as
the one I saw going to Cadiz to have "the water put
upon his head." This missionary question and the
decoying of God-fearing men out of the ranks of the
religion they were born in, is most thorny in every
country like Morocco, where the religion of the land
is one to which the people are attached. An earnest
missionary, a pious publican, a minister of the crown
who never told a lie, are men to praise God for continually. Honour to all of them, labouring in their
vocations and striving after truth as it appears to
them. I, for my part, have found honest and earnest
men both in the Scottish missions in Morocco and in
the ranks of the Franciscan Friars from Spain.
Amongst both classes, and in the missions sent by
other churches, good men abound; and in so far as

* Nearly all the Protestant missionaries in South Morocco are Scotch,
and I take this opportunity of acknowledging the unfailing kindness I have
received from all of them. I only wish I could say I thought their missionary efforts were creating much effect, for they have worked hard.

these good men confine themselves to giving medicines, healing the sick, and showing by the example
of their lives that even Christians (whom Arabs all
believe are influenced in all they do by money) can
live pure, self-denying lives for an idea, the good they
do is great; but that by living, as they do, amongst
the Moors, they do more good than they could do at
home by living the same lives, that I deny. Amongst
Mohammedans plenty of people lead good lives, as
good appears to them—that is, they follow out the
precepts of their faith, give to the poor, do not lend
money upon usury ; and, to be brief, practice morality,* and believe by doing so that they are sacri-
ficing to some fetish, invented by mankind, to make
men miserable.   When, though, it comes to marking
sheep—the object, after all, for which a missionary is
sent—I never saw a statement of accounts which
brought the balance out upon the credit side.   The
excuse is, generally, " Oh, give us time ; these things
work slowly ; "—as indeed they do ; and if the missions think it worth their while to send men out to
doctor syphilis, cure gonorrhœa, and to attend to
every form of the venereal disease, their field is
wide; but if they wish to convert Mohammedans let
them produce a balance-sheet, and show how many
of the infidel they have converted in the last twenty
years.   Not that I blame them for endeavouring to
perform what seems impossible, or try to detract an
atom from the praise due to them for their efforts,
but when so many savages still exist in Central
Africa and in East London—not to speak of Glasgow
and the like—it seems a pity to expend upon a
people, civilised according to their needs, so much

* Morality from *mores*, customs ; therefore, as the customs of all nations
are different, so is their theory of morality.

good faith, which might be used with good effect upon less stony ground.

Prophets, reformers, missionaries, "illuminated" folk, and those who leave their homes to preach a faith, no matter what it is, are people set apart from the flat-footed ordinary race of human kind; of such are missionaries and the dream world they live in. How many an honest, hard-working young man, who gets his education how he can, by pinching, screwing, reading at bookstalls, paying for instruction to those who live perhaps almost as poorly as he himself, thinks when he reads of Livingstone, Francisco Xavier, the Jesuits of Paraguay, and Father Damien, that he, too, would like to take his cross upon his back and follow them. It seems so fine (and is so splendid in reality) a self-denying life, lived far away from comforts, without books; Bible and gun in hand, to show the heathen all the glories of our faith.

Then comes reality, mocker of all best impulses, and the enthusiastic spirit finds itself bound in a surgery (say in Morocco city), finds work increasing, and his dreams of preaching to a crowd of dusky cate-chumens dressed in white, with flowers in their hair, and innocence in every heart, turned to Dead Sea Fruit, as with motives misunderstood, with caustic, mercury, sulphate of copper and the rest, he burns the fetid ulcer, or washes sores, and for reward can say after a term of years that he has made the people of the place look upon European clothes with less aversion than when first he came.

If the mere fact of getting accustomed to the sight of Europeans were a thing worthy of self-congratu-lation, then indeed missionaries in Morocco have achieved much. But as I see the matter Europeans

are a curse throughout the East. What do they bring
worth bringing, as a general rule?

Guns, gin, powder, and shoddy cloths, dishonest
dealing only too frequently, and flimsy manufactures
which displace the fabrics woven by the women, new
wants, new ways, and discontent with what they
know, and no attempt to teach a proper comprehension of what they introduce; these are the blessings
Europeans take to Eastern lands Example certainly
they do set, for ask a native what he thinks of us, and
if he has the chance to answer without fear, 'tis ten
to one he says, Christian and cheat are terms synonymous. Who that has lived in Arab countries, and
does not know that fear, and fear alone, makes the
position of the Christian tolerable. Christ and
Mohammed never will be friends; their teaching,
lives, and the conditions of the different peoples
amongst whom they preached make it impossible;
even the truce they keep is from the teeth outwards,
and their respective followers misunderstand each
other quite as thoroughly as when a thousand years
ago they came across each other's path. But if the
Arabs constitute a stony vineyard, the Jews are
worse, and years ago when first the missionaries
appeared in the coast towns of southern Barbary,
they fleshed their maiden weapons on the Jews. It
struck the chosen people that the best weapon to em-
ploy against their new tormentors was that of irony,
and so they cast about to find a nickname calculated
at the same time to ridicule and wound, and found it,
made it stick and rankle, so that to-day every new
missionary on landing has to accommodate his
shoulders to the burden of a peculiarly comic cross.

Almost all Europeans in Morocco must of necessity
be merchants, if not they must be Consuls, for there is

hardly any other industry open to them to choose. The missionaries bought and sold nothing, they were not Consuls; still they ate and drank lived in good houses, and though not rich, yet passed their lives in what the Jews called luxury. So they agreed to call them followers of Epicurus, for, as they said, "this Epicurus was a devil who did naught but eat and drink." The nickname stuck, and changed into "Bikouros" by the Moors, who thought it was a title of respect, became the name throughout Morocco for a missionary. One asks as naturally for the house of Epicurus on coming to a town as one asks for the "Checquers" or the "Bells" in rural England. Are you "Bikouros," says a Moor, and thinks he does you honour by the inquiry; but the recipients of the name are fit to burst when they reflect on their laborious days spent in the surgery, their sowing seed upon the marble quarries of the people's hearts, and that the Jews in their malignity should charge upon them by this cursed name, that they live in Morocco to escape hard work, and pass their time in eating and in quaffing healths a thousand fathoms deep.

Often at night, awake and looking at the stars and trying to remember which was which, I have broken into laughter when I thought upon the name, and laughed until the Arabs all sat up alarmed, for he who laughs at night laughs at his hidden wickedness, or else because a devil has possessed his soul.

Cargo, of course, was not expected in the *Rabat*, and as by four o'clock in the afternoon the last few passengers had come aboard, it might have been expected that the ship would put to sea. Not so, the captain gave it as his opinion that it was best to wait till midnight so as to arrive in Mazagan by breakfast time; so for eight hours we waited in sight of Casa

Blanca, swinging up and down, giddy and miserable, and in the intervals of misery tried to fish.

Next morning we were off Djedida (New Town), as the Arabs call Mazagan. A yellowish town, peopled by Jews, Moors, and innumerable yellow dogs. Camels blocked all the streets, and above the Consul's flagstaffs a single palm-tree reared its head, fluttering its feathers over the sandstone walls built by the Portuguese in the days when they were navigators, adventurers, and over-ran the world, after the fashion of the modern Englishman. The batteries built by the Moors or by the Portuguese are most ingeniously constructed to expose the gunners, and to batter down the town they are supposed to guard. Outside a street of beehive-looking huts of reeds, each with its little garden, its ten or twelve dogs, thirteen or fourteen children, three or four donkeys, and a score of mangy fowls, and with a bush or two of castor oil plants sticking up in the sand at every corner of the street, gives quite an air of equatorial Africa or Paraguay.

Right in the middle of the Plaza a squadron of some fifty Arab irregular soldiers guard about two hundred prisoners. These latter, heavily ironed and half-starved, were of the tribe of the Rahamna, who for the past twelve months had been in open rebellion against their liege lord the Sultan, Abdul Aziz, whom may God defend. The system in Morocco when a Sultan dies is for the tribes who think they may be strong enough, to refuse to pay all taxes, and then the Sultan is obliged to come in person with an army to discusss the matter, to fight, and if he wins send baskets full of heads to be stuck up on the chief cities' gates, and squads of prisoners like the band I saw in Mazagan to rot in prison till death relieves them

of their miserable lives. Every one of the prisoners
in the Plaza must have known that any chance of
his release was small, indeed, they knew they were
going to be half-starved, either in a dark cellar-like
prison, or in an open courtyard exposed to sun and
cold, for the Morocco Government allows no rations
to its prisoners, and those who have no friends soon
die of hunger.*   Still they were not apparently much
put about. People stood talking to them, flies settled on
their eyelids, dogs licked their sores, horses and camels
jostled against them, the sun poured on their heads,
and still they did not suffer in the way our prisoners
suffer, for they were not cut off in sentiment from
those, their brothers in Mohammed, who stood round
and talked to them to pass the time.   Pious old ladies,
young philanthropists and novelists in search of
" copy" who visit Tangier go into "visibilio," as
the Italians say, over the prisoners in the prison, with
its flat horseshoe arches at the door, so similar in
style to those at Toledo in the old synagogue, now
turned into a church.†

All those good people and each journalist, all have
their word about the darkness, chains, and the want
of air ; the misery, the crowding at the door to take
the chocolate (which should have been tobacco)
which the pious lady brings.   Each tourist sends
home his badly written paragraph to his favourite
paper, and goes away lamenting over the barbarism
of Mohammedans ; and, if he is a " glorious empire"
man, thinks of the time when, under the Union Jack,
the Moorish prisoner shall have a number and a cell,

---

* Shortly before we left Tangier, my interpreter, Mr. Lutaif, took a
man out of the prison who had been five days without food. His offence
was the possession of a good Djellaba (hooded cloak) and fifteen dollars.

† Santa Maria la Blanca.

tin pan to wash in, Bible to read, and all shall be apparelled in Queen Victoria's livery, until they purge themselves of their contempt and promise to amend their naughty lives.

One thing they all forget when writing of a Moorish prison, that, in spite of dirt, of chains, of want of air, of herding all together in a den, that they are happier than prisoners with us, for they can speak, exhale their misery in conversation; they still are men, and leave the prison men, instead of devils, hating all mankind like those who, under our inhuman silent plan, eat out their miserable " terms," cursing the fools who in their foolish kindness hit on a device to turn men into stone.* And so I leave the prisoners in the square, thinking as an old Arab says: " It looks as if the Sultan wished to finish with all the Mussulmen." At any rate, since the last Sultan's death, three years ago, thousands must have been killed in war, died by starvation, or rotted miserably to death in prisons underneath the ground.

It being a feast day of the Jews all stores were closed in Mazagan, for in Morocco all the retail business is in Jews' hands, and no religion that I know of seems to have so many days on which men may not work ; and therefore it is strange that men have not yet flocked to join their faith.

At last the steamer shakes itself free from the allurements of Mazagan and steers almost due west to clear the reef, which, jutting out about six miles, makes Mazagan the least exposed of all the open harbours on the coast. As Mazagan is distant only

* Elizabeth Fry never ceased remonstrances against the silent and solitary plan. In a communication sent to M. de Beranger, of Paris, she urges, under the 7th head, "the impossibility of fitting the prisoners for returning to society under the system."

three days from the city of Morocco it may be destined
some day to a glorious commercial future, with
railways, docks, smoke, pauperism, prostitution
in the streets, twenty-five faiths instead of one,
drunkards, cabs, bicycles and all our vices, so different in their nature from those the Arabs brought from
Arabia and have clung to in the same way they cling
to their religion, dress, speech, their alphabet, and
their peculiar mode of life.

As we steamed out, the town of Azimur was seen
under our lee, about twelve miles from Mazagan,
situated on a hill close to the river Um er R'bieh,
once an important harbour but long silted up by sand.
The harbour, once the resort of pirates, is now silted
up, and the remembrance of the pirates' deeds is still
kept fresh in people's memories by a great store of
old Delft plates, either taken by pirates in the merry
days gone by, or sent from Holland* in the times
when vessels from the Dutch ports traded along the
coast. To-day the foreign merchants buy them or
exchange them for modern china, and their inglorious
end is to hang on a wall beside the so-called artistic
"plenishings" of ladies' over-gimcracked drawing-
rooms.

As we turn southwards, after clearing the long reef,
it seems as if we had already entered another zone.
The hills along the beach become more arid, the
plains all stony or covered with low, thorny scrub.
Saffi, the hottest place on all the coast, melts past,
merely a fi m of white against the reddish background,
and in the distance the foot-hills rising to the Atlas

---

* It was from Azimur that one of the companions of Alvar Nuñez came,
in his captivity in Florida, for he says, " el quarto era negro alarabe de
Azimur, se llancaba Estebanico." The Moors call the place Mulai
Bushtir.

now appear. The largest of them Jebel Hadid, the Mount of Sion standing out like an enormous box* above the coast.

A Yemeni Jew has come on board, bound for Mogador, the city of the Jews. Short, black-eyed, greasy-locked, and with a red fez bound round with a woman's shawl, he, like St. Paul, is of a mean appearance. Still he has much to tell about Arabia, and the province from which he comes. It appears that near Sunnaar, in South Arabia, there is a land called Beni-Mousa. In this favoured spot the inhabitants are all Jews, and none of them are known to speak untruths, at least so says their representative on board the ship. This tribe, he says, is that of Shebatat. A river, which bounds their country, has so fiercè a current that rocks and stones are moved along by it, and no mere Gentile can cross the stream. Upon its banks grow two tall trees (Sandaracs, he thinks), which bend across to one another and salute by saying, "Shabat Sholom." On Saturday they do not bend over to one another, and keep no watch; therefore, on Saturday alone can Gentiles cross the wondrous river, as on that day only does the stream abate its force. All this is true, and I myself am much confirmed in my opinion of its truth, because at night this same veracious Jew produced out of a bag a bottle of spirit (majia) made from dates, and, drinking it, got most uproarious, shouting and singing, falling repeatedly upon the winch to the great delight of all the Moors, and towards midnight avowing his intention of swimming back to the Yemen so that my henchman Haj Mohammed es Swani, who had been a sailor, had to make him fast to a ringbolt in the deck. And as in

* The Cofre de Perote, in Mexico, is also box-like in appearance, as the name indicates.

Arabic without a particle, after the fashion of a child
or negro, I tried to express my astonishment at
such a line of conduct in so grave a man, to a young
Arab who stood near me, without a smile he
answered, in most perfect English, "I am not certain
if I understand all that you say, sir, but I speak
English pretty well." In outward visible appearance
he was an Arab of the usual kind, bare legs and
yellow slippers, shaved head and fez with rather
grimy turban, dirty white drawers, and brown djellaba*
with the hood of it over his head after the fashion of
a friar. It seemed he was an acrobat from the province of the Sus, from the celebrated Zomia† of Si
Hamed O' Musa, the patron saint of all the acrobats
throughout Morocco. Not far from the Wad‡ Nun
is situate the district called Taseruelt, and in that
district the famous patron saint of acrobats is buried
at the above named Zomia. From thence a large proportion of the Arab troops of acrobats, who tumble at
our music-halls, set forth.

My English speaking acrobat had terminated an
engagement at the South London Music Hall, and
was returning to resteep himself in the true faith at
home, and also, it is possible, to rest. He told me that
his ambition was to marry a European girl, and that
his choice would be a German, for he said, "German
girls mind the house and sew; English are prettier,
but will not sew, and, besides that, they are always
drinking plenty." Out of the mouths of babes and

* Djellaba is the hooded garment shaped like a sack, much worn in
Morocco, and apparently of Berber origin, as it is unknown in other Arab
countries.

† Zomia is the house and district of some Sheik or Sherif.

‡ Wad, in Morocco, means river. It is the same word as the Egyptian
Wadi, a dry valley. It appears in many Spanish names of places, as
Guadalquivir, Guadalimar, Guadarrama, etc.

heathens I think a reflection on our national femininity comes with some force. As we stand talking of the "Empire," "Pavilion," "Oxford" and other "halls," both in the provinces and the Metropolis, the island which half shelters the roadstead of Mogador came into view.

Kissed by the north-east trade which just envelopes Mogador, and about half a league of country outside the town, the city, dazzling white, lies in the sun, well meriting the name of Sueira, that is, the picture, given by the Moors. Founded in 1760, by order of the Sultan Sidi Mohammed, the plan made by an engineer from France, whose name, according to the Arabs, was Cornut, the city (supposed by some to be the ancient Erythræa) is the most regularly built and most commercial of all the empire. A little desert, varying in breadth from three to thirteen miles, cuts off the city from the fertile lands. Sand, and more sand, fine, white, and almost always altering in position, gives an idea of the Sahara made in miniature. The little river Wad el Gli Ored runs near the town, and in the middle of the water a former Sultan has built a palace founded on the sand, but though the north-east trade blows almost all the year, and when it rains the rain comes down in torrents, the palace has not fallen, and, as it never was inhabited, it remains a monument of human folly, surmounting all the powers of providence. Jews, Jews, and still more Jews possess the place; they make their Kidush, keep their Purim, New Year, Cabañas, eat adafina, broaden their business and phylacteries, are hospitable, domestic in their habits, each man revered in his own house as if he were a prophet, and all the business of the place is in their hands.

Grave, reserved Jews in gabardines, smart up-to-

date young Jews in white straw hats and European
clothes, daughters of Israel with handkerchiefs bound
round their heads and hanging down their backs, others
in Paris fashions, but all with hair like horses' tails, are
everywhere. Donah and Zorah, Renia, Estrella, Rahel,
and Zulica, with Azar, Slimo, Baruch, and Mordejai
are seen in every street; they sit in shops, lean out of
windows, lounge upon the beach, walk about slowly
as if they stepped on eggs, are kind in private life, cruel
in business; they keep up much communication
with Houndsditch, Hamburg, Amsterdam, Jerusalem,
and other centres of the " community," speaking an
Arabic garnished with English, seasoned with Spanish,
peppered with Shillah* words, and rendered as intelligible as Chinook by the thick utterance with
which they speak. An amiable race, business once
over, and charitable amongst themselves; what is
called moral, that is, their customs do not tolerate
prostitution, and husbands love their wives, children
their parents, and their home life resembles that
which writers say is to be seen in England, but which
experience generally shows is oftener found in France,
where families go out together and men are not
ashamed to play with children, and to sit drinking
coffee out of doors beside their grandmothers.

So to this New Jerusalem, after a five days' voyage,
the *Rabat* arrived, anchored inside the island where
the Sultan has a great open prison where his rebels,
amounting to about three thousand, are confined,
and daily die, both those who live and those whom
death releases. An iron steamboat, much like a

* Shillah is the Arabic name for the Southern Berbers, *i.e.* of the Atlas
and the Sahara; Shluoch, in Arabic, meaning "cast out," and Shillah the
cast-out folk. The Shillah call themselves Amazcight, *i.e.* the noble
people. This difference of opinion as to nomenclature has been observed
in other nations.

"tramp" in shape, and armed with four small guns, commanded by a German officer, displays the red flag of Morocco, identical in colour with the well-known flag which in Hyde Park has braved a thousand meetings, and around which the "comrades" flock to listen when Quelch holds forth on social wrongs, or Mr. Hyndman speaks on India, and outside the crowd the bourgeois feels a shrinking in the stomach as he smooths his hat. We bid the microcosmic craft good-bye, and go ashore stuffed in a boat with Moors and Jews, some Spaniards, two Franciscan friars, eight or ten bird-cages, and land to find the Jewish feast proceeding, the hotels all full, shops all shut, and the whole town delivered over to the mercies of Jehovah, who, caring little for a mere Christian, left us to walk the baking street four mortal hours, till just when we were going to buy a tent to sleep in, Lutaif remembered that he had a dear and valued friend who lived in Mogador. Comment upon his memory seemed injudicious, and his friend, Mr. Zerbib, a missionary, received us into his hospitable house, and we forgot our troubles and the Jews' unseasonable feast, and fell discussing with our host whether or not the thing in Europe known as progress had proved a blessing or a curse, sporadically introduced into Morocco by the waifs and strays, the tourists, traders, runaway sailors, and the others who, on the coast, act as the vanguard of the army of the light.

CHAPTER II.

ALL Mogador we found excited about the province
of the Sus, the very province in which the inaccessible Tarudant, the city of our dreams, was situated.
It seemed that about eighteen months ago, one
Abdul Kerim Bey, an Austrian subject, had arrived
and hoisted his flag as Patagonian Consul. Brazil
and Portugal, Andorra, San Marino, Gautemala,
Siberia, Hayti, and San Domingo, Siam, the Sandwich Islands, Kotei, Acheen, the Transvaal, Orange
Free State, and almost every place where there was
revenue sufficient to buy a flag and issue postage
stamps for philatelists, had long ago sent Consuls
to Mogador. Their flag-staffs reared aloft looked
like a mighty canebrake from the sea ; their banners
shaded the streets after the fashion of the covering
which the Romans drew over their amphitheatres,
and half the population were Consuls of some semi-
bankrupt state. Yet Patagonia, even in Mogador,
excited some surprise Jews who had been in
Buenos Ayres (and a considerable quantity emigrate
thence from Mogador) argued that Patagonia was
under the authority of the Argentine Republic.
Those who had been in Valparaiso said it belonged
to Chile. Few knew where Patagonia really was.
The Arabs, whose geography is fragmentary, thought
" Batagonia " was situated somewhere in Frangue-

stan, and that contented them. What struck their fancy most was certainly the colour and design of the new oriflamme. Barred white and blue, a rising sun grinning across three mountain tops, a cap of liberty, and a huanaco ruminant; an Araucanian Indian in his war paint in one corner, and here and there stars, daggers, scales, and other democratic trade-marks, made up a banner, the like of which had seldom been observed in all the much be-bannered town of Mogador. The owner of this standard and the defender in Morocco of the lives and liberties of Patagonian subjects, dressed like a Turk (long single-breasted black frock coat and fez), and spoke a little Turkish, but no Arabic. His age was that of all the world, that is, somewhere between twenty-eight and fifty, and his appearance insignificant, all but his eyes, which some declared to have the power of seeing through a brick, and others that of piercing through cloth and leather, and discerning gold from silver in the recesses of a purse. Be all that as it may, a travelled man, a doctor; that is, " tabib," for the two words, though given in dictionaries as the Arabic and English for the equivalents of the same thing in either tongue, in point of fact, are different. "Tabib," in Oriental lands, is a convenient travelling designation, as " Colonel " in the Southern States, and as "Captain" was in Georgian times; it rather indicates a status than a profession, and, in addition, is not out of place upon a traveller's card.

Dr. el Haj Abdul Kerim apparently enjoyed his designation and his " tabibship " by the grace of God. His consulate he held by virtue of a mandate of an extraordinary potentate.

Some two-and-twenty years ago, a Frenchman, one

Aureille de Lounens, a man of family and an advo-
cate of Bordeaux, succeeded in persuading the
Indians of Arauco that he was their king. This
soon aroused the anxiety both of the Chilians and
the Argentines; for from the time when first Ercilla
wrote his " Araucana," the Indians of Araucania had
been free, and if they had had a king perhaps they
would have taught the neighbouring Republics what
liberty really meant. For a brief space De Lounens
flourished under the style and title of " Orelio
Primero rey de los Araucanos," and then diplomacy
or treachery, or both, ousted him, and he died " i' the
spital" in his own town of Bordeaux. During his
efflorescence he coined money, designed a flag, gave
titles of nobility, and appointed Consuls ; and it appears that one of them was this Kerim Bey, the Turco-
Austrian, who swooped upon Mogador, out-Consuling
all Consuls hitherto known, by the size and pattern of
his flag. It is not likely that Orelio Primero ever
heard of Mogador, still less that from Arauco he sent
a special envoy to such a place. Most probably he
sent out Consuls generally, after the fashion of
bishops *in partibus*, with a roving consulship, and
with instructions to set up their flags wherever they
found three or four dozen fools assembled and a
sufficient roof to bear the pole.

One of these roving consular commissions no
doubt was given to Dr. Abdul Kerim Bey, in days
gone by, in South America. Indeed, I fancy I remember at Bahia Blanca a forlorn Austrian who was
said to have held some illusory employment about
the person of the Araucanian King, such as head
bottle-washer, holder of the royal stirrup, or guardian
of the royal purse, the last, of course, a sinecure
which, in all courts that have no money, should be

abolished in the interest of economy. Our Mr. Abdul,* during his residence in Mogador, having heard that the province of the Sus was rich in mines, and that no port open for European trade existed south of Mogador, the grandfather of the present Sultan having closed Agadhir (formerly 'known as Santa Cruz when in possession of the Spaniards), bethought himself that it would be a master stroke to make a treaty with the semi-independent chieftains of the Sus, open either Agadhir, Asaka, or some other port, and trade direct with Europe. Sus being mainly peopled by Berber tribes, who, it is said, are the descendants of the Numidians, who certainly were in possession of the country at the epoch of the invasion of the Arabs, has always been but ill-affected to the central government. The town of Tarudant and the Zomia of Si Hamed O'Musa have hitherto been the two chief centres of the Shereefian† authority, but recently, from some fancied slight or from ambitious motives, the representative of Si Hamed O'Musa, one Sidi Hascham, has wavered in his allegiance to his lord.

That which is most desired by every Arab intriguer is the possession of good rifles, and it appears that Kerim Bey, Esq., promised to help the chiefs to un-limited supplies of Winchesters. But be this as it may, Kerim appeared in London with a treaty, real or supposititious, a fez, some twenty words of Arabic, several tons of assurance, and the experience of five-and-forty years. With these commodities he got a syndicate together to engage in trade with the pro-vince of the Sus, open a harbour, divert the caravans

* Abdul Kerim means slave of the Merciful, merciful, of course, being an attribute of Allah.

† The Sultan of Morocco is called His Shereefian Majesty, as being a shereef, i.e., descended from the Prophet.

which now come from the interior and the south to
Mogador, supply the ingenious natives with rifles,
bibles, Manchester " sized" cottons, work the real or
hypothetic mines, introduce progress—that is electric
light, whisky, and all that—and give the acrobats of
Taserualt a reasonable music-hall which might spare
them the long voyage to London to seek a fitting
place in which to show their powers.

The necessary gentlemen (tribe of Manasseh) with
money being found, it was incumbent to get a man
de pelo en pecho,* as the Spaniards say, to visit
Morocco, see the Sultan, go to the Sus, and arrange
matters with the various chieftains personally. Like
all the world, Abdul Kerim had many faults, but
amongst them the fault of rashness was not numbered.
In his wildest moments he had never asserted that he
personally had penetrated in the little visited Sus ; it
was thought that if the treaty (which he exhibited,
but could not read) was genuine, that it had been
negotiated by a third person who knew the country
well.

Brave men are not so far to seek in London, and
one, Major Spilsbury, soon volunteered. He was the
kind of man able and willing to walk up to a cannon's
mouth ; the sort of man who risks his life ten times a
day for forty years to gain his livelihood, and dies—
either by an Indian arrow, Malay parang, or Arab
bullet—" one of our pioneers of empire" or else
a "foolish filibuster," according as he succeeds or
fails. Quiet and courteous, a linguist, and brave to
rashness, he was the very antithesis of Abdul; but
such as they were they started out together on their
quest.

* Pelo en pecho—hair on the chest, by inference a brave man, or man of
action.

Sus being the most southern province of Morocco,
Abdul Kerim quite naturally went to the north, and
dragged his wondering companion all round the
empire till at last they found the Sultan, who was in
Morocco city, when it turned out that all the boasted
influence Abdul Kerim had set forth he possessed was
nothing, and the Sultan refused permission to trade
direct with Sus. At Mogador the inevitable quarrel
took place, and Abdul started for Montenegro, Muscat
or elsewhere, and left poor Major Spilsbury alone.
He being determined to see the adventure through,
engaged a Jewish interpreter, went to the Canaries,
chartered a schooner and landed at Asaka after having
entered into negotiations from Mogador as to his
reception with the chiefs.

Eight or ten days he fought with contrary winds
aboard his little unseaworthy schooner, reached
Asaka, landed, was well received, made treaties with
the chiefs, and all went well until an inferior chief,
either being bribed by the Sultan or because he did
not think himself sufficiently regarded, or because of
the old antipathy to Christians, ever so strong amongst
Mohammedans, rode up at the head of fifty horsemen
and spread confusion amongst the assembled natives,
declaring that he would permit no Christian to traffic
in the land. Shots were exchanged, and Spilsbury,
bearing his treaty, as Camoens bore his poems,
had to escape on board his schooner and for the
present leave the enterprise; though, whilst I write, I
should not be surprised to learn that he was near
Asaka with a fresh expedition.* Quite naturally the

* Events proved that I was right, and almost as I was writing news came
that Major Spilsbury. in *The Tourmaline*, had tried to land at Asaka again,
and had been repulsed by the Sultan's troops, and exchanged shots with the
Moorish armed transport, *The Hassam*.
Four of his men were taken prisoners, several of the friendly Arabs were

advent of such a Consul from a new country such as
" Batagonia,"* his flag, his fez, his name, and all the
subsequent proceedings created some excitement in
such a quiet place as Mogador. Consuls assembled,
took counsel, wrote dispatches, charged for stamps, and
generally fulfilled the functions of their office. Long-
bearded Jews, whose talk up to that time had never
strayed from money, now discussed questions of diplomacy, of international law, discoursed on piracy, of
filibustering, wondered if business would have been
improved if Spilsbury had got a footing, but thought
no affair sublunary could be quite rotten if Daniel
Sassoon† had had a finger in the pie.

The Arabs generally were puzzled, but pleased to
think there seemed a chance of good repeating rifles
being in the market ; but all the European residents
saw clearly the hand of all-encroaching England, and
in especial the French were certain that Mr. Curzon
had given his sanction to a plot to extend the dominion
of the empire over Sus.

All things considered, it was a most inauspicious
time to attempt a journey to such a place as Tarudant,
guarded most jealously itself from Europeans both by
the fanaticism of the inhabitants and by the special
prohibition of the Moorish Government to any European to pass south of the Atlas Mountains to the

killed, and many others, including the Sheikh Neharek-on-Ahmed, were
sent in chains to linger in the prisons of Fez and Mequinez ; Major
Spilsbury was detained some time at Gibraltar, and the whole result of the
expedition was that the reputation of England was much damaged in
Morocco, and the country rendered still more difficult of access than before.
I do not hear that those who fitted out the expedition have suffered in any
way except by loss of money, but that is, probably the only kind of loss
they could ever feel.

   * There being no P in Arabic, the Arabs use B precisely as if they were
inhabitants of " Botzen und Bosen."

   † Mr. Sassoon was reported to be interested in the venture.

plains. Hardly well landed in the town, when a report was spread that we were agents of the British Government, or advance couriers in the interest of the syndicate. Our sojourn at the house of so well-known a missionary as Mr. Zerbib in some way allayed the public fear, for no one credited him with any but purely spiritual views of conquest. The fact that we had no arms, suggested our great cunning, for no one doubted that we could lay our hand on stacks of rifles if we chose, though how we could have done so was a mystery, as all the influence of our minister at Tangier proved insufficient to procure me even a pass for a common double-barrelled gun, so much alarmed were the authorities after the recent landing on the coast. No one, except the Turks, more clearly comprehend that only the jealousy of the European nations saves their independence than do the ruling classes of Morocco. They understand entirely the protestations about better government, progress, morality and all the usual "boniment" which Christian powers address to weaker nations when they contemplate the annexation of their territory. On the one hand they see the missionary striving to undermine their faith, and on the other they behold the whisky seller actually sapping their Mohammedan morality; behind them both they see the ironclad arriving in their harbours under frivolous pretences to exact enormous compensation often for fancied injuries, and they well know the official Christian's God is money, or as they say themselves, "amongst the Nazarenes all is money, nothing but money."* The Moors have vices, plenty of them, some of them well-known in London and in Paris, but in their country a poor Mohammedan, unless in case of famine, is seldom left to starve. Even

* "El N'zrani Malshi flus" is a common saying in Morocco.

a begging Christian renegade, of whom there are a
few still left, always receives some food where'er he
goes, and is not much more miserable than the poor
Eastern whom one sees shivering about the docks in
London and imploring charity for " Native Klistian "
with an adopted whine, and muttered national imprecation on the unsuspecting almsgiver.

The Moors all know when once a European gets a
footing in their land, even although that should be
brought about by filibustering syndicates financed by
London capitalists, that the nation to whom the filibusters belong steps in to guard its subjects, and
having once stepped in, remains for ever. They see
Ceuta, Alhucemas, Peñon de la Gomera and Chafari-
ñas all in foreign hands, and like the fact as much as
we should like the Russians in the Isle of Wight.
Therefore, their irritation about the Sus was most
intense, and the jealousy of foreign travellers never
keener.

Much has been said about the badness of the Government of Morocco. Most Governments are bad, the
best a disagreeable institution which men submit to
only because they fear to plunge into the unknown,
and therefore bear taxation, armies, navies, gold-laced
caps, and all the tawdry rubbish which takes from
themselves to furnish living and employment for their
neighbours, under the style and title of national
defences, home administration, and the like.

In countries like Morocco, where men still live
under the tribal system, all government must be des-
potic ; witness Algeria, Afghanistan, and Russian
Tartary. The unit is the tribe and not the individual,
and what we understand by freedom and democracy
would seem to them the grossest form of tyranny on
earth. No doubt no' man in all Morocco is secure in

the enjoyment of his property; but then in order to be amenable to tyranny one must be rich, and as most tribesmen own a horse or two, a camel, perhaps a slave, some little patch of cultivated ground or olive garden, it is not generally on them the extortion of the Government descends, but on the chief Sh-ikh, Kaid, or Governor, who, if he happens to be rich, can never sleep secure a single day, for he knows well some time he will be brought to Fez or to Morocco, thrust in a dungeon underground, and made to give up all he has on earth. True, whilst this very man enjoys his wealth and place he oppresses all the tribe to the utmost of his power; but still I fancy that hardly a Moor alive would change the desultory Eastern tyranny, which he has suffered under all his life, and under which his fathers groaned since the beginning of the world, for the six monthly visit of the tax collector as in Algeria. When people in Morocco speak of Algeria they admit the safety of the roads, the gathered harvests, no hostile intervention coming between the sickle and the wheat; they admire the railroads, laugh at the figure which the French soldiers cut on their horses, but generally finish by saying, "the Arab pays for all, and in that land they tax your dog, your horses, and you yourself, and all are slaves."

Most Europeans point with pride to the curious system known as "protection," and called by the Arabs "Mohalata," which for at least a hundred years has existed in Morocco, as something to be proud of. The system needs a few words, as generally writers on Morocco, without a word of explanation, talk of the custom and state it is a good one, in the same way that free and fair traders each assume their nostrum is the best, or as professors of the Christian or Mohammedan religions look on their dogmas as being alone fitted for honest men to hold. Briefly, the system of the "Mohalata" was invented to obviate the difficulties of trading in a country so badly governed as is Morocco. The word in Arabic means partnership, but the system has been complicated by the habit of protection by means of which the European partner generally contrives to get his Moorish partner made a citizen of the country to which he himself belongs. Thus, "Mohalata" and "Protection" have come to be so mixed together, that it is rare to find a Moor in partnership with any European and not protected by a European Consul. Once protected, the Moor ranks as a Montenegrin, Paraguayan, Englishman, Frenchman, or Portuguese, or what not, and is removed from the exactions of his own Caid (governor), and even is placed outside the jurisdiction of his own Sultan.

So far, so good, for no one can pretend the Sultan's government is good, and under shadow of the protec· tion system many individual Moors have become rich. But in their efforts to escape from their own rule, the wretched Moors often fly from the claws of Moorish tribal feudalism, and fall into the mouth of European commercialism, unrestrained by public opinion, the press, or any of the preventive checks which keep the "cash nexus" system within some sort of bounds in England. The following anecdote may serve to illus- trate how the protection system occasionally works out. Mohammed ——* ten years ago was partner of a European merchant in Mogador. The European (a God-fearing man) purchased three camels on con- dition that Mohammed —— should act as camel-

---

* I will be glad to give names in full to anyone who will take up the poor devil's case.

driver, and take the beasts about the country where-ever it was profitable to take goods. A camel in Mogador may be worth some thirty dollars. For this business Mohammed was to receive a certain portion of the profits made. For several years all went well; Mohammed made his journeys, took his merchandise about, and got his portion of the gains, feeding the camels at his own expense.

One day the Christian (in Morocco all Europeans pass colloquially as Christians) said to Mohammed, " I intend to leave the place and to return to Europe. My intention is to sell the camels, and we can then divide the profits of the sale according to our deed." The Arab answered he was willing, and began to cypher up the sum the beasts should bring when sold.

The Christian then informed him that he had a scheme by which he thought that they might each gain much, and if it prospered, that Mahommed could keep the camels for his pains. Mohammed, nothing loath, sat all attention to hear the expected plan by means of which he was to keep his beasts. "You shall take the camels," said the Christian, "and load them for a journey to the Sus. At some point of the journey thieves shall attack you, and you shall then throw all the merchandise upon the ground, then return home at once, and swear before the Cadi that I entrusted you with two thousand dollars and it is stolen, and I will force the Government to compel the Sheikh of the tribe where the robbery was done, to make all good, and we will share the money, and you can keep the camels for your own." A scheme of this kind always attracts an Arab; it is just the sort of thing he would invent himself. And when his own ideas are returned to

him, passed through the medium of a Christian mind,
he is certain that the thing must be all right.
Curiously enough, although the Moors are never tired
of cursing at the Christian sons of dogs, yet they
are well aware of their superior business capabilities,
and never seem to doubt their word in matters of the
sort. " But," said Mohammed, " if I tell the Cadi that
I had your money and that thieves took it, he will
throw me into prison, and there is little chance I
ever shall come out alive." " Have no fear," said the
merchant, " the imprisonment will be a mere formality.
I will feed you when you are in prison, and in a few
days you will be free."

The camels were duly loaded, and Mohammed set
out upon his journey to the Sus. In a few days he
returned, having torn his clothes, rolled himself in
the sand, and with some self-inflicted bruises, informed his friend the merchant, who took him to the
Cadi to testify on oath.

Most unluckily for the miserable man the place he
chose to pitch upon for the scene of his adventure
was a few miles outside the town, in a district called
Taquaydirt. The Cadi sent for the headman, who
came and swore that he had never seen Mohammed,
and he himself failed to identify any of the natives
of the place, who were presented to him. Seeing
the thing looked grave, he went and took sanctuary in the tomb of Sid M'Doul,* the patron
saint of Mogador, about a mile outside the town.
Inside the sanctuary the man was safe, and every
day his European friend sent him his food, his

* Sid M'Doul is said to have been a Scotch sailor who became a Moor
and after his death, a saint. Be this as it may, from the saint's name
Europeans have made the name Mogador, which is never used by the
Moors, who call the town Sueira, the picture.

" Tajin,"* " Couscousou,"† flat Moorish bread, and green tea (called Windrisi from Windres, that is London, from whence it comes), seasoned with mint and sweetened with enormous lumps of sugar broken with a hammer from the loaf. A week passed by, and every day his wife and children came and talked to him, standing outside the shrine, and much elated at the kindness of their European friend, and of the affluence which, in a day or two, was to burst on them through his influence.

But all their feasting did not suit the European's book, and he contrived to get Mohammed out of the sanctuary, upon the pretext that it was necessary to swear again to the affair before the judge. The swearing and examination over, the Cadi (at the Christian's instigation) threw the poor devil into prison, and then for a few days the Christian sent him his food, as he had done before when in the sanctuary. After a day or two he feigned to think Mohammed had deceived him as to the robbery, and had really taken the two thousand dollars for himself. The supply of food then ceased, and the Christian raised a plea against the Arab for restitution of his money, or, failing that, the seizure of his goods.

The wretched man, seeing himself deceived, confessed the plot, but as he (this time) spoke the truth, no one believed him. The lawsuit ran its course, and the Arab's wife sold off his horse and gun (the most cherished property an Arab has), sold off his camels, their cows, their goats, and sheep, and raised six hundred dollars after selling everything she had.

* Tajin literally means " the dish." It is generally a greasy stew of mutton, soaked with rancid butter and saffron, and seasoned with asafœtida.

† Couscousou is a kind of dry porridge made of grated wheat, stewed, and served up with mutton or chicken, and pieces of boiled pumpkin.

His children begged, the wife worked as she could, the husband, heavily chained in prison, starved.

Five long years passed away, the wife feeding her husband as she could, the children running about like pariah dogs, maintained by charity. Then the good Christian merchant died, and his heirs, of course, still pressed for payment of the debt.

Four more long years went by, and then a thing occurred which makes one think the proverb " that to jump behind a bush is better than the prayers of a good man." * Within the prison were five hundred men, Mohammed one of them ; a mutiny broke out, the guard was overpowered, and a few dozen men got out. Then came Mohammed's turn, and he, thinking that his good deed might win his freedom, seized the key and locked the door, keeping the rest within. News went unto our lord the Sultan in his camp, and people hoped that he might exercise his clemency. Back came a letter praising Mohammed's deed, and saying he deserved his liberty, but that the Sultan could not grant it till the debt was paid.

Ten years have passed away, the merchant is long dead, six hundred dollars paid for nothing, a family reduced to misery, and still the victim of the plot remains in prison, heavily chained and prematurely old; Allah looks down, the call to prayers rises to heaven five times a day, and poor Mohammed, a grey-headed man, resigned and uncomplaining, talks to the casual stranger at the prison gate and says the Christian was no doubt a knave, but that the thing was written (mektub), and that therefore no one was to blame, Allah Ackbar, no God but God, and Lord Mohammed is his messenger.

* " Mas vale salto de mata que ruegos de buenos," goes the adage in Spanish, and it is one that most sensible men will endorse.

The protection system may benefit the Jews, who, once despised and spit upon by every Moor, have of late years become the tyrants of the land. Scarcely a Jew of any property in any Mellah,* in Morocco, who is not a citizen of some foreign state. Perhaps America has made the most use of its protective powers. Both the United States and the Brazils have frequently named Consuls who were quite unworthy of representing either state. These men, in several instances, have sold protection right and left, and nothing is more common than to meet a Moor or a Jew in one or other of the seaport towns, who tells you that he is a Brazilian or an American. To-day the United States seem to have seen the error of their ways, and several of their Consuls are of high character, and fitted to do honour to the post they occupy.

Until quite recently, at times a Consul would "sell a Moor," that is would tell his luckless "citizen" that unless by such a time a sum of money was forthcoming, his protection would be withdrawn. The effect of this would be as a sentence of death to the unlucky man. Generally the protected citizens amass some money, and if the protection is withdrawn, their Caid or Governor falls down upon them, puts them in prison, where they either die or else remain till, as the prisoner in the Gospel, they have paid the uttermost farthing they possess. As to reclamations, how can a Moor, speaking no foreign language, go to Andorra, Montenegro, or San Marino, to appeal. Pay and appeal,† the proverb says ; but fancy an Arabic-speaking man, without a cent, appealing in New York,

* Mellah is the word used to designate a Jewry in Morocco. Literally it means Salt, and I have never heard any explanation of the term, but the salt has not lost its savour, as any traveller not suffering from rhinitis can testify.

† Pagar y apelar.

or in Brazil, in neither of which countries men of dark races are viewed with favour, and justice is a costly pastime even for the rich.

No doubt some few have become rich under protection. Witness the case of Si Bu Bekr, who for so long a time was British Agent, and who, when a few months ago he showed me all his treasures in his palace in Morocco City, tapped on his iron chest, and said, "This one is gold, that is all jewels; this, again, is full of bonds;" and is assumed to have a hundred thousand pounds all safely tied up in Consols.

But, on the other hand, sometimes the partnership and protection is as a shirt of Nessus, and I have heard an Arab say, "Can I not get away from this cursed ' Mohalata?'" rather the exactions of my Caid than the insidious bleeding by my Christian partner. Still it must be confessed that both protection and "Mohalata" are much sought after by the natives, and nothing is commoner than to be asked, whilst on a journey, either to protect or enter into "Mohalata" with a Moor. As in the case of the kindred system which prevails in Turkey, of "capitulation," much abuse creeps in, and as the country is not ripe for mixed tribunals I suppose the chicken will have to live and bear its pip.*

Peacemakers and reformers pass a thankless life, and it appears as almost every ill we see is irremediable, and as the world goes on quite cheerfully (no matter what we do), crushing the weak, and opening wide upon the passage of the strong, that curses are no use; the only course the wise man can adopt is to stand well away and keep his own opinions to himself, unless, indeed, after the fashion of the man in Joseph

* " Viva la gallina con su pepita."

Conrad's story,* he prefers to hang himself, and then put out his tongue at the world's managing directors.

Finding myself the observed of all observers in Mogador, I transferred my residence to Mr. Pepe Ratto's International Sanatorium, about three miles outside the town, which passes generally under the designation of the Palm-Tree House. There I essayed to live my filibustering character down, and for a day or two went sedulously out shooting in the hottest time of day, to show I was a European traveller; collected "specimens," as butterflies and useless stones; took photographs, all of which turned out badly; classified flowers according to a system of my own; took lessons in Arabic, and learned to ride upon the Moorish saddle. A few days of this exhilarating life made all things quiet, and the good citizens of Mogador were certain that I was a *bona-fide* traveller and had no design to attack the province of the Sus.

The International Sanatorium de la Palmera was a sort of hotel of the next century. Everything in it was "*en construction.*" The Managers, two little Marseillais, of the bull-dog type, spent almost all their time either in practising *la boxe Marseillaise*, in playing on the concertina, an instrument which, when I am in Europe (dans les pays policés,) I fancy absolete, but which, in days gone by, set my teeth often aching in the River Plate and in Brazil. After so many years when first again I heard its wheezy tones, upon a moonlight night in the Palmera, with camels resting under the great palm tree, and Arabs lying asleep, their faces covered in their haiks, horses and mules champing their corn, hyenas growling in the

* "Outpost of Progress," Cosmopolis, June, 1897. Story of an outpost of Progress told without heroics and without spread-eagleism, and true to life; therefore unpopular, if indeed, like most other artistic things it has not passed like a " sheep in the night."

distance, jackals yelping, and the frogs croaking like
silver cymbals, as they never croak to the north of
latitude forty, it set me wondering why men must
go about on a calm, clear night grinding an instrument to make their unoffending fellows' stomachs
ache. Besides the concertina and "la boxe" (Mar-
sellaise), the brothers, curly-headed and pleasant
little sons of La Joliette or La Cannebière, devoutly
entered everything into a ledger, large enough for
Lombard Street, by double entry; and besides that
had an infinity of talents *de société*, kept chameleons,
understood botany, were cooks and linguists, speaking
most languages including "petit nègre" quite fluently,
were civil, educated, ignorant, and thoroughly good
fellows to the full length of their respective five feet
four and five feet seven inches.

The hotel was on a hill and had a view over a sand
hill, on which grew oceans of white broom, dwarf
rhododendrons, gum cistus, thyme (which in Morocco
is a bush), and mignonette, and in whose thickets
wild boars harboured and from which sand grouse
flew whirring out. The owner of the place, a mighty
sportsman, having slain more boars, and had more
adventures in the slaying than any one, since Sir
John Drummond Hay laid down his spear. Born
in Mogador, of English or Gibraltarian parents, and
speaking Spanish, English, Arabic, and Shillah quite
without prejudice of one another, Mr. Ratto, known
to his friends as "Pepe," fills, in South Morocco, the
place that Bibi Carleton fills in the north. No book
upon Morocco is complete without a reference to both
of them. How the thing comes about I do not know,
but not unfrequently the sons of Europeans born in
hot countries turn out failures, either in person or in
mind, or both, but when the contrary occurs and the

transplanting turns out well, the type is finer than is common in the mother country. Both of my types would, walking in a crowd in any town of Europe, attract attention. Tall, dark, brown-eyed, erect and lithe, clear brown complexions, open-handed and quick of apprehension, good horsemen, linguists, and yet perhaps not fitted to excel in England or in France, or any country where continuous work is necessary, they have had the sense to stay at home, and become as it were "Gauchos," that is a sort of intermediate link between the Arab and the European, and at the same time to incorporate most of the virtues of the two races. Put them in Western Texas, Buenos Ayres, or South Africa, and they must have made fortunes; as it is both are as rich as kings when mounted on a good horse, a rifle in their hands, and a long road to travel for no special cause.

Not far away begins, sporadically, the district of the Argan Tree,* in fact, outside the door of the Palmera stands a small specimen, the roots almost uncovered and bent towards the east by the prevailing wind.

Not far away, still lives a patriarch of this restricted family, flat topped and gnarled and like a Baobab its branches taking root all round the stem, and running on the ground for fully fifty feet, goats climbing on its limbs, snails clinging to the leaves, pieces

---

* The Argan Tree, the Elœodendron Argan of some and the Argania Sideroxylon of other commentators, for botanists like doctors often disagree, seems to belong to the family of the Sapotaceæ. Its habitat is very limited, being apparently confined to the sandy district between Mogador and Saffi, in which it forms a dense wood stretching for forty miles. In habit it resembles an Acacia, being thorny, twisted in trunk and limbs, and able to survive the longest droughts without apparent suffering. It produces a nut about the size of an olive, from which an oil is extracted and used in cooking by the Moors. It is unpalatable to those Europeans who have never eaten a Turkey Buzzard.

of rag tied to the boughs by passing Arabs, reminding one of the Gualichu* tree in the South Pampa of Buenos Ayres.   After long years of life it seems to rest, putting forth leaves and shoots, and bearing fruit, as if it were by habit, and as a protest against the decay which has overtaken all its fellows.   The passing Arab, though he may break a branch to light his fire, still reverences it in a vague way, never forgetting as he passes to praise God for it, as if Allah had set it there to tell him of his power.

The choice of guides became a difficulty.   Few men in Mogador cared to attempt a journey to Tarudant in company with a European, even though disguised.   Arabs who knew the way were terrified at venturing alone into the territory of Berbers, and Arabs feared to be found out upon the road and put in prison by the Sultan's governors.

All were agreed the journey was hazardous, although to what extent they were not sure.   Sometimes in travelling in Arab countries it is possible to take a guide into a certain part, and then to get some tribesmen to accompany you.   In our case this was impossible, as I could not speak Arabic sufficiently to pass off as a native of the place.   Even to say I was a Georgian, a Circassian, or Bosnian, for any of which I might have passed as far as type goes, would have aroused suspicion, for why should an inhabitant of such a country journey to Tarudant?

---

* Gualichu is the god (or devil), of the Pampa Indians.   At any rate, he is the spirit they propitiate by tying rags, cigars, pieces of hide, tin cups— or anything they may have useless enough to be offered to a deity—to its branches.   The tree which I take to be a Chañar or Gurliaca Decorticans, though others, perhaps wiser than myself, say it is a Tala, stands on a little eminence, and is the only tree for leagues.   Darwin remarked and camped close by it, and it is known all over the South Pampa from Tandil to Patagones.

Although the place I wished to visit is tabooed for Europeans, still Arabs, like other men, delight in doing what they know they should not do, with the full consciousness of doing wrong.

To the illiterate Moor or Arab nothing seems so wrong as to eat bacon, pork, or touch a pig, and yet at times they say " I ate some pork the other day, it was magnificent," after the fashion that boys smoke at schools, pretend to like it, and are sick behind a hedge. An Arab says no wonder Christians are so red in the face and look so well, do they not feed on pork and drink strong wine ? It seems to be implanted in the human mind that anything a man is bidden not to do, must, of necessity, be the one thing that if he did it, would make him happy all his life.   If this be so, and clergymen (all of the highest moral standing) have assured me that is the case, surely the general concensus of the opinion of mankind is towards doing everything they like, and if that is the case it must be right, for anything which can secure a majority of votes is sent from heaven, for God himself is quite uncertain of the justice of his acts till men have voted on them.

Still, guides for such a journey did not abound. One was too old, a second too religious to go with Christians, or a third too big a rogue even to go with Christians ; till at the last a man, Mohammed el Hosein, came forward of his own accord.

Report averred he was a slave-dealer, but the best muleteer in the country. In person he was thin and muscular, age thirty-eight, just married, a first-rate horseman, cunning and greedy, but to be depended on if once he gave his word. All his delight, as he himself imformed me, was to drink green tea and smoke tobacco, and, therefore, like the old Scotch lady, who, when a cook was recommended to her for her good moral character, exclaimed, " Oh, damn her morals, can she mak guid broth ?", I did not boggle at his slave - dealing, but took him on the spot. Strangely enough he had been employed by missionaries, who spoke well of his capacity touching his muleteership, but lamented over the hardness of his heart. By nationality he was a Berber, with the flat face, small eyes, and high cheekbones of all his race. He sang in Shillah, in a falsetto voice, a quavering air, both in and out of season, and seated on a mule, a packing needle in his hand to act as spur, got over more mortal leagues of country in a day than any other mule driver whom I remember this side of Mexico.

After the muleteer, came choice of roads, for three were open to us ; the first along the coast passing the town of Agadir.* This road is flat and sandy, and follows close to the coast right down to Agadir, and by it Tarudant can easily be reached within five days from Mogador. The disadvantages of following this road were three; firstly, we had to pass the town of Agadir, in which the Sultan had a governor; and secondly, Agadir once passed, we had to traverse the country of the Howara tribe, which bears an evil name for turbulence. Journeying, as I proposed to do, in Moorish dress, two difficulties lay in my path.

---

* Agadir Ighir (Ighir means a fort in Shillah) was once held by the Spaniards, and called Santa Cruz. It is situated on a slight eminence near Cape Gher, has a tolerable port and is the natural outlet for the trade of the Sus, but it is closed to trade by order of the Sultan, and the merchants in Mogador do all they can to keep it closed, as they themselves depend much on trade with the same province. In the last century Agadir had a flourishing trade with Europe, but the closing of the port killed the place, and there are now not above a thousand inhabitants. Amongst these there are a good many Jews, and it is reported that amongst these Jewish families there are to be found the handsomest women in Morocco. One regrets that there is no trade with Europe, on account of these daughters of Israel.

Firstly, I might be recognised, and if so recognised by an official of the central government I should have been turned back at once, as has already happened to other travellers in South Morocco. Again, dressed as a Moor and not discovered, I had to run all the risks a Moor must run in travelling, from robbers and from violence. These risks do not beset a European travelling in European dress to the same degree, as Moors in general are chary of meddling with Europeans. It may be asked, why then did I adopt the Moorish dress, and not go boldly as a European after having got a permit from the Sultan, and taken a guard of Moorish soldiers.

These were my reasons: the Sultan of Morocco, when he gives a European a permit to travel in his territory always writes on it, after the usual salutations to his various governors, " we recommend this Christian* to you, see that he runs no danger." The Moor, reading between the lines, sees that the Sultan wishes him to stop the Christian visiting any unfrequented place, and naturally he puts a lion in the path. Thus, had I gone to Agadir furnished with guard and Sultan's letter, the governor would have received the letter, kissed it, duly placed it on his forehead, called to his scribe to read it, made me welcome, and informed me that it was quite impossible for me to go farther, as certain bastards,† who feared neither God nor Sultan, would be sure to kill me on the road. I should have told him : " well, my death be on my own head," and he would straight have answered, " be it so in God's name, if it were only yours, but who will shelter me from the anger of

---

* Rumi. Roman, is the polite word for a Christian. N'zrani or Nazarene is half-contemptuous.

† Oulad el Haram.

our Lord the Sultan if you are killed?" Persuasion,
bribes, and everything would have been in vain, and
had I then insisted, I should have found myself
politely escorted back by a guard of cavalry, as all
the Sultan's governors are well aware that their liege
lord admits of no mistakes, but punishes mistakes and
faults alike.

Just as I had determined to risk the journey by the
way of Agadir, news came that the Howara tribe
was in rebellion, and that the road was shut.   There
still remained two mountain passes through the Atlas,
one starting from a place called Imintanout, and
going by Bibouan to Tarudant, and still another from
Amsmiz, a town close to Morocco city, which crossed
the Atlas at its greatest breadth and led to Tarudant,
across the River Sus at a place called Ras el Wad, a
whole day's journey from Tarud nt.   Needless to say
both roads were longer and much more difficult than
the coast route, and by either of them I should have
employed at least eight days to reach my destination.

Choosing the shortest road I then determined to
go by Imintanout, and set about at once to make my
preparations for a start.

Mohammed el Hosein brought his own mule, and
with it another belonging to one Ali of the Ha-Ha*
tribe, that is to say Mohammed hired a mule from Ali
who accompanied us (as I learned upon the road) to
see his animal was not ill-treated.   Ali I suspect
received no pay, but was a sort of general *homme de
peine*, and quite contented so that he received his food
and that his mule was fed, and even thought himself
quite fortunate when he received a pair of cast-off
shoes.   He had no idea where we were going to, and

* Ha-Ha is the name of the province in which Mogador is situated; it is
also the name of the tribe.

when we told him, wished to return, and would have done so had we not laid hands upon his mule, which seeing, he resolved to brave all dangers rather than trust it to the tender mercies of Mohammed el Hosein. For the rest Ali was a muleteer, which race of men, whether Spaniards, Mexicans, Turks, or Brazilians is all alike, singing all day while sitting sideways on their beasts, smoking continually, eating when there is food, and sleeping quite contentedly (as the unjust all sleep), their heads resting upon a pack saddle, feet to the fire, and with a tattered blanket covering their faces from the dew at night. Lutaif, following his character of a man of letters, rode on a mule, perched on a high red pack saddle, which, loosely girthed, after the Moorish fashion, swayed about and made it quite impossible to mount or to dismount without assistance. By this time we had bought our Moorish clothes, in which Lutaif, being a Syrian, looked exactly like one of the figures on the outside of a missionary journal, which assume to represent biblical characters, and really are a libel on the Syrian race. Having arranged to represent a Turkish doctor, I put on the clothes with some mis-givings, and left my room in the Palmera with the air of one who has assumed a fancy dress. On my appearance all declared that I need never say I was a Turkish doctor, for I looked so like a man from Fez, in type and colouring, that it was better to say nothing as to who I was, and that the passers-by would take me for a travelling Sherif. A Sherif being a holy character, generally rides upon a horse, and so I purchased one through the good offices of Mohammed el Hosein, who happened to know of " the best horse in all the province which his owner wanted to dispose of—with saddle and bridle all complete—for a mere

nothing, being short of cash." I purchased the whole
" outfit" at nine-and-twenty dollars, a third more
than a native would have paid. The saddle was
rotten, and felt like riding on a bag of stones, but
the horse, though lean in condition, was full of quite
unsuspected spirit, sure-footed, and excellent upon
the road. And thus equipped with horse, high
Moorish saddle covered with red cloth, dressed all
in white with a blue cloth cloak to cover all, a fez
and turban, head duly shaved, and yellow slippers,
with, of course, a pair of horseman's boots (called
temag by the Arabs) buttoned up the back with green
silk buttons, embroidered down the side with silk
and silver thread, a leather bag to sling across the
shoulders and act as pocket, I was ready for the start.

Tents and the general camp equipment of a European journeying in Morocco, did not trouble me. We
had a little tent packed on a mule, just large enough
to serve as sleeping quarters for myself and for
Lutaif. The men had to sleep by their mules after
the Moorish fashion, and if it rained to come for
shelter under the lea side of our tent. Cooking
utensils were but a kettle and an iron pot, no forks,
no spoons, as being dressed as Moors we had to eat
after the Moorish fashion with our hands, our only
luxury being a rather gim-crack brass tea tray, a
pewter German teapot, and six small glasses to drink
green tea flavoured with mint, and made as sweet as
syrup. In my anxiety to be quite the native, I even
left my camera, an omission which I regret, as had I
taken it I might have published a book of views
of the Atlas, and saved much trouble to the public
and myself.

A European who came to see us off looked at our
modest equipage with some disgust, and said that

he had never seen a Christian start like a Susi
trader, and that we should soon repent the want of
European comforts. Your European comfort when
in Europe is in place, but on the march in a wild
country everything additional you take is as the
grasshopper in the adage, which I think soon made
its presence felt. It is customary for fools and serious
men, when setting out on any journey (say to
Margate), finishing books, entering into the more or
less holy state of matrimony, becoming bankrupt
or entering holy orders, going to sea, meeting their
first love, burying their most disagreeable relation, or
being jilted, thrown from a bicycle, or being kicked
or knighted, in fact in any of the disagreeables, which
like rain fall on the just and the unjust, but always
show a preference for the poor honest man, to sit
down and record exactly how they felt, what thoughts
occurred to them, and generally to disport themselves
as if another mortal in the world cared they were even
born, except their mother and themselves.

Time-honoured institution, from which no scribbling
traveller should depart. If you have nought to say,
why write it down, extend it, examine into it, and
write and write till after writing you persuade yourself you have written something; and if upon the
other hand you happen to have aught worth writing,
keep it to yourself, and go to bed remembering that
to-morrow is another day, that thoughts will keep
and mules are ever better saddled about an hour
before the sky on the horizon begins to lighten, and
the first faint flush of dawn spreads slowly like a
diurnal Aurora Borealis and drives the morning star
back to its night; for then, as mules are cold and
empty, they cannot swell their stomachs out so much,
and stop the muleteers from drawing home the girths.

CHAPTER III.

LEAVING the International Sanatorium of the Palmera at the hour that Allah willed it, which happened to be about eight in the morning of the 12th October, dressed in Moorish clothes, our faces far too white, and our ample robes like driven snow, the low thick scrub of Argan, dwarf rhododendrons, and thorny sandarac, and " suddra "* bushes after five minutes' riding swallowed us up, quite as effectually as might have done a forest of tall trees. Mohammed el Hosein, fully aware of the importance of getting accustomed to the Moorish clothes before at once emerging on the beaten track which leads from Mogador to Morocco City, engaged us in a labyrinth of cattle tracks, winding in and out for full two hours through stones and bushes, following the beds of water courses, dry with the twelve months' drought, which had caused almost a state of famine, and calling to us to hold ourselves more seemly, not to let our " selhams "† hang too low, not to talk English, and when dismounted to walk as befits Arab gentlemen, to whom time is a drug.

* Suddra is the Zizyphus Lotus of botanists. It is extremely thorny, and is much used by the Arabs to make the enclosures known as " Zerebas " round their houses; when dry it takes a curious grey-blue tinge, very effective in certain lights. It is of this plant, I think, that the Soudanese make the temporary " Zerebas " round their camps, which on occasions have given so much trouble to our troops.

† Selham is the hooded cloak worn as an outer garment; it is made of blue cloth or white wool. It is the " burnouse " of Algeria.

After much threading through the tortuous paths, getting well torn and sunburned by the fierce sun, we emerged at the crossing of the river El Ghoreb, which runs into the sea at Mogador.

Here we encountered the usual stream of travellers always to be met with at the crossing of a river in countries like Morocco; grave men on mules going to do nothing gravely, as if the business of the world depended on their doing it with due precision. Long trains of mules laden with cotton goods going up to the capital; a travelling Arab family, the father on his horse, his gun cased in a red cloth case, balanced across the pommel of his saddle; his wife, either on foot or seated on a donkey following him, the children trotting behind, a ragged boy or two drawing a few brown goats, a scraggy camel packed with the household goods on one side, and on the other with a pannier from which a foal sticks out its head; and, lastly, two or three grown-up girls, who, as we came upon them crossing the stream, lift up their single garment and veil their mouths according to the laws of Arab decency. We sit and eat under a tree as far away as possible from all the passers-by, and our clean clothes and look of most intense respectability, secure us from all danger of intrusion on our privacy.

No sooner seated than Swani seized my legs and pulled them violently, and rubbed the knee-joints after the fashion of a shampooer in a Turkish bath. On my enquiry he assured me he knew I must be suffering agony from the short Moorish stirrups and cramped seat. I had indeed felt for the past half-hour as if upon the rack; but a horseman's pride and acquaintanceship with many forms of saddles had kept me silent. The rubbing and pulling afforded intense relief, and I acknowledged what I had endured, on his assurance that no one escapes the pain, and that the most experienced riders in the land are sometimes kept awake all night, after a long day's march, owing to the stiffness of their legs.

In mediæval Spain, good riders were often designated as " Ginete en ambas sillas,"* that is accustomed to either saddle, *i.e.*, the Moorish and the Christian, and I now understood why chroniclers have ta en the trouble to record the fact. Strangely enou h the high-peaked and short-stirruped saddle does not cross the Nile, the Arabs of Arabia riding rather flat saddles with an ordinary length of leg. The Arab saddle of Morocco, in itself, is perhaps the worst that man has yet designed, but curiously enough from it was made the Mexican saddle, perhaps the most useful for all kinds of horses and of countries that the world has seen.

The Moors girth loosely and keep their saddle in its place by a broad breast plate ; so that it becomes extremely difficult to mount, and to do so gracefully, you have to seize the cantle and the pommel at the same time, and get as gingerly into your seat as possible. Like all natural horsemen, the Moors mount straight, and bend their knees in mounting ; thus, in their loose clothes, they appear to sink into the saddle without an effort. Once in the saddle a man of any pretension to respectability has his clothes arranged for him by a retainer, as being so voluminous, it is quite an art to make them sit.

Swathed in the various cloaks and wrappings which constitute the Arab dress, the feet driven well

* This phrase often occurs in Spanish chronicles, after a long description of a man's virtues, his charity, love of the church, and kindness to the poor, and it is apparently inserted as at least as important a statement as any of the others. In point of fact, chronicles being written for posterity, it is the most important.

home into the stirrups, and gripping your horse's sides with all the leg, the seat is firm, though most uncomfortable at first. After a little it becomes more tolerable, but few men can walk a step without enduring agony when they dismount after three or four hours on horseback, especially as it is a superstition amongst the Moors to mount and dismount as seldom as the can, for they imagine the act of getting on and o﹍ fatigues the horse far more than the mere carrying the burden on his back. Of course, both getting on and off are done in the name of God, that is after the repetition of the sacramental word Bismillah, used on eating, drinking, riding or performing any action for which a true believer should give thanks to Him who giveth benefits to man. It is the fashion amongst Europeans to sneer at Arab riding, and no doubt an Arab in the hunting field would not look well; and it is possible that a hunting man might also find himself embarrassed to ride a Moorish horse in Moorish saddle fast downhill over a country strewn with boulders, or at the "powder play," to stand upon his saddle and perform the feats the Moors perform.

Horsemen and theologians are both intolerant. Believe my faith, and ride my horse after my fashion, for no Nonconformist, Cossack, Anglican, Gaucho, Roman Catholic, or Mexican can see the least redeeming point about his fellows' creed, his saddle, horse, ox, ass, or any other thing belonging to him.

Lunch despatched, green tea drunk, and cigarette carefully smoked behind a bush, for men in our position must not give offence by " drinking the shameful "* in the face of true believers, we mount again,

---

* "Drinking the shameful" is smoking tobacco, not drinking new whisky as in some civilised lands.

and plunge into an angle of the Argan forest, which extends from Mogador to Saffi.

Goats climb upon the trees, and camels here and there browse on the shoots; under the trees grow a few Aras (*Callitris Quadrivalvis*), and in the sandy soil some liliaceous plants gleam like stars in the expanse of heaven. After an hour the trees grow sparser and we emerge into a rolling country, and pass a granary, which marks the boundary between the provinces of Ha-Ha and Shiadma, and take our last look of the sea.

The Argan trees become more scarce as we cross into the fertile and well-cultivated province of Shiadma. Sand now gives place to rich red earth, and Swani, pricking his mule with his new dagger, which he had wheedled me to buy him under pretence that it did not befit my follower to go unarmed, comes up and asks if, even in England, there is a better cultivated land. I answer, diplomatically, that there is none, although perhaps the soil of England in certain parts is just as rich. Being an Arab he does not believe me for a moment, but ejaculates, with perfect manners, "God is Great, to him the praise for fertile lands, whether in England or Morocco."

The Caid's house on a hill stands as the outward visible sign of law and order, and Mohammed el Hosein imparts the information that the prison is always full. 'Tis pleasant to go back, not in imagination, but reality, to the piping times when prisons were always full,* maidens sat spinning (I think) in bowers, and the gallows-tree was never long without its "knot." This leads me to consider whether, if all

---

* I would not be taken here as wishing to disparage the prisons of my own country, or to insinuate that they are often empty.

the world were regulated by a duly elected county council, all chosen from a properly qualified and democratic, well-educated, pious electorate, and all men went about minding each other's business—with fornication, covetousness, evil concupiscence, adultery, and murder quite unknown, and only slander and a little cheating left to give a zest to life—they would be happier upon the whole than are the unregenerate Moors, who lie and steal, fight, fornicate, and generally behave themselves as if blood circulated in their veins and not sour whey? Despite the Sultan's tyranny, with every form of evil government thrown in, with murder rampant, vices that we call hideous (but which some practice on the sly,) common to everyone, the faces of the poor heathen Moors, whom we bombard with missionaries, are never so degraded as the types which haunt the streets of manufacturing towns. And if the face is the best index to the mind, it may be that the degraded heathen Moor is at the heart not greatly worse than his baptised and educated rag-clad English brother in the Lord.

As evening falls we pass a shepherd close to the high road, sitting down to pray, beside him are his shoes and crook, and not far off his dog looks on half cynically, and up above Allah preserves his attitude of "non mi ricordo," which is excusable where men worry him five or six times a day. Still the shepherd must have been genuine, and could not have known that infidels would pass his way.

The country here is chiefly composed of red argillaceous earth, the rock limestone, and the general configuration round-topped hills rising towards the Atlas. The Argan trees become more rare, and within sight of our destination we see the last of them.

The Argan, like the Cacti of the Rio Gila, in Arizona, seems to be able to resist any drought. Strange that all-wise Providence failed to endow Africa with either the Cactus or the Aloe, both plants so eminently suited to its climate. It was, however left to poor, weak, erring human reason to supply the want.

It is pleasing to reflect that for once the powers * generally opposed to one another should have united in endowing a country with two non-indigenous plants, which have taken to the soil as if they had been originally found there. Is it reason after all that is infallible?

Meskala reminded me curiously enough of an "hacienda" in Mexico, with an almost similar name, Amascala, the same white walls, the same two towers of unequal height over the gateway, almost the same corrals for animals outside, formed in both cases of the branches of a prickly shrub, goats feeding by the same turbid stream flowing through a muddy channel, and the gate once opened, which in our case took at least a quarter of an hour's entreaty mixed with objurgations, the self-same twisting passage of about twenty yards in length, through which the stranger enters before ariving at the great interior court.

The court, about two hundred feet across, was full of animals, belonging some to the Sheikh himself, and others to the various travellers who had sought shelter for the night within his walls.

We had a letter from the Consul in Mogador setting forth that we are friends of his, but not descending to particulars, so that we were ushered into an airy upper room, and bread and butter, in a toler-

* Reason, I fancy, filtered into man's composition after the original plan was completed, and was may-be the work of the serpent.

ably lordly dish, was set before us. We were uncertain whether Sheikh el Abbas penetrated my disguise, but if he did he made no sign ; nor did it matter much, as I intended to be taken for a Christian travelling in Moorish dress to escape observation (as is often done), till near the place where we break off into the wilds, and leave the main road to Morocco city. Had all gone well, I hoped this would confuse the hypothetic persons, and jumble up their substance to such an Athanasian extent as to make recognition quite impossible.

Lutaif discourses much of eastern lands and reads el Faredi, an Arab poet, to the admiration of the assembled elders.

Swani makes tea and Sheikh el Abbas drinks the three cups prescribed by usage, lapping them like a dog, and drawing in his breath like a tired horse at water, to show his great content. The upper room looked out upon the court; and in the moonlight I saw a shepherd, assisted by a little ragged boy, engaged in separating the goats from amongst the sheep, and ranging them in separate little flocks, after the fashion that the good are to be divided from amongst the wicked, when this foolish affair of life is finished with ; though with this difference, that whereas in this case the two flocks were nearly equal, who can suppose but that after the last count, the goats will not exceed the sheep by ten to one. In a corral hard by the horses eat, some camel drivers crouch round a fire, and as I look at the unchanging Eastern life, the call to prayers reminds me that Allah has blessed it by continuity for a thousand years.

The Sheikh sat long, talking of things and others, of the decline of British prestige, the advance of

Russia, the new birth of Turkey, and of the glory of
the Moorish kingdoms in the "Andalos" (Spain); and
then of business, and how the "Brus" (Germans), a
nation which he says seemed to have come into the
world but recently, from some high mountains, are
bidding fair to be the first of Franguestan. The
German Emperor strikes him as being a great king.
He is a Sultan, says the Sheikh, after the fashion that
the Spaniards used to say when Ferdinand VII.
had perpetrated some atrocity, " es mucho rey," that
is, he is indeed a king.*

I fancy that he knows I am a Nazarene, although
my conversation is quite evangelical, that is, yea and
nay, and now and then a pious sentence muttered
very low to hide the accent. Lutaif and Swain
answer for me, as if I were an idiot, and step in, so to
speak, between me and the Sheikh, as when he asks,
for instance, if I have seen the war ships of the
Christians, when they at once respond I have, and
give particulars invented at the moment, and I learn
that ships steam more than fifty miles an hour, guns
carry twenty miles, to all of which I nod a grave
assent, and the Sheikh sips his tea 'and praises God
for all his mighty works.

Lutaif tells of a vessel at Beirout, a Turkish war
ship, sent by the German Emperor to the Sultan (he
of Brus), so large that two young Syrians of his
acquaintance, who had shipped as sailors and got
separated, vainly sought each other for seven years,
at night climbing to the masthead, by day descending
to the hold, but all in vain, because the vessel was so

---

* Others of his subjects admired his procedure so much that their catch-
word was reported to have been " Viva Fernando y vamos robando," which
after all, is but a practical application of the old Spanish aphorism " Viva
el rey daca la capa."

huge; the Sultan could step aboard of her out of his palace on the Bosphorus and after walking all day land in whatever country he desired. This meets with great approval, and I have to confirm it to the letter, and do so with a nod.

The night is hot and the mosquito hums in his thousand; but the Sheikh as he goes warns us to bar the door, because, he says, " Sleep is Death's brother," meaning that when one sleeps death may be near and yet the sleeper be unconscious of it.

The muleteers retire to sleep beside their mules. Swani wraps up my feet in the hood of one " djellaba," and draws another up to my head ready to cover it when I feel sleepy, and as we lie upon the floor, on sheepskins, watching the moon shine through the glassless window, Lutaif puts out the flickering wick, burning sustained by argan oil in a brass bowl, exclaiming, as he did so, " Oh, Allah! extinguish not thy blessing as I put out this light." How much there is in names; fancy a deity, accustomed to be prayed to as Allah by Arabs, suddenly addressed by an Armenian as Es Stuatz, it would be almost pitiable enough to make him turn an Atheist upon himself. I feel convinced a rose by any other name would not smell sweet; and the word Allah is responsible for much of the reverence and the faith of those who worship him.

We left Meskala early and in rain, which soon was over, and entering on a little bit of desert country, the Atlas range appeared like a great wall of limestone capped with white in the far distance.

For three hot hours we passed through a miniature Sahara, rocky and desolate, stones, stones, and still more stones and sand, a colocynth or two lying amongst the rocks, some orange-headed thistles,

Ziziphus Lotus here and there, some sandarac bushes now and then ; the horses stumbling on the stones, mules groaning in the sand, and no great rock in all the thirsty land to shelter under from the sun. Three hours that seemed like six, until a line of green appears, a fringe of oleanders on the margin of a muddy stream in which swim tortoises, and by which we lie and lap like dogs, and understand wherefore the Psalmist so insisted on his green pastures where his Allah made him lie.

In England your green pastures have no significance, and call to mind but recollections of fat cattle and sheep, with backs as square as boxes, in the lush grass between the hedges, as the express whirls past and the stertorous first class-passengers hold up their wine glasses against the light and praise the landscape as they eat their lunch.*

But in Morocco and Arabia green grass means life, relief from thirst, and still to-day their poets stuff their verses full of allusions to the pastures rare to them, but which with us make one at times long for a bit of brown to break the sea of dull metallic green. Fig trees and olives, oleanders† with pomegranates, and a few palms make an oasis in the little desert, and on a sheepskin spread on some cobblestones close by a rock, exactly like the one that Moses is depicted striking in old-fashioned Sunday books, the water

---

* It is true that Herrick saw a certain beauty in our " Meadows," or he would not have written the following stanza, but in his days there were no patent manures :—

> Ye have been fresh and green,
> Ye have been filled with flowers ;
> And ye the walks have been
> Where maids have spent their hours.

† " Difla " in Arabic, from which the Spaniards have taken their word Adelfa, as from " Dib " jackal they have formed Adibe " Berk " a pond Alberca and the like.

rushing out in a clear stream, we lie and smoke and
fall a-talking of our chances of reaching Tarudant.

Mohammed el Hosein gave it as his opinion that if
he could conduct a Rumi* there, he would make his
name in Mogador as the best muleteer in all the
south, and all his previous fears seemed to vanish as
he descanted on the line of conduct to pursue when
once inside. He seemed to think the risk, if known
to be a Christian, was considerable, and counselled
that we should encamp outside the gates and reach
the town a little after dawn when people were arriving
to sell provisions, and then go instantly to the
Governor's house which was close to the gates, and
claim protection from him. Swani, who, as a native
of Tangiers, though he had seen the world and twice
performed the pilgrimage to Mecca, yet was a little
uneasy in South Morocco, and thought it best that
we should go to some caravansarai (called in Morocco
fondak) and try our best to escape detection, I shamming ill, and Lutaif giving out he was a Syrian doctor.

Ali the muleteer, who learned for the first time our
destination, was in an agony of fear, and said he must
return at once; but when we pointed out to him that
he would then not only lose his wages but perhaps
his mule, he made his mind up, on condition I pro-
cured him a letter of protection from the English
Consul in Mogador. Mohammed el Hosein, before
he left the town, had made me sign a paper stating I
had engaged him for all his life, and, fortified with
this protection, I understand he now bids all his
governors and masters absolute defiance, wrapped, so
to speak, within a tatter of the British flag. Lutaif,

* *I.e.*, Roman is generally used by Arabs in North Africa when they
wish to be civil to a Christian. "Caballer el rumi" has a pleasant sound,
even when uttered by a man who, in his heart, thinks you a Christian dog.

who knew the Governor of Tarudant, one Basha
Hamou, who had been Governor of Mequinez—a negro,
and a member of the famous Boukhari* Pretorian
bodyguard—gave his opinion that Mohammed el
Hosein was right, and that though Basha Hamou
might not be pleased, he would be obliged to give us
protection, and that he, probably after the first excitement of the natives had subsided, would send us back
under escort to Mogador. I held my tongue, resolv-
ing that if we got there I would not return without a
good look at the place.

About a mile from where we sat was situated the
castle of the local Caid, a castle set upon a rock, and
strong enough apparently to set tribal artillery at
defiance ; but our Lord the Sultan being " unfavourable" to him, the castle was deserted, cattle stolen,
crops all destroyed, and an air about the place reminding one of some of the Jesuit Missions (destroyed
to show the Liberalism of Charles III.) which I have
seen in Paraguay. In fact the Caid is only Caid *in
partibus*, and it is understood a Sheikh in Fez has
offered the Sultan 100,000 dollars to be made
Governor, providing he (the offerer) might have a
" free hand " with the tribe ; this means to oppress
them, and in a year or two to take the 100,000 dollars
out of them to pay the Sultan, and as much more for
himself. Strange that the Arabs, though so warlike,
should in all ages have endured so much oppression.
It may be that the tribal system renders them specially

---

* The Boukharis were first raised by Sultan Muley Ismael, one of the
most powerful rulers the country has ever had; he flourished in the
eighteenth century, and sent an ambassador to Louis XIV. to demand the
hand of his daughter, which, perhaps through religious intolerance, or some
other reason, was not accorded to him. The Boukharis were all negroes
from the Soudan, who, belonging to no Arab tribe, were devoted to the
person of the Sultan alone.

liable to this, for inter-tribal jealousies make them an easy prey to any Sultan who can command money enough to set them at one another's throats.

Jhu Jaldun (in the introduction to his history) says: "The Arabs are the least fitted men to rule other nations, for they demolish the civilisation of every land they conquer. They might be good rulers, but they must first change their nature." This no doubt arises from their incapacity to govern themselves, still with all their faults they are a fine race, and if they have demolished the civilisation of several countries, they have in return left their own type wherever they have conquered, and what type in the world is finer. I say nothing of the more doubtful of their legacies, their system of numeration, and the thoroughbred horse.

The grateful spring, fruit trees, and shady little oasis where we rested rejoice in the name of Aguaydirt el Má, a compound of Arabic and Shellah, Má in Arabic meaning the water, and Aguaydirt, no doubt having some meaning of its own in the weird tongue it comes from.

As we ride through a bushy country with some straggling farms, we pass a Sheikh on a good horse, long gun across the saddle, and a tail of ragged followers on foot. It seems he is a tax collector, gathering the taxes in person, and no doubt quite as effectually as the Receivers' General used to do in France, including even he who sleeps (his bubble burst) under a flagstone in the door of San Moisé, in Venice, with a brief dog-Latin epitaph, setting forth the usual lack of virtues of a man who fails.

Curious to observe (again per usual) the fatness and good clothes of the collector, and the mean estate of the poor "taxables," their downcast looks, and all the

apparent shifts and wiles they are putting forth to
escape the worst outrage that a free man can bear,
that is to have his money taken from him under the
pretext of the public good.

Pleasant to gather taxes on a good horse, well
armed, a horse I mean that could do his ninety miles
a day for several days and carry something heavy in
the saddle bags.

I had a friend who, being for a short time Governor
of a province in a Central American Republic, and
finding things became too hot for him, collected all
the public money he could find, and silently one night
abdicted in a canoe down to the coast, and taking
ship came to Lutetia ; and then, his money spent,
lectured upon the fauna and the flora of the country
he had robbed ; and, touching on the people, always
used to say that it was very sad their moral tone was
low ; the reflection seeming to reinstate himself in his
own eyes, for he forgot apparently that in his
abdication he but followed out the course which law
had pointed out to him in his official days.

Night catches us close to el Mouerid, a dullish pile
of sun-dried bricks, the lord of which, one Si Bel Arid,
is an *esprit fort*, and knowing me for a Christian,
ostentatiously walks up and down talking on things
and others to show his strength of mind. Though
disapproving of them, most Moors like to be seen with
Christians, in the same way some pious men are fond
of listening to wicked women's talk, not that their
conversation interests, but to show the asbestos quality
of their own purity, and to set forth that, as in
Rahab's case, no imputation can attach itself to men
of virtuous life. Therefore, as maiden ladies are said
to love the conversation of rakes, clergymen, that of
(*pour le bon motif*) fallen women, so do Moors love to

talk with and be seen in public with the enemies of
God.

El Mouerid looks miserable in the storm of rain and
wind, in which we leave it as the day is breaking.
The Arab dress in windy weather teaches one what
women undergo in petticoats upon a boisterous day,
but still their pains are mitigated by the fact that
generally men are near at hand to look at them,
whereas we could not expect to find admiring ladies
on the bleak limestone plain. Curious striations on
the hills, as if the limestone " came to grass " in
stripes, give an effect as of a building to the rising
foot-hills, into which we enter by the gorge of
Bosargun, a rocky defile which gradually becomes a
staircase like the road from Ronda to Gaucin, or that
to heaven, almost untrodden of late years. We pass
a clump of almond trees, by which a light chesnut*
mare is feeding; she looks quite Japanese amongst
the trees, buried up to the girths in aromatic shrubs;
a little bird sits on her shoulder, no one is near her,
though, no doubt, some sharp-eyed boy is hiding
somewhere watching her, for in this district no animal
is safe alone. From the top we get our first view of
the Atlas in its entirety; snow, and more snow marking the highest peaks, the Glawi, Gurgourah, and the
tall peaks behind Amsmiz. No mountain range I ever
saw looks so steep and wall-like as the Atlas, but this
wall-like configuration, though most effective for the
whole range, yet robs the individual peaks of dignity.

To the east the stony plain of Morocco, cut into
channels here and there by the diverted water of the
Wad el N'fis (a river I was destined to follow to its
very source), under the highest peaks of Ouichidan,

* Light chesnut in " Spanish " is " ruano "; the proverb says " Caballo
ruano para las putas." Query: Does that hold good of a mare ?

upon the very confines of the Sus.   Here, for the first
time, we see, though far below us, the curious subter-
raneous aqueducts, looking like lines of tan pits, with
which the plain of Morocco is intersected everywhere.

These aqueducts, called " Mitfias," are a succession
of deep pits, dug at varying distances from one
another ; the water runs from pit to pit in a mud
channel, and the whole chain of pits often extend for
miles.   Men who undertake such herculean labour in
order to irrigate their fields cannot be well called
lazy, after the fashion of most travellers who speak,
after a fortnight's residence in Morocco, of the "lazy
Moors."   The truth is that the country-people of
Morocco are industrious enough, as almost every
people who live by agriculture are bound to be. Only
the Arabs of the desert, and the Gauchos of the
southern plains, and people who live a pastoral life,
can be called lazy, though they, too, at certain seasons
of the year, work hard enough.   The Arabs and Berbers of Morocco work hard, and would work harder
had they not got the ever-present fear of their bad
government before them.   When one man quarrels
with another, after exhausting all the usual curses on
his opponent's mother, sister, wife, and female generation generally, he usually concludes by saying : "May
God, in his great mercy, send the Sultan to you"—for
he knows that even Providence is not so merciless as
our Liege Lord.

About three miles below us are two curious flat-
topped hills, looking like castles.   Mohammed el
Hosein pronounces them to have been the site of
two strong castles of the Christians. What Christians,
then ?—Roman, or Vandal, or Portuguese ?   Perhaps
not Christian at all, but Carthaginian; for in Morocco,
any old building, the builders of which are now for-

gotten, is set down to the all-constructing Christians, in the same manner as in Spain, the Moors built all the castles and the Roman bridges, and generally made everything which is a little older than the grandfather of the man with whom you speak. Not but at times the person questioned puts in practice, to your cost, the "pawky" Spanish saying : " Let him who asks be fed with lies." What Christians could have been so foolish as to build two castles in a barren plain, far off from water, does not appear. At any rate, after a careful search, we can discover no trace of building, and put the castles down with the enchanted cities Fata Morgana, Flying Dutchman, and the like phenomena, which seem more real than the material cities, ships, and optical illusions, which, by their very realness, appear to lose their authenticity, and to become like life, a dream.

Passing the castles, we emerged again upon a desert tract, which took almost two hours to pass, and at the furthest edge of it a zowia of a saint, Sidi Abd-el Mummen, with a mosque tower, flanked by palms, rising out of a sea of olives twisted and gnarled with age, and growing so thickly overhead that underneath them is like entering a southern church, out of the fierce glare of the sun.

History has not preserved the pious actions which caused Si Abd-el Mummen to be canonised. In fact, Mohammed, if he came to life again, would have a fine iconoclastic career throughout the world of the Believers ; for though they have not quite erected idols, graven or otherwise, yet all their countries are stuck as full of saints' tombs, zowias of descendants of saints, and adoration of the pious dead prevails as much as in the Greek or Latin churches. True, the custom has its uses, as it serves to indicate the dis-

tance on roads, and men as naturally enquire their
way from Saint (Sidi) to Saint, as from church to
church in Spain, or public-house to public-house in
rural England.   In other countries Saints, before
becoming free of the fellowship, have to show their
fitness for the post; but in Morocco no probation
of any kind—that is, according to our ideas—seems to
be necessary.

I knew an aged man, who used to sit before the
Franciscan Convent, in the chief street of Tangier—a
veritable saint, if saint exists—and, sitting there,
dressed in a tall red fez,* given by some pious soldier,
a long green caftan, clean white drawers, and a
djellab of fine blue cloth; long hair descending on
both sides of his face in locks like bunches of chry-
santhemums; eyes piercing, and yet wavering; for
the poor Saint was nearer to Allah than the common
herd by the want of some small tissue, fibre, or
supply of blood to the vessels of the brain: thus
clothed and mentally accoutred for his trade, a basket
by his side, and in his hand a long pole shod with
iron, for he belonged to the sect called the Derkowi,
he sat and told his beads, and took his alms, with an
air of doing you a favour: for who gives to the poor
does them no favour, but, on the contrary, insures his
own eternal happiness, and but gives out again that
which Allah entrusted to him for the behoof of
man.

---

* A tall peaked fez in Morocco is the outward visible sign of a soldier or
man of the Mahksen Government, from the Arabic word Mahksen, which is
not used in other Arab-speaking countries in the sense of the Government,
but simply as signifying a "Store," come the Spanish word "Almacen," a
store, and some say also our word, "magazine."   The inward spiritual
grace is a swaggering demeanour to show the soundness of his faith, an
insolence of manner not quite unknown among soldiers of other powers ;
and a firm determination to obtain for nothing everything that the wretched
"Pekin" has to pay for in the debased copper currency of the realm.

I happened one day, with European curiosity, to enquire what made the venerable man so venerated, and was told that, having suddenly gone mad, he killed his wife, threw off his clothes, and then marched naked through the land—justice not interfering—for the mad are wise; and then, the violence of his madness over, had quietly sat down and made himself a sort of "octroi" upon passers by, after the fashion of blind Bartimæus, who sat begging at the gate. The explanation pleased me, and in future when I passed I laid up treasure in that mothless territory, where no thieves come, by giving copper coins; and was rewarded even here on earth, for once I heard an Arab say: "This Kaffir, here" (speaking of me) "fears neither God nor devil, yet I have seen him give to the old Saint; it may be, God, the merciful, may save him yet, if but to show His might."

And so it is that Saints' tombs stud the land with oven-shaped buildings with a horse-shoe arch, a palm-tree growing by, either a date palm or a chamcerops humilis, in which latter case pieces of rag are hung to every leaf-stalk, with running water near; and the place serves as a re-union for pious folk, for women who pray for children, for gossipers, and generally holds a midway place betwixt a church and club. In order that the faithful wayfarers, even though idiots, shall not err, in mountain passes, as in the gorge of Bosargun, at four cross roads, passes of rivers, and sometimes in the midst of desert tracts the traveller finds a number of small cairns, in shape like bottles, which show—according to the way they point—where the next Saint's tomb lies; for it is good that man should pray and think about himself, especially upon a journey—prayer acts upon the purse; alms save the soul; and

Saints, though dead, need money to perpetuate their fame.

After nine hours of alternating wind and heat we reached Imintanout, the eastern entrance of the pass which, crossing a valley of the Atlas, leads to Sus. So to speak Tarudant is within hail, three (some say two) days and we are there, if ——, but the if was destined to be mortal, as it proved. The straggling village almost fills the gorge through which the road enters the hills. Above it towers the Atlas; a little stream (then dry) ran through the place, which had an air between a village in Savoy, and a Mexican mining town lost in the Sierra Madre. Brown houses built of mud, stretches of Tabieh* walls, the tops of which crowned with dead prickly bushes, which look steely and bluish in the setting sun, the houses generally castellated and looking (though browner) like the houses near the border in Cumberland and Northumberland; gardens hedged in with aloes, amongst which grow blackberries, and in which stand palms and pomegranates, a few flowers, some fig-trees, olives, and through which ran rills of water in little channels, so that the gardens had the two chief requisites to an oriental paradise, water and shade. Further up the gorge the Mellah (Jewry), in which we catch a glimpse for the first time of the Atlas Jews, servile and industrious, wonderfully European-looking as to type, superior to the Arabs and Berbers in business capacity, and thus at once their masters and their slaves.

The Caid's house, perched upon a rock, I avoided like a plague spot, fearing to be recognised and sent

---

* Tabieh, the "tapia" of the Spaniards and the "pisé" of the French, is merely mud run into frames till it hardens, and then left to dry in the sun. It figures in the saying "Sordo como una tapia," deaf as a wall, and seems to be at variance with the northern proverb, "Walls have ears."

back to Mogador, and made, instead, for the house of one Haj Addee, a Sheikh,* which being interpreted may stand in his case for country gentleman.

The Sheikh has been in Mecca, Masar el Kahira (Cairo), carries a rosary, has some knowledge of the world (Mohammedan), and is not quite unlike those old world Hidalgos of La Mancha, they of the "Rocin flaco y galgo corredor," whom Cervantes has immortalised in the person of Don Quixote.

Friends interested in my journey in Mogador had recommended the Sheikh to me as a safe man in whom to trust, before engaging myself in the recesses of the Atlas. So, riding to his house, I sent in Swani with a letter from an influential man in Mogador, and Haj Addee soon appeared, and, after asking me to dismount, led me by the hand to his "guest house." This was an apartment composed of three small rooms, one serving as a bedroom, the second as a place in which to store our saddles, tent, and camping requisites, and the third, which had no roof, as sitting-room. All round the sitting-room ran a clay divan, a fire burned in one corner, and overhead the stars shone down upon us, especially the three last stars in the Great Bear's tail, so that, take it for all in all, it was as pleasantly illuminated a drawing-room as any I have seen. Hard by the door stood an immense clay structure, shaped like a water barrel, which served for storing corn† in during the winter,

---

* Sheikh is a most indefinite word, and is generally held to mean a chief, but often only means gentleman. Scribes, especially if Easterns, *i.e.*, from Syria, Damascus, or Bagdad, often use the title. Lutaif upon our journey figured as Sheikh Abdul Latif el Shami (the Syrian), and, when convenient, I was styled Sheikh Mohammed el Fasi, at other times simply " el Tabib " (the Doctor), sometimes " Sherif," anything, in fact, to distract attention from my white face and extremely small knowledge of Arabic.

† The usual system of storing grain is either in earthen jars buried in the ground, or in funnel-shaped pits known as " Metmoras," from which word

and in the spring broken to pieces when the corn was used.

Seated on the divan, I watched an enormous copper kettle try to boil upon a brass tripod* in which a little charcoal glowed, whilst in a small brass dish a wick fed with raw mutton fat made darkness manifest. As I look round the room it strikes me that there seems to be a sort of dominant type of Mohammedan formed by religion, in the same way that in the north of Ireland you can distinguish a Catholic from a Protestant, across the street. Mohammed el Hosein, though of a different race, and from thousands of miles away, presents the perfect type of an Afridi, as depicted in the columns of the illustrated papers. Ali, our muleteer, with his thin legs, beard brushed into a fan, and coppery skin, might sit for the picture of a Pathan; it may be that an Oriental would discern a great resemblance between a Dutchman and a Portuguese which had lain dormant to our faculties, and if this was the case my theory would be as well confirmed as many other theories which have revolutionised the scientific world.

We talk of Mecca and Medina, of travelling from Jeddah, stretched in "shegedefs"† upon a camel's back, of Gibel Arafat, the Caaba, and of the multitude of different classes of Mohammedans who swarm like bees, Hindoos and Bosnians, Georgians, Circassians, the dwellers in the Straits, and the Chinese believers, whom my host serves up all in a lump as Jowi, and

the Spanish word "Mazmora" has been taken, and from which we again took our old-fashioned word "Massymore," used for a dungeon.

* This tripod is used all over Spain, and called, in Andalusia, "Anafe," from the Moorish words "En Nar fi," the fire is in it.

† A Shegedef is a kind of long pannier in which the richer pilgrims lie or sit one on each side of a camel. There is an awning over all, and pilgrims have assured me that the pleasantest part of the whole journey is the portion which is performed in this manner.

says that they are little, yellow, all have one face, and that their mother in the beginning was a Djin. It appears that at the sacred places, the town of tents is of such vast dimensions that it is possible to lose yourself and wander for miles if you forget to take the bearings of your tent. It must be a curious sight to see the various nationalities, the greater part of whom have no means of communication other than a few pious sentences, and a verse or two from the Koran.

Swani, who is a double pilgrim, having twice been in Mecca, comes out most learnedly as to nice points in Mohammedan theology. Though he can neither read nor write, and is, I fear, not all too strict in the mere practice of his religion, yet he can talk for hours upon the attributes of God, and as judiciously as he had been a graduate of St. Bees, so well he knows the essence, qualities, power, majesty, might, glory, and every proper adjective to be applied. The object of his hopes is to induce me to perform the pilgrimage. He assures me that it is quite feasible, has even arranged for my disguise, and tells me that in Mecca he can take me to a friend's house, who is as big a Kaffir as myself. His idea is that I shall go as a Circassian, which people I resemble as to type, and when I say, " What, if I fall upon a real Circassian ?" he only answers, " That is impossible," in the same manner as when asked what they would do if they discovered me; he answers, " they would not discover you, you look so like a man from Fez." What annoys him is that I make no apparent progress in the language, and I fear that I shall have to take a longer pilgrimage before I am fit, even with such a guide, to throw the stones on Gibel Arafat. Sometimes our talk ran on the wonders of the West; the steamships in which the pilgrims sail from Tangier to Jeddah, and on board of one of which, our host informs us, once when he was praying, the Kaffir Captain touched him on the arm, and, pointing to the compass, informed him he was not head on to the proper point. This conduct seems to have impressed Haj Adee, and he remarks, "God, in his mercy, may yet release that 'captain' from the fire." As we were talking, neighbours dropped in, in the familiar Eastern way, and sat quiet and self-contained, occasionally drinking from one of the two long-necked and porous water-jars, known as "Baradas," or the "coolers," which stand, their wooden stoppers tied to them with a palmetto cord, on each side the divan. Swani concocts the tea, using the aforesaid weighty copper kettle, a pewter cone-shaped tea-pot, made in Germany, a tin tea-caddy, painted the colour of orange marmalade, with crude blue flowers, which kind of merchandise Birmingham sends to Morocco, to be sold at one-and-sixpence, to show how much superior are our wares to those of all the world. The host knocks off great pieces from a loaf of cheap * French sugar with the key of the house, drawing it from his belt, and hammering lustily, as the key weighs about four ounces, and is eight or nine inches long.

Imintanout being, as it were, the gate of Sus, and the end of the first stage of our journey, we ask most anxiously as to the condition of the road. The way we learn is easy, so easy that trains of laden camels pass every day, and the whole distance across the mountains is a short two days. So far so good, but when we intimate our intention of starting early next morning, then bad news comes out.

It appears the tribe called Beni Sira, sons of burnt

* It is actually sold cheaper in Morocco than in Marseilles.

fathers, as our host refers to them, have stopped the
pass, not that they are bad men, at least our host is
sure of this, or lives too near them to venture on
a criticism, but because they are dissatisfied with
the new governor recently appointed, and wish to
get him into bad odour with the Sultan by causing
trouble. It appears those mis-begotten folk have
fired upon a party only the day before, and wounded
a Jewish merchant, who is laid up in a house not far
from where we sit. A caravan of twenty mules was
set upon last week, two men were wounded and the
goods all carried off. A most ingenious system of
proving that the Governor is incompetent to preserve
order, and therefore must be changed.

Suspecting that the story was untrue, and only
got up to prevent my entering the Sus, I sent two
messengers, one to see the Jewish merchant, and tell
me if he is really wounded, and another to a
Sheikh, asking if a traveller, going to pray in Tarudant, and skilled in medicine, can pass that way.
The report of fighting seriously alarms our muleteers,
and even Swani, though brave enough, looks grave
at having to fight so far away from home. Haj Adee
—to show goodwill, or to impress us with his power—
offers, should the local Sheikh of the Beni Sira return
an unfavourable reply, to get his men together and
fight his way right through the pass. I thank him
with effusion, but resolve not to incontinently place
myself alone in the middle of a tribal battle without
a rifle, on a half-tired horse, and deprived even of a
Kodak with which to affright the nimble adversary.

And so I lose a day, or perhaps gain it, talking to
the curious people, and prescribing wisely for ophthalmia, dividing Seidlitz powders into small portions
to be taken at stated times to serve as aphrodisiacs,

and watching an incantation which seems to cure our
host of rheumatism.

Haj Adee was a sort of " Infeliz," as the Spaniards
call a man of his peculiar temperament.   I am
certain that in whatever business he entered into he
must have failed, he had so honest a disposition, and
his lies were so unwisely gone about, they would not
have deceived a Christian child. His rosary, each
bead as big as a large pea, was ever in his hand ; he
said it was made from the horn of that rare beast, the
unicorn, and he had bought it with a price at Mecca,
from a " Sherif so holy that he could not lie."   It
looked to me like rhinoceros horn, and so, perhaps,
the Sherif had lied less than he had intended when
he sold the beads.   In the middle of the string were
four blue beads, and between these four beads a piece
of ivory standing up like a cone, and called " el
Madhna," * that is the " erect one."   Besides the
" Madhna " there was a little comb, shaped like a
stable mane comb, and made of horn, which
dangled from the rosary, and which Moors use to
comb their beards after performing their ablutions,
and which they seldom carry in Morocco, except they
have performed the pilgrimage.

Haj Adee suffered from rheumatism in the left
shoulder. This he called simply " el burd," "the
cold," and complained that he had exhausted all
lawful medicine and was about to try an incantation.†
So to us entered a " fakih," that is a holy man, fat
and white-bearded, and with the half-foolish, half-

---

* " The Madhna " may be a relic of phallic worship, many relics of which
have lingered even at Mecca, as Burton, in his chapter on Mecca in his
celebrated " Pilgrimage to Medinah and Mecca," relates.

† I offered him quinine, but he looked coldly at it as a man in the time
of Molière might have disdained the futile drugs of the licensed practitioner
knowing that he had orvietan at his command.

cunning look, so often to be found in "holy men" who are professors of some faith either inferior to, or differing from, our own. The man of God gave me a scowl, and, I fancy, saw I was a misbeliever, then sat down, after the fashion of his class, in the best seat, and, mumbling something, drew out a dagger and wrote upon it, with the juice of a plant he carried in his hand, some mystic characters. The master of the house, together with a friend, stood up and held two pieces of split cane about a yard in length. Both had the air the Italians call "compunto," that is, they looked like people walking down the aisle of a crowded church (as if they trod on eggs) after partaking of the Holy Communion, and conscious that it is not impossible they may have eaten and drunk their own damnation, and that before a crowd of witnesses.

The Levite, sitting in a corner, kept on muttering, and underneath the cane rapidly passed the cabalistic dagger to and fro, just in the middle of the reeds, touching them lightly, as the dagger moved almost like a shuttle in his hands. The look of concentration and air of being accomplices after the fact was kept up for almost five minutes, and quite insensibly I find I joined in it, and, looking at Lutaif (a Christian, if such a man there be) at Swani and Mohammed el Hosein, I found that they too were fascinated, much like a rabbit in a snake-house moves towards the snake.

It seems, of all the forces which move mankind, humbug is the strongest, for humbugs are always taken in by humbug, and the very men who practice on the folly of mankind fall easy victims to the manoeuvres of their brothers in the art. Gradually the movement of the dagger grew slower, then stopped, and then the mystery man struck the patient gently with the blade upon the arm, broke the two canes across, tied them together in a bundle, and put them on a ledge just where the thatch is fastened to the mud walls of the house.

Admirable to observe the look of faith of all the standers-by. If ever I witnessed a religious action, that is, taking "religio" and "superstitio" (as I think the Romans did) to be synonymous, I did so then. Even the Salvation Army, at its most unreasonable, never succeeded in bringing such a look of ovine faith upon the faces of its legionaries. The patient says that he is greatly benefited, and for the first time in my life I see a religious ceremony begun, continued, and concluded (with the result successful), and without apparent sign of a collection being taken up.

Faith should not be divorced from its true spouse, the offertory. What man has brought together, even the act of God should not disjoin, for faith is so ethereal that, left alone, it pines and languishes in a hard world, unless sustained by pennies in a plate, in the same manner as the soul, which, as we all know (nowadays), is eternal, takes its departure when the body dies, and lies unquickened if the head receives a knock.

The function over, we sit and talk, look at one another's arms, lie as to our shooting powers, and, after careful examination of my pistol, to my astonishment, our host produces a large-sized Smith and Wesson revolver, which it appears he bought in Kahira (Cairo), and seems to think the most important result of all his pilgrimage. Hours pass, and still no messenger, and a fat "Saint"* rolls in, and salutes Swani as an acquaintance of the pilgrimage.

* The word "Sherif" is often rendered by Europeans, in Morocco, as "Saint," they having most likely taken the word from the Spanish word "Santon."

They kiss and embrace, hugging one another and alternately placing their beards over one another's right and left shoulders. As Burton observes, the Arabs are by far the most emotional of the Oriental races. Poetry, or a well-told lamentable tale, moves them to tears, and friends who meet often weep for joy.

Swani privately imparts to me, in Pigeon Spanish, which he tells the "Saint" is Turkish, that the "Saint" is a humbug, and that when they last met he would hardly speak to him, for he (Swani) was working as a sailor on board an English pilgrim steamer, and dressed "a la inglesa, saber del trousers, catchy sea boots y todo."

Still waiting for the messenger, I fall to observing the difference between the Arabs and the Berber race. It is the fashion amongst travellers in Morocco and Algeria to exalt the Berbers, and run down the Arabs. "The noble Shillah race" has become quite a catch-word with every one who sees a Berber and writes down his impressions. Curious that no one talks of the "noble Tuareg race," yet the Tuareg's are Berber of the Berbers, and their language, known as Tamashek, merely a dialect of the Berber language, which spreads over the vast area of territory from Tripoli to the Atlantic Ocean, and from the Mediterranean to Timbuctoo. Undoubtedly the oldest known inhabitants of the countries which now are called the Barbary States, they seem to have kept their type and customs unchanged since first we hear of them in history. The Arabs found them in possession of all Morocco, and drove them into the mountains and the desert beyond, and though they forced Islam upon them still the two peoples are anti-pathetic to one another, have blended little, and you can tell them from one another at a glance.

The Arab, one of the finest types of all the races of mankind, tall, thin, fine eyes, aquiline noses, spare frames; walking with dignity; a horseman, poet; treacherous and hospitable; a gentleman, and yet inquisitive; destroying, as Ibn Jaldun assures us, the civilisation of every land they conquer, and yet capable of great things, witness Granada and Damascus; a metaphysician and historian; sensual and yet abstemious; a people loveable, and yet not good to "lippen to," as Scotchmen say; and yet perhaps of all the Orientals those who have most impressed themselves upon the world.

The Berbers, short, squat figures, high cheekbones, small eyes, square frames, great walkers, only becoming horsemen by necessity, as when the Arabs have forced them to the desert; as fond of mountains as the Arabs are of plains; in general agriculturists, whereas the Arab in his true sphere prefers a pastoral life: the Berbers, little known outside their mountains, look rather Scottish in appearance, that is, Scotch, as ordinary mortals see that race, and not as seen through "kailyard" spectacles. It may be that the Berbers are a noble race, but personally I should apply the adjective " noble " to the Arabs, and to the Berbers give some such qualifying phrases as " relatively honest," "tenacious," or perhaps, best of all, " bourgeois," which, to my way of thinking, best expresses the characteristics of those Berber tribes who, in the north side of the Atlas, are dominated by the Sultan's power. Where they touch one another to the south upon the confines of the desert, it would be hard to give the palm for savagery; and the great Berber tribes, Ait Morghed Ait* Hannu, have become

* Ait corresponds to the Arab   Ibn " or " Ben," and the Scotch " Mac."

practically Arabs in their customs and their use of horses. The Tuaregs,* on the other hand, have remained absolutely Berber, and indiscriminately attack Arabs and Christians, and all who cross their way.

As to the name of Berber, ethnologists, after the fashion of all "scientists," have disagreed, taken one another by the beards, and freely interchanged (and I suppose as faithfully received) the opprobious names which render the disputes of men of science and of theologians so amusing to those who stand aside and put their tongues out at both sorts of men.

Breber, Baraba, Berber, all three phases of the word are found. Some learned men derive the word from the Greek, and make it simply stand for "Barbarian." Others, again, as stoutly make it Arab, and say it means "People of the Land of Ber."†

Ibn Jaldun (always an innovator) has his theory, which seems just as good as any other man's. He makes the Berbers to descend not from Shem, but Ham (Cam as the Arabs call him), and relates that Ham had a son called Ber, whose son was called Mazirg, and that from Ber came the Beranis, who, in time, and by corruption of the word, turned into Berberes. If not convincing, the theory shows invention, and smacks (to me) of the derivations I have heard

* It was the Tuaregs who killed the French explorer, the Marquis de Morès, and they have killed many explorers of almost every European nation. From their habit of going veiled to protect themselves against the sun and dust in the desert, some have supposed that the mysterious " veiled men" referred to in the Spanish Chroniclers as having accompanied the Almohades in their invasion of Spain in 1146, were Tuaregs. The leader of the Almohades was Mohammed-ibn-Abdullah, King of Fez, or Morocco as some say, for the kingdoms were not joined in those days. In either case, he might have brought the Tuaregs. The word "Almohade" is said to mean "Unitarian," a title of honour in lands where "miscreants" either reject or do not fear the doctrine of the Trinity.

† Grüberg 'di Hemsö. "Speechio Geographico e Statistico di Marocco," page 72.

hacked out, so to speak, with a scalping knife round the camp-fire; for, uncivilised and semi-civilised men waste as much time in seeking to find out how the form of words got crystallised as if they had diplomas from their universities.

Strangely enough, the people we call Berbers do not know the name, and call themselves "Tamazirght," that is, "the noble." Their language is called "Amzirght," and resembles closely the "Tamashek" spoken by the Tuaregs, the dialect of the tribes of the Riff Mountains, and that of the Kabyles of Algeria.* The Arabs neither use the word "Tamazirght" nor the word "Berber," but call the Berber tribes "Shillah," that is, the "outcasts"; the verb is "Shallaha," and the term used for the speech Shluoh,† a sort of "Shibboleth" in European's mouths, for very few even of those (who, like the Germans and the Spaniards can pronounce the guttural) ever attain to the pronunciation of the Arabic and Berber semi-gutteral, semi-pectoral aspiration of this word.

Till the last twenty years the greater portion of the Berber tribes, although Mohammedans, owned but a nominal allegiance to the Sultan of Morocco, and lived almost quite independently under their "Omz-

---

* For list of "Amzirght" words collected at Gundaffi, see notes.

† Mr. Walter Harris, in his "Tafilet," says the word Shillah = "noble," but he has probably been informed by a Berber. He also, after the fashion of most European travellers, "finds out immediately how infinitely superior the one (the Berbers) in morals and character are to Arabs. Their every word and look speak of greater honesty and truth than one finds in a month amongst the Arabs" ("Tafilet," p. 62). Certainly Mr. Harris has every right to speak, as few men know the mountaineers better than he does, and dressed in their clothes, his head shaved, and a string of camel's hair bound round his forehead, bare feet and legs, and wrapped in a brown djellaba, he could pass anywhere for one of those "moral" and "honest" folk. I wish, though, that he had stated plainly what he understands by Shillah "honesty" and "morality," for, as in theological discussions, the greatest difficulty is to define terms.

arghi" (lords), Amacrani (great one), and Amrgari
(elders), but nowadays, even in Sus and in the desert,
the Sultan's authority is much more felt. In fact,
until quite lately they lived as their forefathers—the
Getulians, Melano getulians, and Numidians—lived
before them, with the exception that being driven to
the mountains they had greatly lost the horsemanship
which made them famous to the ancient world. Even
to-day it is not rare to see them ride, just as the
Roman writers said the ancient Numidian cavalry
rode, without a saddle or a bridle, and guiding their
horses with a short stick, which they alternately
change from hand to hand to make them turn.

The words Mazyes, Maziriciæ and Mazyces occur in
many Greek and Roman writers, and seem not quite
impossible to be derived from " Amazirght," or from
" Mazig," the most ancient form known of their
appellation. Leo Africanus, himself a Moor,* calls
them " Amarigh," and says of them " they are strong,
terrible, and robust men, who fear neither cold nor
snow; their dress is a tunic of wool over the bare
flesh, and above the tunic they wear a mantle.
Round their legs they have twisted thongs, and this
serves them also for shoes. They never wear anything
on the head at any season ; they rear sheep, mules
and asses, and their mountains have few woods.
They are the greatest thieves, and traitors, and
assassins in the world——†

Even to-day this picture of them holds good in
most particulars. The Berbers of the mountains

* He was born in Granada, and fled to Fez after the capture of Granada
by the Catholic Kings. Being taken prisoner by Christian pirates, he was
brought to Rome, received into favour by the Pope, was baptised, and
died at Rome after translating his work on Africa into Italian.

† " Noble Shillah race " of modern travellers. " Moral and honest "
folk of Mr. Harris, &c. &c.

seldom wear turbans or anything but a string tied round their foreheads.   Generally they have a linen shirt to-day, but often wear the tunic as Leo Africanus says, and now and then one sees them with the twisted leg bandages like Pifferari.   As to their moral character, after some small experience, I rather hold to the view of Leo Africanus, than that of Mr. Walter Harris.   One thing is certain, that they cannot lie more than the Arabs do, but then the Arabs lie so prettily, with so much circumstance, and such nice choice of words, that it all comes to be a matter of individual taste, for there are those who had rather be deceived with civil manners by an Italian, than be cheated brutally by a North Briton, for the love of God.

The first of all the tribes we hear of in history as living in Morocco are the Autoloti of Ptolemy, who seem to be the " Holots," who now live in "El Gharb," that is, the country between Tangier and the Sebu. In Hanno's Periplus, the same word occurs, and the description of their country seems to tally with the territory where they live.

Luis de Marmol, who was long prisoner with the Moors in the sixteenth century, places a people called " Holots," near to Cape Azar.   Now it is certain that the " Holots " are Berbers, and the testimony of the writers referred to goes to prove the long continuance of the Berbers in the land, and also seems to prove that in ancient times, as now, the Berbers were not nomads, as the Arabs were, but stationary, as they are to-day.   Graberg di Hemso, in his curious " Spechio Geographico di Marocco," says, " Questi Mazighi della Tingitana fabbricarono, ne quella costa in vicenanza del capo Bianco la citta di Mazighan, che porta ad oggi il loro nome di nazione."   He

quotes no authority for his statement, and it is
certainly at variance with fact, for Mazagan was
founded by the Portuguese in 1506, and is called
Djedida, *i.e.*, New Town, by the Arabs; still the name
of Mazagan may yet commemorate an older town
under the style of Mazighan.

Be all that as it may, the "Tamazirght" inhabited
Morocco ages before the Arabs conquered the land,
and gave them the religion of the sword. Tradition
says they were once Christians, and certainly in their
embroideries and decorations the cross is used. Yet,
looking at the matter from an artistic point of view,
discounting (for the nonce) "morality," the "cross,"
and "honesty," it seems to me that noble is not a
term to use in speaking of the Berber, and I submit
it better fits a race such as the Arabs, who, in the
persons of their horses and themselves, have done so
much to refine the type of all those peoples, equine and
biped, whom they have come across.

As night was falling, and a whistling wind spring-
ing up from the mountains, the messenger appeared
bringing the news that the Sheikh refused to let anyone cross the pass, and that there had been a pretty hot
exchange of shots that afternoon between the men of
the Beni Sira, and a troop of cavalry crossing from
Sus. This was a stopper over all, for it was evident
we could not force our way through a road winding
by precipices, held by a mountain tribe. Remembering the Arab proverb which runs, "Always ask
counsel from your wife, but never act on what she
says," I held a long palaver with Haj Adee, Lutaif,
and my men, on what was best to do. Two courses
were now open to me, either to wheel about and follow
the shore road by Agadhir, or else to try the upper
and more difficult pass to Sus, which starts above

Amsmiz. This place was situated about two days' journey further on, the pass, according to all reports, took three good days to cross, and having crossed it, we should still be a long day from Tarudant.

Lutaif had no opinion, and as the rest all counselled Agadhir, except Haj Swani, who gave it his opinion that he would go wherever I did, I "opted" for Amsmiz, arguing that to turn back would certainly dishearten my companions, and if the Howara had been fighting a week ago, they would be fighting still, and thinking that even if taking the upper road I failed, I should see more of the interior of the Atlas, than I was likely to do by any other route. After having cursed the Beni Sira thoroughly in all the languages we knew, drank gallons of green tea, sat for an hour or two listening to stories of the Djinoun, smoked cigarettes and Kiff, and generally tried to imagine we were not disappointed, we retired to bed, so as before first light to be upon the road. Our bedroom had no window, and gave on the *al fresco* drawing room I have referred to; all round the walls were little recesses in which to put things, made in the thick-ness of the wall, pouches and powder horns hung from goat's horns forced underneath the thatch, three long "jezails," all hooped with silver, one with a Spanish two-real piece, depending from the trigger-guard, stood in the corner, a lantern made of tin with coloured glass, gave a red light, upon the floor of mud a Rabat carpet in pattern like a kaleidoscope or Joseph's coat, was spread; nothing of European manfacture in the whole room, except a large-sized (navy pattern) Smith and Wesson pistol, which, hang-by a red worsted cord upon the wall, seemed to project the shadow of the cross upon the room.

CHAPTER IV.

My journey all next day lay through low hills of reddish argillaceous earth, cut into gullies here and there by the winter rains, and clothed with sandaracs, Suddra (Zizyphus lotus) and a few mimosas. The hills sloped upwards to the wall-like Atlas, and on the left the desert-looking plain of Morocco, broken but by the flat-topped hill known as the Camel's Neck (Hank el Gimel), and bounded by the mountains above Demnat, and the curve the Atlas range makes to the north-east so as to almost circle round Morocco city. We search our hearts, that is, I search my own and the others' hearts and try to persuade myself that we have acted prudently in not attempting the Imintanout road. But when did prudence console anybody? Rashness at times may do so, but the prudent generally (I think) are more or less ashamed of the the virtue they profess. The Moors, of course, were glad we had risked nothing, for though no cowards when the danger actually presents itself, indeed, in many cases (as at the battles with the Spaniards in 1861) showing more desperate courage than anyone except the Soudanese, still they are so imaginative, or what you please, that if men talk of danger they will take a five days' journey to avoid the places where hypothetic peril lurks. Mohammed el Hosein, being in his character of ex-slave dealer, what the French call a "lapin," talked of his adventures in the past, told how he had smug-

gled slaves into the coast towns almost before the
Christian Consul's eyes, sung Shillah songs in a
high, quavering falsetto, and boasted of his prowess
in the saddle, occasionally bursting into a suppressed
chuckle at the idea of taking a Christian into Tarudant.

Almost before we are aware of it, on going down a
slope between some bushes, we found ourselves right
in the middle of a crowded market. These country
markets are a feature of Morocco, and, I think of,
almost every Arab country. Often they are held miles
away from any house, but generally on an upland
open space with water near. When not in use they
reminded me of the " rodeos," on to which the Gauchos,
in La Plata, used to drive their cattle to count, to
mark, part out, or to perform any of the various
duties of an " estancieros* " life. The markets usually
are known by the day of the week on which they are
held, as " Sok el Arba," " Sok el Thelatta," " el
Jamiz," and so forth; the Arabs using " Arba,"
" Tnain," " Thelatta," " one, two, three " &c., to designate their days. This market, in particular, I knew
to be the " Sok es Sebt," but thought we had been
some distance from it, and all my assurance was
required to make my way amongst at least two thousand people with the dignity which befits a Moorish
gentleman upon a journey. Arabs and Berbers, Jews
and Haratin (men of the Draa province, of mixed
race), all talking at the fullest pitch of strident voices,
all armed to the teeth, ovens with carcases of sheep
roasting entire inside them, knots of sheep, of cows,
some camels, lines of small brown tents made to be

---

* Estancia is the Argentine term used to denote a cattle farm. In Spain
it is rarely or never used in such a sense, and the word " Cortijo," is the
usual term for a farm.

packed upon a mule and called " Kituns," dust, dust, and more dust, and the peculiar smell, as of wild beasts, which emanates from a crowd of Arabs ; Moors from Morocco city in white fleecy haiks, these I avoided, as being my equals in suppositious rank, and, therefore, likely to address me ; Berbers in striped brown rags, and wrapped in the curious mantle, called an " ach-nif " in Shillah, made of black wool with fringes and an orange-coloured eye, about two feet in length, woven into the back ; through them I shoved my horse, not even looking down when the poor fellows lifted my cloak and kissed the hem, and, passing through majestically, I heard some mutter "that Sherif is very proud for one so thin," fat being amongst Moors a sign of wealth, as it was evidently amongst the Jews, if we are to take the testimony of the Old Testament as worth belief.

To ride right through a market and pass on would have looked suspicious, as markets in Morocco form a sort of medium for exchange of news, in the same manner that in old times the churchyard was a kind of club ; witness the story of the elder who was heard to say—" he would not give all the sermons in the world for five good minutes of the churchyard clash." So, after having gone about a quarter of a mile, we got under some olive trees (zeitun, from whence the Spanish aceituna, an olive), and, sitting in the shade sent Swani to the market to buy some " Schwah," that is, most of the carcase of a whole sheep roasted " en barkecue," Various poor brothers in Mohammed came to assure themselves of my complete good health but Mohammed el Hosein informed them the Sherif was ill, and, giving them some copper coins, they testi-fied to the existence of the one God, and hoped that he might in his mercy soon make me well. Being

schooled as to the form to be observed, I looked up
slowly, and, raising one hand, muttered as indistinctly
as I could that God was great, and that we all were
in his hands. This pleased Mohammed el Hoesin so
much that when we were alone he assured me I must
have been born a Sherif, and could I but speak
Arabic a little less barbarously that our journey would
have been productive, as Sherifs make it a practice,
whilst giving small copper to the poor, to cadge upon
their own account from the better classes, of course,
for Allah and His Holy Prophet's sake. Lutaif, who
in his character of Syrian, talked almost incessantly
to anyone we met, elicited that this particular market
called "Sok es Sebt," the "Sixth Day Market," is
one of four held in Morocco on a Saturday, thus
showing that the Jews have got most of the trade
into their hands, and do not care that markets should
be held upon their holy day. We tore the "Schwah"
between our fingers in the "name of God"; it tasted
much like leather cooked in suet, we passed the
ablutionary water over our hands moving them to
and fro to dry, drank our green tea, and were preparing for a siesta when it was rumoured that an
English Jew was soon expected to arrive. Having
as little, or even less, acquaintance with Yiddish than
with Arabic, and being certain that the English
Israelite would soon detect me, and falling on one
shoulder exclaiming "S'help me, who would 'ave
thought of meeting a fellow countryman out 'ere," I
saddled up and started as majestically as I felt I could,
upon my way. The start was most magnificent,
Swani and Mohammed helping to arrange my clothes
when I had clambered to my seat, and all went well
with the exception that no one happening to hold
Lutaif's off stirrup, and the huge Moorish mule saddle,

called a "Sirijah," being so slackly girthed, that it is almost impossible to scale it all alone, he fell into the dust, and Ali coming up to help with a broad grin received a hearty "Jejerud Din" (curse your religion), which caused a coolness during the remainder of the journey, for Lutaif, though a good Christian and as pious as are most dwellers on the Lebanon, yet came from the country where, as Arabs say, "The people all curse God," referring to the imprecation on their respective creeds, which is most faithfully taken and received between Maronite and Druse, Christian and Moslem, and all the members of the various jarring sects who dwell under the shadow of the cedars on those most theologic hills.   Nestling into the gorges of the hills, and crowning eminences, were scattered villages of the true Atlas type, built all of mud, flat roofed, the houses rising one over the other like a succession of terraces or little castles, and being of so exactly the same shade as the denuded hills on which they stand as to be almost impossible to make out till you are right upon them.   At times so like is village to hill, and hill to village, that I have taken an outstanding mound of earth to be a house, and many times have almost passed the village thinking it nonexistent.

Riding along and dangling my feet out of the stirrups to make the agony of the short stirrup leather, hung behind the girths, endurable, it struck me what peaceful folks the Arabs really were.   Here was a traveller almost totally unarmed, for the Barcelona and Marseilles "snap-haunces" we had borrowed at the Palm-Tree House were hardly to be called offensive weapons; without a passport, travelling in direct defiance of the Treaty of Madrid, in Arab clothes, asserting that he was an Arab or a Turk (as seemed

convenient) and unattended for defensive purposes
and yet apparently at least as safe, and running less
temptation to commit offence, than when crossing
Regent Street at night.

What was it that stopped a band of Arabs on the
look-out for plunder? what stood between us and a
party of the "Noble Shillah race?" either or both
could easily have plundered us and thrown our bodies
into some silo and nobody the wiser. The truth is, in
Morocco, when one reflects upon the inconveniences
of the country, the lonely roads, the places apparently
designed by Providence to make men brigands, and
the fact that almost every Arab owns a horse and is
armed at least with a stout knife, that the inhabitants
are either cowardly to a degree, are law abiding to a
fault, or else deprived by nature of initiative to such
extent as to be quite Arcadian in the foolish way in
which they set about to rob. When I remember
Mexico not twenty years ago, before Porfirio Diaz
turned the brigands, who used to swarm on every
road, into paid servants of the government; and how
men on starting on a journey, say, from the Rio
Grande to San Luis Potosí, all made their wills and
started weighted down with Winchester pistols and
bowie-knives, besides a stout machete stuck through
their girths; and how, sometimes the tramways running to bull fights outside Mexico itself were robbed,
the trains "set up," and how the whole republic was
delivered up to the tender mercies of the "road agent,"
Morocco seems to me a paradise. Throat cutting,
plenty of it; murder committed every day, oppression
rampant, tribal battles frequent and bloody; but then
the throat cutting is chiefly legal, the murder private
vengeance, and the oppression committed by the
government, and as for tribal battles do we not un-

derstand that foxes and carted stags, pheasants and
rabbits, grouse, roe, with partridges, snipe, wood-
cock, capercailzie, and those birds and beasts, who,
by the virtue of the Act are "Game," enjoy the sport,
then why not Moors? But highway robbery seems
not to flourish; occasionally you hear a Jew returning
from a market has been robbed, and men point out
with awe the place where robbers (Haramin)* slew
such a one, and on enquiry it turns out it happened
almost fifty years ago.

The above, of course, refers to all those portions of
Morocco where Christians travel; that is to Fez, to
Tetuan, from Mazagan to the city of Morocco, and
generally about Tangiers, the coast towns and the
Gharb,† outside those spheres the case is different;
and in the Riff, the Sus, Wad Nun, or even a few
miles outside of Mequinez, a Christian's life, or even
that of a Mohammedan from India, Persia or the East,
would not be worth a "flus."‡ We rested for our
mid-day halt upon the open plain under the shadow of
a great rock, the heat too great to eat, and passed the
time smoking and drinking from our porous water
jars, till the "enemy," as the Arabs call the Sun,
went down a little; and in the cool went on until a
wilderness of cactus, olives, oleanders, almond and
fig trees, olives, and palms, and apricots, and little
sandy paths zig-zagging between aloe hedges and a

* Literally "Bastards."

† El Gharb is a prairie territory stretching from Tangier to the river
Sebu. The word "Gharb" means " the west," and Algrave in Portugal
was simply the west of that country. The word "Trafalgar" is com-
pounded from "Tarf" a headland and "El Gharb" the west.

‡ Flus is a small copper coin, a donkey load of which about makes change
for a sovereign. It has come in Morocco to mean money generally, and
was evidently so used in Spain under the Moorish domination, for I remember seeing a coin, the inscription on which was "this flus was coined in
Andalous," *i,e.* Spain, which the Moor generally referred to as "Andalous.'"

few tapia walls backed by a ruined castle, betokened we were near Asif-el-Mal. Asif means river in the "noble Shillah" tongue, and at the foot of the crumbling walls a river ran, making things green and most refreshing to the eyes after ten hours of fighting with the enemy, enduring dust, and kicking at our animals after the fashion which all men adopt upon a journey, not that it helps the animals along, but seems to be a vent for the impatience of the traveller. Norias* creak, a camel with a donkey and a woman harnessed to one of them, water pours slowly out of the revolving "Alcuzas," and at the trough the maidens of the village stand waiting to fill their water jars, shaped like an amphora, which they carry on the shoulders with a strap braced round their hands. Asif-el-Mal boasts a Mellah, and Jews at once came out to offer to trade with us, to talk, and hear the news. Intelligent young Jews, Moisé, Slimo, and Mordejai with Baruch, and all the other names, familiar to the readers of the Old Testament, flock round us. All can read and write, can keep accounts, as they were born in Hamburg; most have ophthalmia, some are good-looking, white with great black eyes, and every-one of them seems to be fashioned with an extra joint about the back. Yet hospitable, civil and "prevenant" and a link with Europe, which they have never seen, but about which they read, and whose affairs they follow with the keenest interest, all knowing Gladstone's name and that of Salisbury; that France protects the East, that the Turks have fought with Greece; and longing for the day, when they can put on European clothes and blossom out arrayed after

---

* Noria is the Persian water-wheel, Naurah in Arabic, which literally means a machine, and as it probably was the greatest machine at the time of its invention (say B.C. 5,000), the name has remained.

the gorgeous fashion of the tribe in Mogador.   Each
of them wears a love-lock hanging upon his shoulder,
and, without doubt, if they were but a little bit more
manly looking, they would be as fine young men as
you could wish to see.

Their race almost controls the town, few Shillah
and hardly any Arabs, but the Sheikh and his immediate following live in the place.   A proof
the land is good, the soil productive, and the water
permanent; for when did Jews set up their tabernacles
on an unproductive soil, in a poor town, or follow the
fortunes of any one who was not rich?   Their chief,
Hassan Messoud, a venerable man, dressed in a long
blue gown, a spotted " belcher " pocket handkerchief
over his head and hanging down behind in a most
unbecoming style, advanced to greet us.   Perhaps
the finest Eastern Jew I ever saw; a very Moses in
appearance, as he might have been on Sinai a little
past his prime, and yet before the ingratitude of those
he served had broken him.   Beside him walks his
daughter, a Rebecca, or Zohara, bearing fresh butter
in a lordly tin dish, and bread baked upon pebbles,
and with the impression of the stones upon the under
side.   Such bread the chosen people have left in
Spain, and still in Old Castille amongst the " Cris-
tianos Rancios," who hate the very name of Jew, and
think that the last vestige of their customs has long
left Spain, the self-same bread is eaten at Easter, if
I remember rightly; and so, perhaps, the true believer
(Christian this time) unwittingly bakes bread which
yet may damn him black to all eternity.

Hassan comes quickly into the tent, and bids us
welcome in Jewish Arabic; and waiting cautiously
till even our own Moors have left the tent, breaks
into Spanish and asks me of what nationality I am.   I

tell him from "God's country," and he says "Ingliz,"
to which I answer, "yes, or Franciz, for both are one";
and he grins, squatting close to the door of the tent,
servile but dignified, full six feet high, his black beard
turning grey, and hands large, fat, and whitish, and
which have never done hard work. We talk, and then
Hassan takes up his parable. Glory to Allah he is
rich, and all the Governors are his dear friends, that
is they owe him money; and as he talks the old-time
Spanish rhyme comes to my memory, which, talking
of some Jews who came to see a certain king, speaks
of their honied words, and how they praised their
people and boasted of their might.

> " Despues vinieron Don Salomon y Don Ezequiel,
>   Con sus dulces palabras parecen la miel,
>   Hacen gran puja, de los de Israel."

And yet he was but easy of dispense, wearing the
clothes of an ordinary Morocco Jew, with nothing to
indicate his wealth.

As we sat talking to him of the exchange in
Europe, about the Rothschilds, Sassoons, Oppen-
heims, and others of the "chosen" who bulk largely
in the money columns of the daily press of Europe
(all of whom he knew by name), and interchanging
views about the late Lord Beaconsfield, whom Hassan
knew as Benjamin ben Israel, the daughters of God's
folk came out upon the house-tops, dressed in red
and yellow, with kerchiefs on their heads, eyes like
the largest almonds, lips like full-blown pomegranates,
and looked with pride upon their headman talking to
the "Sherif" or "Christian Caballer," whichever he
might be, on equal terms. Strange race, so intellectual, so quick of wit, so subtle, and yet without the
slightest dignity of personal bearing; handsome, and

yet without the least attraction, conquering the Arabs as they conquer Saxons, Latins, or all those with whom they come in contact upon that modern theatre of war—the Stock Exchange. Hassan Messoud having protested that by the God of Abraham we were all welcome, retired and left us to pitch our tent upon a dust-heap in a courtyard, between some ruined houses and the village wall,

Under the moonlight, the distant plain looking like a vast steely-blue sea, the deep red roads all blotted out, and the palms and olives standing up exactly as dead stalks of corn stand up in an October wheat-field; the omnipresent donkeys and camels of the East asleep, hobbled or straying in the foreground beneath the walls, and the mysterious, silent, white-robed figures wandering about like ghosts, the town appeared to me to look as some Morisco village must have looked in Spain when the Mohammedans possessed the land, and villages brown, ruinous, and hedged about with cactus-like Asif-el-Mal, clung to the crags, and nestled in the valleys of the Sierra de Segura, or the Alpujarra.

At daybreak, Hassan Messoud appeared with break-fast at our tent, olives and meat in a sauce of oil and pepper, most appetising upon an empty stomach, but not to be refused without offence, Then, throwing milk upon the ground from a small gourd, he blessed us, and invoked the God of Israel to shield us on our way. A worthy, kindly, perhaps usurious, but most hospitable Israelite, not without guile (or property), a type of those Jews of the Middle Ages from whom Shakespeare took Shylock, and in whose hands the lords, knights, squires, and men-at-arms were as a Christian stockbroker, who, cheat he as wisely as he can, is to-day in the hands of any Jew, who, a few months ago, retailed his wares in Houndsditch, but who, the Exchange attained to, walks its precincts as firmly as it were Kodesh, and he a priest after the order of Melchizedec. Riding along the trail which runs skirting the foothills of the Atlas, and forces us to dive occasionally into the deep dry " nullah," for there are only six or seven bridges in all Morocco, and none near the Atlas, the vegetation changes, and again we enter dwarf rhododendrons, arbutus, and kermes-oak, and pass into a zone of plants like that of southern Spain, with the exception that here the mignonette becomes a bush, and common golden rod grows four feet high, with a thick woody stem. White poplars, walnuts, elms, and a variety of ash are planted round the houses ; and from the eaves hang strings of maize cobs ; bee hives like those the Moors left in Spain, merely a hollow log of wood, or piece of cork bark, lie in the gardens ; grape vines climb upon the trees, producing grapes, long, rather hard, claret-coloured, and aromatic, the best, I think, in all the world, and which have fixed themselves upon the memory of my palate as have the oranges of Paraguay.

About mid-day, upon a little eminence, we sight the tower of the Kutubieh, glory of Morocco, but the city is, so to speak, hull down, and the white tower seems to hang suspended in the air without foundations ; indeed, it looks so thin at the great distance from which we see it, as to be but a mere white line standing up in the plain and pointing heavenwards, that is, if towers built by false prophets do not point to hell. All day my horse, really the best I ever rode in all Morocco, had been uneasy, wanting to lie down ; so disregarding the advice of Mohammed el Hosein to prick him with my knife and pray to God, somewhat prosaically I got off, and, unsaddling him, found his shoulder fearfully swollen, and saw at once how I came possessed of a horse, the like of which few Christians, even for money, get hold of from a Moor. I saw at once he had a fistulous sore right through the withers, and incurable without an operation and a long rest. Then I believed what Mohammed el Hosein had told me, that the horse was from the other side of the Atlas and had been used in ostrich hunting, for a better and more fiery beast I never rode, and though thin, rough, and in the worst condition, had he been sound about the back, quite fit to carry me to Timbuctoo.

The Arabs have an idea upon a journey that a man should dismount as seldom as he can. They say dismounting and remounting tires the horse more than a league of road, they therefore sit the livelong day without dismounting from their seat. The Gauchos, on the contrary, say it helps a horse to get off now and then and lift the saddle for a moment, loosening the girth so that the air may get between the saddle and the back. This the Moors hold to be anathema, and Spaniards, Mexicans, and most horsemen of the south agree that the saddle should not be shifted till the horse is cool, on pain of getting a sore back. Who shall decide when horsemen disagree? However, the Gauchos all girth very tightly, and the Arabs scarcely, draw the girth at all, their saddles repose on nine (the number is canonical) thick saddle cloths, and are kept in their place more by the breast-plate than the girth. It may be therefore that given the loose girth, short stirrup leathers, and their own flowing clothes, that personal convenience has more to do with the custom of not getting off and on, than regard for the welfare of their beast. The Arabs in Morocco, though fond of horses, treat them roughly

and foolishly; at times they cram them with unnecessary food, at times neglect them; their feet they
almost always let to grow too long, their legs they
spoil by too tight hobbling, and if upon a journey
their horse tires they ride him till he drops.

Across the mountains and amongst the wilder
desert tribes, this is not so, and travellers all agree
that the wild Arab really loves his horse; but he has
need of him to live, whereas inside Morocco horses are
used either for war or luxury, or because the man who
rides them cannot afford a mule. The pacing mule,
throughout North Africa, is as much valued as he was
in Europe in the Middle Ages, and commands a
higher price than any horse; yet whilst allowing that
he is dogged as a Nonconformist on the road, sober
and comfortable, to my eye, a man wrapped in a
white burnoose, perched on a saddle almost as large
as the great bed of Ware, looks fitter to be employed
to guard a harem than to enjoy the company of the
houris inside. Necessity (in days gone by) has often
forced me to ride horses with a "flower" * on their
backs or with a sore which rendered every step they
made as miserable to me as it was hell to them; but
as on these occasions I rode either before an Indian
Malon,† or for the dinner of a whole camp, so I at once
determined that, notwithstanding any risk, I would
purvey me a new horse at the next stop. As it
turned out, the changing horses and the talk which
ensued, as the owner of the horse and I tried to
deceive each other about our beasts, was the occasion

* The Gauchos used to call a sore on a horse's back "una flor," a flower,
and they certainly rode their horses no matter how red the "flower" was,
as if their own withers were unwrung.

† Malon was the word used on the Pampa to designate an Indian invasion. I put it to casuists if it was permissible on these occasions to ride a
sore-backed horse, and still be called a humane man.

of my never reaching Tarudant. At least I think so, and if it was, some better traveller will do that which I failed in doing, write a much better book than any I could write, and if he be a practical and pushful man spare neither horses on the road, nor stint the public of one iota of his "facts," for to the pushful is the kingdom of the earth. As to what sort of king-dom they have made of it, it is beyond the scope of this poor diary to enquire.

And so we crossed the Wad el Kehra, and early in the afternoon tied up our animals under a fig-tree, with a river running hard by, a stubble field in front, and Amsmiz itself crowning a hill upon our right. Amongst the "algarobas," * fig trees and poplars, swallows flit, having come south, or perhaps migrated north from some more southern land.

At the entrance of the town stood the palace of the Caid, an enormous structure made of mud and painted light rose-pink, but all in ruins, the crenelated walls being overthrown, the machicolated towers blown up with gunpowder. The Caid it seems oppressed the people of the town and district beyond the powers of even Arabs and Berbers to endure; so they rebelled, and to the number of twelve thousand besieged the place, took it by storm, and tore it all to pieces to search for money in the rose pink-walls.

Most people in Morocco if they have money hide it in the walls of their abode, but the Caid of Amsmiz was wiser, and had sent all his to Mogador. He fought to the last, then cutting all his women's throats, mounted his favourite horse and almost un-attended " maugre all his enemies, through the

---

* "Algaroba" is one of the words the Spaniards have taken from Arabic. The word in that language being " El Karoub " or as some spell it " El Keurroub."

thickest of them he rode," leaving his stores well-
dressed with arsenic, so that, like Samson in his
fall, he killed more of his enemies than in his life.
To-day he is said to live in Fez, greatly respected, a
quiet old Arab with a fine white beard, whose greatest
pleasure is to tell his rosary.

Curious how little the Oriental face is altered by
the storms of life. I knew one, Haj Mohammed el
————, —a scoundrel of the deepest dye—who, in his
youth had poisoned many people, had tortured others,
assassinated several with his own hand, and yet a
kindly, courteous, venerable gentleman, whose hobby
was to buy any eligible young girl he heard of, to
stock his harem. One day I ventured to remark that
he was getting rather well on in years to think of
such commodities. He answered: "Yes, but then
I buy them as you Christians buy pictures—to adorn
my house; by Allah, my heirs will be the gainers by
my mania." Yet the man's face was quiet and serene,
his eyes bright as a sailor's, his countenance as little
marred by wrinkles as those one sees upon the
Bishops' benches in the House of Lords; and as he
stroked his beard, and told his beads, he seemed to
me a patriarch after the type of those depicted in the
Old Testament. Perhaps it is the lack of railways,
with their clatter, smoke, and levelling of all mankind to the most common multiple; but still it is the
case—an Eastern scoundrel's face is finer far than
that a Nonconformist Cabinet Minister displays, all
spoiled with lines, with puckers round the mouth, a
face in which you see all natural passion stultified,
and greed and piety—the two most potent factors in
his life—writ large and manifest.

An orange grove, backed by a cane-brake, with the
canes fluttering like flags, was near to us; cows,

goats, and camels roamed about the outskirts of the town, as in Arcadia—that is, of course, the Arcadia of our dreams—or of Theocritus, unlike the chequer-board, wire-fenced and widely-roaded land, where "Swipes" is king, and where the rich shoot corn-fed pheasants, whilst their womenkind pursue their friends who have remained at home, and about which we cant, whilst taking care to visit it as little as we may.

Jews went and came, saluting every one, and being answered: "May Allah let you finish out your miser-able life"; but yet as pleased as if they had been blessed. Their daughters came, like Rebecca, to the well—all carrying jars—-unveiled, and yet secure, for in this land no Moor so vile as to cast eyes upon the daughter of a Jew.

Upon the ramparts, shadowy white-robed figures, with long guns, go to and fro, guarding the town from hypothetic enemies; and through an arch, be-tween two palm trees, the Kutabieh rises, distant and slender, and the white haze around its base shows where Marakesh lies. On every hedge are blackberries and travellers' joy; whilst a large honeysuckle, in full flower, smells better than all Bucklersbury in simple time; a jay's harsh cry sounds like the howl of a cayote, and Europe seems a million miles away. And in the evening-light, the foot-paths, which cut every hill, shine out as they had all been painted by some clever artist, who had diluted violet with gold.

Nothing reminds one that within half-a-mile a town, in which three thousand people live, is near, except the footpaths which zig-zag in and out, crossing the fields, emerging out of woods, and intersecting one-another, as the rails seem to do at Clapham

Junction. A fusillade tells that a Sherif from the Sus
has just arrived; all Amsmiz sallies forth to meet
him mounted upon their best, fire off their guns,
charging right up to the Sherif, and firing close to
his horse—wheeling and yelling like Comanches—
and presenting, from where we stood, a picture,
shadowy, fantastic, and unbelievable to one who but
three weeks ago had left a land of monotones. The
Sherif's people open fire, and when the smoke clears
off the Sherif himself, mounted upon a fine white
horse, rides slowly forward, holding a green flag; and
all the people fall into a long line behind him, which,
by degrees, is swallowed up under the horse-shoe
gateway of the town. Mohammed el Hosein, whom
I had sent to look out for a horse, appears with
a little, undersized, and brachycephalic Shillah,
leading a young black horse, unshod, with feet as
long as scoops, in good condition, and sound in wind
and limb, and with an eye the blackest I have seen in
mortal horse—a sign of perfect temper; incontinently I determine in my mind to buy him at all cost.
We praise our horses—that is, the Shillah praises his
—but I, as a Sherif, am far too grand to do so at first
hand; but Swani lies like a plumber about mine—
which stands and kicks at flies, and looks—like horses
do, when one is just about to part with them—much
more attractive than one ever thought before.
The Shillah leads up his horse, which I pretend
hardly to notice; and, luckily for me, he speaks no
Arabic. Then he looks at my horse, and, I imagine,
runs him down, for Swani springs upon the horse's
back, and runs him *ventre à terre* over the rough
stubble, and, stopping with a jerk—the horse's feet
cutting the ground like skates—gets off, and says
that, help him, Allah, the horse is fit for Lord Mo-

hammed, and that I only sell him because I am so tender-hearted about his back.

This makes the Shillah think there is a "cat shut up inside,"* for no one sells a horse for a sore back amongst his tribe. We try his horse—that is, Mohammed el Hosein makes him career about the field without a bridle; and then I mount him, and display what I consider horsemanship. Nine dollars and the horse? By Allah, seven; but the Shillah, who has not tried my horse, looks at his colt, and says: "I brought him up, fed him with camels' milk, rode him to war, and he is six years old; nine dollars and the horse." We shake our heads; and he, mounting his horse, yells like a Pampa Indian, and charging through the cane-brake bare-backed, and with nothing but a string on one side of his horse's neck, rushes up a steep bank and disappears, riding like a Numidian. I say it was a pity I did not give the nine, but am assured all is not over, and that the man has probably gone to bring back "a bargain-striker" to complete the sale. Throughout Morocco, when animals change hands, the bargaining lasts sometimes for a week; and at the last a man appears, sometimes a passer-by, who is pressed into the undertaking, who—seizing on the bargainers' right hands drags them together—and completes the deal.

In about half-an-hour our man comes back, bringing the local "Maalem," that is smith, who talks and talks, and as he talks surveys me from the corner of his eye. At last the Shillah yields, takes the seven dollars, counts them with great attention, tapping each one of them upon a stone to see if "it speaks true," and then mounting my horse essays its paces.

* Aqui hay gato encerrado is the Spanish proverb in reference to anything which seems too good to be true.

As it fell out the horse, which galloped like a roe, with Swani set off with a plunge which almost sent the Shillah over one side, and turning flew to the mules and stopping by them refused to move a step. The Shillah thought, of course, he had been done, and I had most reluctantly to mount the horse and make him go. We give our word the horse is not a jibber, and swear by Allah if he is, and the Shillah will send him back to Mogador, he shall receive his money and his own horse on our return.

He takes our word at once and grasps my hand, puts his own bridle on my horse, and bending down kisses his own horse underneath the neck, and says, in Shillah, that he hopes I shall never ill-treat his horse; I promise (and perform) and bid my own horse farewell after my fashion, and the Shillah mounts and rides towards the town, out of my life. A little dour and fish-eyed, turbanless and ragged man, legs bowed from early riding, face marked with scars, a long curved knife stuck through a greasy belt, hands on a horse as if they came from heaven; his farewell to his horse was much more real than is the leavetaking of most men from their wives, and moved me to the point of being about to call him back and break the bargain, had I not reflected that the pang once over, the poor Shillah would never in his life be at the head of so much capital.*

In less than half-an-hour the Maalem had shod the horse, shortening its feet with an iron instrument shaped like a trowel, and nailing on the shoes, which almost cover the whole foot, with home-made nails; he

---

* The Shillah's black horse is now in the hands of Don José Miravent, the Spanish Consul at Mogador, after having carried me all the journey. As to my grey horse I cannot say, nor yet be certain, if there are birds in last year's nests.

stays to guard our animals (and spy upon us), and we prepare for our first al fresco night.

Unlike America, where travellers sleep out of doors from Winnipeg to Patagonia, in the East, except in crossing deserts, to sleep out of doors without a tent is quite exceptional, and yet one never sleeps so soundly as on a fine night beside a fire, one's head upon a saddle, feet to the fire, and the stars to serve as clock. Even the wandering Arabs generally carry tents, and thus, in my opinion, all through the East much of the charm of camping out is lost. But everything we do is a convention, and Arabs are not savages, but on the contrary even the Bedouins are highly civilised after their fashion, and the civilised man must always have a roof, even of canvas, over his head to shut out nature. Not but that your common Moors, like to "your Kerne of Ireland" in ancient days, do not sleep out, for nothing is more common than on a rainy night, in camping at a village, for the Sheikh to send a guard to watch a traveller's horses, and for the guard to "liggen in their hoods" all the night long. So at Amsmiz, under a fig tree, I made my camp, despite the protests of Lutaif, the Maalem,* and Mohammed el Hosein, who joined in saying that it was not decent for a man of my (Moorish) position to camp outside the town. Swani himself was rather nervous, and, as it turned out, there may have been some risk, for a strong "war-party," as they would say upon the frontiers in America, drove almost every head of cattle belonging to the town that very night. We slept as sound as doormice, and the "Maalem," who kept watch with an old muzzle-loading rifle

---

* "Maalem" literally means a "master" as a master carpenter, master smith, &c. In Morocco it is often used for a good rider who is said to be "Uahed Maalem."

stamped with the Tower mark, slept like a top, knowing the duty of a most ancient guard, for during the night I thought I heard a noise of people passing, and waking saw him fast asleep with the old rifle by his side full cocked, and with a bunch of rushes in its muzzle either for safety or for some other reason not made plain. Darwin relates the peculiar and in-effaceable impression a night he slept under stars, upon the Rio Colorado, in Patagonia, made on him. He says the cold blue-looking sky, the stars, the silence, the dogs keeping watch, the horses feeding tied to their picket pins, and the sense of being cut off from all mankind, appealed to him more than the beauty of the tropics, the grandeur of the Andes, or anything that he remembered in his travels. And he was right, nothing appeals to civilised and to uncivilised alike, so much as a fine night when one sleeps near one's horse, and wakes occasionally to listen to the noises of the night. Men from the counter, from the univer-sity, riff-raffs of towns cast out like dross into a frontier territory, all feel the spell. The Indians and the Arabs feel it, but do not know exactly what they feel; still, in a house, under a roof, they pine for something which I am certain is the open air at night.

'Tis said some ancient wise philosopher once took an Indian from the southern Pampa and showed him all the delights, the pomps and vanities, of Buenos Ayres, showed him the theatre with Christian girls dancing half naked, took him to mass at the cathe-dral, led him along the docks, let him fare sump-tuously, and then accompanied him to gaze upon the multifarious faces of strange women, who used to lean from almost every balcony and beckon to the stranger in that town; and then the Indian, fed, instructed, with his mind enlarged by all the pomp and circumstance of a Christian town, asked him to say if he liked Buenos Ayres or the Pampa best. The story goes that, after pondering a while, the Indian answered : " Buenos Ayres very large, beautiful things, very wonderful, Christian women kind to poor Indian, but the Pampa best." A brutish answer of a brute mind, 'tis patent that the man was quite incapable of understanding all he saw, no doubt our gospel truths were all unknown to him, the philosopher who took him round to haunts of low debauchery either a fool or knave ; but on the other hand, riddle me this, how many men of cultivation, education, and the rest, have seen the Pampa, prairie, desert, or the steppes, and putting off the shackles of their bringing-up stayed there for life, and became Indians, Arabs, Cossacks, or Gauchos ; but who ever saw an Indian, Arab, or wild man of any race come of his own accord and put his neck into the noose of a sedentary life, and end his days a clerk ?

And so of faiths, the missionary for all his preaching would never mark a sheep, had he but gospel truths alone to draw upon. What brings the savage to the fold is interest, guns, cotton cloth, rum, tea, sugar, coffee, and the thousand things for which a commentator might search the Scriptures through from end to end and not find mentioned. In Central Africa the Christian and the Moslem missionary are both at work marking their sheep as fast as may be, and each one as much convinced as is the other of the justice of his cause. With a fair field, without the adventitious aids of Christian goods, the Moslem wins hands down.

The Christian comes and says " My negro friends, believe in Christ," and the poor negro, always eager to believe in anything, assents, and then the Christian sets him to black his boots, and all that negro's life he never rises to an equality with his converter. Then comes the Mussulman and cries "Only one God." The fetish worshipper who has had a dozen all his life, thinks it a little hard to give them up, but does so, becomes a Moslem, and is eligible to be Sultan, Basha, Vizier, Caid, Sheikh, or what not; so that, put rum and rifles on one side, and preaching be the test, in fifty years from the Lake Chad to Cape Town there would not be a single negro, except a few who stuck to their old gods, outside Islam.

I slept but fitfully, knowing if I could leave Amsmiz without suspicion that I was sure to reach my journey's end. The night wore on, the sapphire sky changing to steely-blue; as the "muezzin" called at the "Feyer,"* great drops of dew hung from the leaves; up from the river rose the metallic croaking of the frogs; Canopus was just setting; across the sky, the mirage of the dawn stole stealthily, the mules stood hanging down their heads upon the picket rope, a jackal howled somewhere out on the plain; Allah perhaps looked down, and not far off from me baited quite peacefully my (new) destrere on "herbes fine and good."

* "El Feyer" in Morocco is the call to prayers about three in the morning.

CHAPTER V.

PLEASING to wake up under the fig trees with all our cloaks and blankets wet with dew, to find our guard, the "Maalem," still sound asleep, and be accosted by a tracker who informed us that many of the cattle of the town had been driven off the night before, and who would hardly believe that all our animals were safe. Soon parties from the town, armed and muffled up in cloaks against the morning air, rode out from underneath the horseshoe gateway, and spread in all directions, trying to strike the trail of the "mad herdsmen," as they were called along the Highland Border in the days before prosperity had rendered Scotland the home of commonplace.

Though sharp of eye, it did not strike me that the Arabs and Shillah were experienced trackers. They rode about too much, and must have crossed the trail of the lost cattle a hundred times, and I kept thinking that an "Arribeño"* from the River Plate would have done better work than the whole tribe. Still, as they scattered on the hills, their white clothes just appearing now and then behind the clumps of trees, as they "quartered" all the ground, they fell effectively into the middle distance, and no doubt, if they never found their cattle, on the first fine night

* An "Arribeño" is a man from the upper provinces, some of which have long hard names, as Catamarca Jujuy Rioja, &c.; so, to save adjectives, they are lumped as "Arribeños."

they would recoup themselves from some neighbouring
village in the hills. Cattle and horse-stealing, with
an occasional higher flight into the regions of abduc-
tion of young girls, seem to be staple industries in all
pastoral countries, and nowhere but in western Texas
are taken very seriously, but there the horse-thief
hangs. Camped once outside a village called Bel-a-
rosis, on the road from Tangier to Rabat, a raid-
ing party attacked the place upon a rainy night,
fought quite a lively action, the bullets coming
through my tent, drove off some horses and several
yoke of oxen, and in the morning the Caid rode up
on horseback, his followers behind him, in just the
spirit that a gentleman at home starts out to hunt.
He praised his God for his good luck, and said he
reckoned (by Allah's help) to retake all the " Creagh,'
and drive above a thousand dollars' worth of sheep,
of cattle, and horses, from the weakest neighbours
of the nearest hostile tribe he met.

In all the actions that take place consequent upon
these cattle raids, but few are slain, for though both
Arabs and the Berbers all have guns, their style of
fighting is a survival from the time they carried bows.
They rarely charge, and never engage hand-to-hand,
but gallop to and fro and fire their guns with both
eyes shut, or, turning on their horses, fire over the
tail; so few are killed, except the prisoners, who
generally are butchered in cold blood, if they are
not of such account as to be worth a ransom. A
merry, pleasant life enough for able-bodied men,
and not unhealthy, and one that makes them
singularly bad subjects for missionary work. So
stony is the ground in the vineyard of the tribes, that
up to now I never heard of any missionary so bold or
foolish as to attempt to dig. A day will come, no

doubt, when their hearts will prove more malleable ; but I fear before that time their bodies will have to be much wrought upon by rifles, revolvers, and the other civilising agents which commonly precede the introduction of our faith.

Leaving Amsmiz, the road to Sus leads over foot-hills all of red argillaceous earth and fissured deeply here and there by winter rains. Now and then strange effects of coloured earth, blue, yellow, green, and mauve, diversify the scene. The road leads through a straggling oak wood and emerges at a village, where, in the middle, the county council is assembled in a thatched mosque. Mosques serve for council chambers, meeting places, and in villages, for travellers to sleep in, for throughout Morocco the sanctury is never closed, and thus the people feel their God is always there, and not laid up in lavender for six days in the week.

The " Maalem," who had accompanied us as guide, and as a guarantee that we were creditable folk—for in the wilder districts of Morocco, travellers take a man in every district to convoy them to the next—had reached his limit, and, laying down his gun, entered the mosque to get another man. What he said there I do not know ; if he had doubts perhaps he uttered them, at any rate, after a most unseasonable wait, which kept us all on pins and needles, he emerged, bringing a most ill-favoured tribesman, who came up to me and, kissing my clothes, asked for my blessing. I gave it him as well as I was able, but fancied he was not satisfied, as he retired muttering in Shillah, of which I did not understand a word. The "Maalem" bade us good-bye, and asked for cartridges, which, of course, we gave, but how they benefited him is a moot point, for they were intended for a small-size Win-

chester; he drew his charge and crammed the four
or five cartridges we gave him into his old "Tower"
gun, but as I did not pass by Amsmiz on my return, I
have no information how he fared when he touched off
the piece.

Little by little the road got worse until we entered a
tremendous gorge, just like a staircase, which made the
worst roads in the Sierra Morena look like Piccadilly
by comparison. Only a mule, an Iceland pony, or a
horse bred in the mountain districts of Morocco
could have coped with such a road, and, as it was,
the efforts of the poor brutes were pitiable to see.
Under our feet, at a great depth below, the Wad el
N'fiss boiled furiously amongst the stones, winding
and rewinding like a watch spring, and forcing us to
cross it many times, when its swift current proved so
formidable that, although not more than three feet
deep, we had to enter altogether in a group to keep
our feet. As we were toiling up a steep incline, a
shouting brought our hearts into our mouths, and,
looking back, we saw two mountaineers rushing to
intercept us, from a neighbouring hill. No time for
any consultation, or to do more than cock our miserable guns and sit quite meekly waiting for the worst.
On came the mountaineers, bounding from stone to
stone till they appeared upon the road and blocked
our way. Long guns, curved daggers, and almost
naked save for their long woollen shirts, their side
locks flying in the wind, they looked most formidable,
and poured out at once a volume of guttural Shillah
which sounded menacing. Mohammed-el-Hosein,
who with Ali the muleteer spoke Shillah, interpreted
to Swani who, half in Arabic and half in Spanish
(which he called Turkish) informed me what they
said.

It seemed the desperadoes wanted us to stop until a little boy brought down some Indian corn and milk, for it appeared it was the custom of those hills never to let a well dressed Moor pass without some little offering. Of course a poor man, or anyone to whom the maize and milk would have been of great service passed by unnoticed, as in other lands. I graciously assented, and in due course a boy appeared carrying a wooden bowl, from which I drank and passed it to my followers after the usual grace.* The tribesmen would accept no money, but asked me to say a word for them about their taxes, which were not paid, to their liege lord. As might be expected of me I said I would, and should have done so had I known who their lord was or where he lived, or had I chanced to meet the lord in a more seasonable place. Little by little we entered the zone of Arar trees (Callitris Quadrivalvis) about which Hooker says :—"this tree has no congener, its nearest ally being a South African genus of Cupressus (Widdingtoniana.)†" Various writers, as Shaw‡ and Daubeny,§ have attempted to indentify this tree with the " Θυια," of Theophrastus, and the Thyine Wood of the Apocalypse. Daubeny makes both Martial and Lucian refer to it under the name of Citrus, and Hooper is of opinion that the "Citrea mensa" of Petronius Arbiter was made of Arar-wood. An ingenious writer (Captain Cook, " Sketches in Spain ") is almost certain that the roof of the Mosque of Cordova is of Arar, because the Spaniards refer to it as being made of " Alerce."

* Bismillah is the Arab " grace before meat." In rendering thanks to the " Great Giver " they say, " El Ham du lillah," " Praise be to God." Poor heathens, what can be the use of their troubling *our* Creator.

† " Hooker's Morocco," page 389.

‡ " Travels in Barbary."

§ " Trees and Shrubs of the Ancients."

"Alerce" happens to mean larch in Spanish, but when did a derivation hunter ever allow that the people of any country really understood the meaning of words in their own paltry language. It is perhaps well not to question too closely the dogmas of science, and what prudent man would aver that anything might not be found in the veracious pages of the Apocalypse?

The Arars spread all over the mountains in a dense low scrub, rarely attaining more than ten feet high, on account of the frequent fires which the inhabitants light in the spring to obtain pasture for their goats and sheep. In an angle of the road I passed four fine old trees, perhaps forty feet in height, immensely branchy, and with trunks measuring possibly two and a-half feet in diameter. In the glades between the cedars patches of Indian corn were ripening, some was dead ripe, but no one dared to gather it, for the Caid of Kintafi, into whose territory we now had passed, had issued orders that he would give the signal for the harvest, and had not yet seen fit to give the word. Well do the Spaniards say that "fear, not walls protect the vineyard,"* for not a house stood within several miles of some of the maize patches and still not a head of corn was touched.

The Caid of Kintafi, who was destined to be my captor, had some years before waged war with Muley-el-Hassan, the late Sultan of Morocco. The Sultan had invaded the mountain territory of Gundaffi, and destroyed most of the villages, but not being able to reduce the fortress of the Caid had won him to his side by offering him the hand of either his sister or his daughter, and had departed after having brought the war to a conclusion, on the peace-with-honour plan.

* Miedo guarda viñas y no vallados.

The Caid rendered him henceforth a limited obedience, responding to his overlord's demands for taxes, and for assistance in the field when he thought fit, but taking care not to rebuild his villages, so that the aforesaid overlord might find a desert through which to pass if the fit took him to again commence hostilities. El Kintafi, for after the Scottish fashion he is designated territorially, is of the Berber race, and although speaking Arabic he speaks it as a foreigner, and is reckoned one of the greatest chieftains of the Berber people in the south.

Eight or nine months of drought had rendered the plain country through which I passed up to Amsmiz almost a desert, and it was pitiful to see the people digging for a kind of earth-nut, locally known as "Yerna," white in colour and semi-poisonous till after many washings. The plant I have not been able to identify, the leaves are something like one of the umbelliferæ. Hooker does not seem to notice it in his Botany of Morocco, and perhaps, when he was in the south, famine had not forced the people to dig for it, or the small thin leaves had all been withered by the heat.

Crawling along the mountain roads I found myself trying to estimate which of the two entailed most misery upon mankind, the old-time famine, which I saw going on all round me in Morocco, caused by want of water and failure of the crops, or the artificial modern and economic famine so familiar in all large towns, where in the West End the rich die from a plethora of food, and in the East End the poor exist just at subsistence limit by continual work. No doubt, in modern towns, the poor enjoy the doubtful blessings of improved sanitation, gas, and impure water, laid on in insufficient quantities to every

house; of education, that is, illusory instruction to
the fifth standard, to fit them to drive carts and tend
machines; but, on the other hand, they have but
little sun, either external or internal, in their lives,
and know their misery by the help of the education
which they pay for through the rates.

The sufferer by famine, as in Morocco, suffers
enough, God knows, stalks about like a skeleton, dies
behind a saint's tomb, but in the sun, with a belief in
Allah to the last, and dies a man, his eyesight not
impaired by watching wheels whirr round to make
a sweater rich, his hands not gnarled with useless
toil (for what can be more useless than to work
all through your life for some one else), and his
emaciated face still human, and not made gnomish
by work, drink, and east wind, like the poor
Christian scarecrows of Glasgow, Manchester, and
those accursed "solfataras," the Yorkshire manufacturing towns. But place it where you will, either in
tents, on some oasis in the desert, wandering as the
Indians used to wander before America was but one
vast advertisement for pills, or in the sweaty, sooty,
noisy "centre of industry" (may man see fit some
day to destroy his handiwork, as God seems impotent), mankind is made to suffer; so, perhaps, Tolstoi
has the root of things when he suggests that marry-
ing, giving in marriage, and all licensed or illegitimate propagation should cease, and man by non-
existence at last attain to bliss.

So in a pass between two walls of earth, with
bands of shale crossing them transversely, and roots
of long dead Arars sticking through the ground,
I came upon the human comedy fairly played out by
representative marionettes of every age and sex.
First, father, a fine old Arab, gaunt, miserable, grey-

headed, ragged, hollow-cheeked, without a turban, shoes, or waist-belt, and carrying a child which looked over his shoulder, with enormous black and starving eyes; the mother on foot, in rags and shoeless, and still holding between her teeth a ragged haik to veil her misery from the passer by, a baby at her back, and in her hand a branch torn from an olive-tree to switch off flies; then three ophthalmic children, with flies buzzing about their eyelids; lastly, the eldest son stolidly sitting in despair beside a fallen donkey carrying salt, and rubbed by girth, by crupper, and by pack ropes, and an epitome of the last stage of famine and of overwork. And as we came upon them, from a saint's tomb near by, a quavering call to prayers rang out, and the whole family fell to giving praise to Him who sendeth hunger, famine, withholds the rain, and shows His power upon the sons of men, infidel or believer, Turk, Christian, Moor, and Jew, with such impartiality that at times one thinks indeed that He is God. As for the donkey; Bible, Koran, and the rest of sacred books were writ for man, and the galled jade may wince until the end of time for all Jehovah, Allah, Obi, and the rest of the Olympians seem to care. All our bread, dates, and tea, went to the owners of the donkey, and had I been in European clothes I should have bought the starveling beast and put a bullet through his head.

Cistus and heath with mignonette, dwarf arbutus and stunted algarobus, with thyme and sweet germander, made a thick underwood upon the hills; and yet, as is the case in all Morocco, and, I think, everywhere throughout the East, footpaths crossed here and there, men seemed to be eternally coming and going, donkeys, more or less wretched in appearance,

wandered here and there, and in the air, above the
scent of flowers, hung the stench of human excrement,
the "bouquet d'orient," the perfume which, I fancy
scents the breeze in Araby the blest.

Along the desert trails, in the Sahara* and the Soudan,
I fancy, man is rarely long unseen, and camels and
donkeys must have been struggling across the sands
before the first instant of uselessly recorded time.
Still, as in India, wild beasts thrive almost alongside
cultivated fields, and in the sandy paths which ran
through the thick undergrowth tracks of wild boar
appeared ; and on the borders of the bare hills, above
the vegetation, "moufflon" † skipped, looking so like
to goats that I could scarcely credit they were wild.

All the streams we crossed had whitish beds, and a
white sediment clung to the grass upon their banks.
It seemed there was a salt mine in the neighbourhood
which supplied all the province, and underneath us
far below, looking like ants, we saw long strings of
mules and donkeys meandering along the paths
towards the mine. The road gradually got worse
and worse, and in few places averaged above four feet
wide, so that I rode one stirrup brushing the mountain side and in great terror that I should lose my
yellow slipper down the precipice, five or six hundred
feet in depth upon the other side, which went sheer
down into the Wad N'fis. Occasionally we had to
call to trains of mules advancing to stop till we could
get into one of the hollows scooped here and there

---

* Sahara is a dactyl in Arabic.

† The "moufflon" of the Atlas is called "Oudad" by the Berbers.
No doubt when duly stuffed and labelled in a museum he has his proper
Latin name, without which no self-respecting beast can die. People then
gaze at him through dusty glass, and the less educated, seeing the Latin
ticket, go away wondering at the depth of wisdom men of science seem
to descend to.

into the hillside to allow the travellers to pass. The
mules in nearly every instance had their packs
covered up in the striped blankets made in Sus, and
woven in a pattern of alternate black and white bars,
fringed edges, and curious cabalistic-looking figures
in the corner of the web. Now and again a Sheikh's
house, perched upon a hill and built like a castle, with
turrets, battlements, and " Almenas,"* all in mud,
and looking as like a properly constituted fortalice
as the difference of income of their owners and that
of the owners of the modern stucco fortalice outside an
English town permits. Along the road one constant
interchange of " Peace be with you" was kept up,
as we met other parties of believers going or coming
from the Sus, for the other two main highways being
closed by the outbreak of hostilities, all traffic had
converged upon the road which started from Amsmiz.

Rounding a corner and dipping down a steep incline,
almost before we were aware of it, we found ourselves
between a castle and a small mosque ; all round the
" perron" which led to the gate groups of muleteers
sat resting ; by a side door were lounging several
attendants armed with long guns, the barrels hooped
with silver and with brass, and, to complete the picture,
the Sheikh himself in shirt sleeves, so to speak, that is,
without a haik, and dressed in a long white garment,
sat in the shade studying the Koran. His air of
patriarchal simplicity so impressed me that only with
an effort I remembered that I too was one of the same
faith, and rather rudely I fear, according to Moorish
ideas of etiquette, I mumbled a low " Peace be with

* Casa de Almenas (a house with battlements) is in rural Spain a
euphuism for a gentleman's house. I fancy, like the torch extinguishers
in the regions about Berkeley Square, that these " almenas " occasionally rise in a single night in houses where owners in the past have
neglected to be legally constituted and known as gentlemen.

you" as I passed. From the mosque windows and the door came out a sound of voices as of children shouting all at once, it was the children of the place learning to read, for amongst Arabs no place too small, no " Duar" of six tents, lost in some far remote oasis of the Soudan, without its schoolmaster. About a league further along the road, and leaving the castle which rejoiced in the appelation of "Taguaydirt-el-Bur," we got off under some oleander and olive trees by the side of a clear stream to wash and eat.

Mohammed-el-Hosein swears by Allah no infidel has ever seen the place, and asks, if so, let him describe it. A thing indeed which Maupassant himself could hardly have achieved without inspection.

" Give me the signs of such a place" is a common Arab question if, in talking of some place, he doubts you have been there. Most of the famous places in the Mohammedan world are well known by description to all believers, and nothing is more common than to hear one man "giving the signs" of Mecca, Medinah, or some other holy spot with the minuteness of a lady novelist describing scenery. As we sat eating under our olive trees, people kept passing on the road continuously. Thus in the heart of one of the most unknown ranges of mountains (to the Nazarene) in the whole world, there is no solitude, no sense of loneliness, and all, apart from the grandeur of the hills, the snow, the precipices and brawling streams, as little interesting and appealing as little to the imagination as Hampstead Heath, or that alambicated quintessence of Mark Lane, the Scottish deer forest.

Though I know no single Oriental country but Morocco, and that is known to all Mohammedans as Mogreb-el-Acksa (the Far West) I yet imagine that

words with my understanding; but no doubt, the gift of tongues and all duly allowed for, he had often found himself similarly situated when on the tramp. Just at the crossing of this stream we paid and dismissed the guide who had accompanied us from the wayside mosque; he straight departed by a road fit for but partridges alone, across the hills, and I think somehow or other in conjunction with the "Maalem" from Amsmiz, contrived to pass the word along the road, of their opinion of my adherence to the Christian faith.

Struggling along over the shingly bed of the Wadd N'fiss for about two miles, we came again to a funnel-shaped gorge, which led by degress to a terrific staircase of rocks, known to the local muleteers as N'fad Abu Hamed, "the Knees of Father Hamed," as being so steep that no one could ascend it except upon all fours, or from its effects upon the knees of the unlucky mules, or from some other reason as to which commentators have disagreed. Just at the top I looked back over the finest range of mountain scenery I remember to have seen, and thought that with good luck and patriotism some few score Afridis in such a place might hold in check a regiment of marauding "Britishers," but on reflection I saw clearly that the word "patriotism" was out of place when used against ourselves. To the west towards the Sus the mountains seemed to dip, and Ouichidan, the highest peak in all the Southern Atlas, towered right above us a little to the east of where we stood, whilst far away in the dim distance rose the far distant mountains of the anti-Atlas, which rise above the province of the Draa, and on whose snow no Christian has ever trod. Descending rapidly we passed a strath in which some country people were engaged in burning down a tree, an ancient poplar which the wind had partly shifted from its place, and which, when it fell, must fall inevitably across the road. In a small patch of Indian corn an aged Negro was at work, dressed all in white with a red fez, and illustrating (in the middle distance) the mystery of creation in a fantastic fashion of his own.

Stumbling and tripping, leading our exhausted beasts, we came long after nightfall to a miserable house perched on a ledge of rocks over a river, and with a garden between the hillside and the stream; the place is called in Shillah, Imgordim. Nothing was to be had either for love or money, and we went supperless to bed save for green tea, sadly reflecting that had I been a Moor indeed, food would have been obtainable, for I could have sent a man to take it in the usual way, by force; and as it was, perhaps the people thought me a fool for not following out the course adopted by all " respectable Sherifs " when travelling about. Throughout Morocco " Sherifs," especially from Fez, are a positive curse to the poorer class of Moors; for being " holy " they behave exactly in the same way that the two Jewish " Sherifs " Hofni and Phineas behaved in Holy Writ; but most unfortunately, the people are so unresisting, that punishment which overtook their prototypes seldom is meted out to them, and they pervade the land, begging and taking contributions from the poor for Allah's sake. One of the really wise laws the French have made in Algeria is that forbidding the "Sherifs" to go round "sorning" on the people. Imagine if religion had the same hold in England as it has in Morocco, and recognised descendants of St. Paul*

---

* I fear they would have to be descended from St. Peter, who carried a wife about with him, as his great rival somewhat tartly remarks. At

perambulated up and down, taking by force when the
faithful were disinclined to give, and you may have
an inkling of how onerous the burden was upon the
poorer villagers before the French put down the practice in Algeria. All the night long the people keep
passing on the road, and a small black mosquito,
resembling the "Jejen" of Paraguay, was most impertinent.

Next morning (October 20th) we were early upon
the road, as is most generally the case in travel when
one goes supperless to bed and rises to get on horseback with but a cup of weak green tea for breakfast.
The animals had eaten well as we had barley with us,
and, as on the day before, we started climbing stair-
cases of rock, crossing and re-crossing the Wad el
N'fiss, passing deserted villages, and interchanging
greetings with the various parties of travellers upon the
road. A precipitous descent over red sandstone rocks
and through a thicket of tall oleanders, brought us to
an open space, where the bed of the N'fiss spread out
about a quarter of a mile in width. To right and left,
at the distance of a mile or two, on either hand
perched upon hills were fortalices, and further up the
valley a castle which I was destined to become better
acquainted with by night. The mountains, about ten
miles away, formed a most perfect semi-circle, and Tisi
Nemiri, upon our right, appeared to rise sheer from
the river into the clouds.

Mohammed el Hosein, who, all the morning, after
the fashion of a hungry man, had been exceedingly
ill-humoured, now produced from the recesses of his

---

any rate, even the Ebioim have never ventured to cast any doubt on
St. Paul's private character. This is consolatory when one recalls the
case of Burns and other poets, including King David.

    * Tisi = hill, in Schluoh. Nemiri means " stones."

saddle-bags four rather small pomegranates, which all five of us proceeded to devour with great alacrity. Whilst eating, he informed us that the semi-circle in front was the last ridge between us and the Sus, and that with luck we ought to camp well in the province of the Sus by evening.

Again we fell discussing our plan of action on reaching Tarudant. All now depended upon passing the guard at the N'Zala,* where an official of the Sultan was reported to be permanently sitting at the receipt of such custom as might come his way. Mohammed el Hosein was confident that, for a dollar, he could get us past without much risk, I shamming ill and sitting a little apart under a tree, whilst he bargained with the official, the danger being that the man should, out of civility, put some question to me which I must answer, and thus, by my poor Arabic, betray myself, for Mohammed el Hosein was sure that no one on the road had for a moment questioned my identity.

In fact, about an hour before we camped, whilst riding along one of the shingly stretches over which the road went following the bed of the N'fiss, I had been put to a pretty strong test, and had emerged triumphantly. About a quarter of a mile in front of us we saw a band of twenty people sitting on a grassy slope and watching apparently for our passing by. Of course we thought it was a detachment of tribesmen who had penetrated my disguise and were about to attack us, but, as to turn back was quite impossible, and even consultation difficult, by reason of a party of travellers who followed us, we had to

---

* N'Zala is a sort of post-house established by the Government. At the N'Zala we contemplated passing there was a sort of custom-house put up to swindle travellers, as is usual in all well-governed countries.

face the difficulty, after having deliberated briefly
upon my dropping my handkerchief to give Mohammed el Hosein the opportunity to get off and
ride beside me to consult.   As we came closer I saw
the people had no arms and were chiefly young men
of from eighteen to twenty years of age.   Swani
passed on the word it was a "Tolba," that is, a band
of wandering students, in fact, an "Estudiantina,"
and then I knew what line of conduct to adopt.   Just
as we crossed the river they came all round my horse,
wading in the fierce current above knee deep, and,
catching my cloak, kissed it most fervently, invoking
blessings on the Sherif from Fez, and calling upon
Siddi bel Abbas, the patron saint of travellers, to
guard me from all harm.   I knew of course that that
meant money, and blessed them in my best Arabic,
whilst luckily for me the splashing of the horses and
the men crossing the stream made so much noise I
might have spoken in Chinook for all they knew.   I
signed to Swani who advanced and gave them a
peseta, and some of them kissed my knees, which I
permitted graciously as to the manner born, and,
stooping down, touched with my right hand the head
of one who seemed the cleanest, and rode on, looking
as ineffable as a man desperately anxious and
engaged in crossing a shingly, violent-running river
can be supposed to look.   Mohammed el Hosein and
Swani, the danger past, and the travellers behind us
having halted, laughed till they almost fell off their
pack saddles; Lutaif, I think, gave thanks after the
fashion of the Lebanon, and Ali looked at me, thinking, I verily believe, I really was as holy as I hoped I
looked.

Naturally, this little passage raised our spirits, as
the students of the Tolba, though beggars, were all

educated men, had wandered much about the country, and must have seen Christians at the coast towns a thousand times. I recommend to educational reformers a peripatetic university after the Tolba system. The students might beg their way along on bicycles, listen to lectures in convenient places—upon commons, under railway arches, beside canal locks, and the like—play football, as the members of the Tolba in Morocco play, by the roadsides, and thus high thinking with low diet, football, and bicycle, might all conduce to scholarship, to health, and know- ledge of the country roads. In Morocco the system works well enough, although some say that in the Tolbas those customs flourish which have led scholars in England to Malebolge ; but even of Oxford and of stationary universities, ill-natured things—about mon- astic vices, relics of mediæval habits, and the like— have been preferred. Be all that as it may, a merry life to lounge along, to read under the olive trees, camp near some village, write charms for folk who want them, and recite whole chapters from the Koran, at night yelling them out in chorus, after the way of children learning their lessons in a kindergarten.

So, thinking on the Tolba, our spirits rose, and we determined to send Ali to the nearest house to buy provisions. Lucky we did so, for it provided us with a square meal which we were destined not to enjoy again for several days. It appeared, the N'Zala once passed, that a sharp descent of some three hours led into the plain beyond. There, according to Mo- hammed el Hosein, the people were all armed and very warlike; and the road to Tarudant led through the main streets of several villages. He did not look forward to much risk in passing them, but thought there might be a chance of falling in with robbers by the way, who naturally would rob a Moor (they being Berbers) quite cheerfully, and would without doubt kill any Christian whom they came across, not being restrained by fear of the authorities, as are the people in the settled parts of the country across the mountain. However, Mohammed el Hosein finished up always by saying, " We are in Allah's hand; but leave it all to me, for if danger should occur it is not for nothing I am called the cleverest muleteer upon the southern road." And as he spoke his little Shillah eyes sparkled like live coals, his thin, black, pointed beard wagged to and fro, and his face and muscular arms twitched and contracted as he shook with laughter in the enjoyment of the joke. To deceive anyone is always pleasing to a Moor (sometimes to Christians also), and to take in a town and pass an infidel upon it as a Sherif from Fez appeared to him the greatest piece of humour of his life. To our enquiries as to what was best to do if, in a village, I was recognised, his answer was invariably the same, so that at last I did not bother him, seeing him confi· dent, and feeling almost certain in my mind the worst was past. Ali returned laden with bread and mutton, eggs and fruit, and we sat down to eat our last repast in freedom in the jurisdiction of the Caid of Gundaffi, whom Ali told us lived like a Sultan, and that he had had to wait full half an hour with other travellers before being permitted to purchase food.

Lunch over, we got on the road in great good humour, and for an hour crossed a bare stony plain, till, winding round a little hill, we came suddenly into full view of a deserted house on one side of the road, and about half-a-mile away upon the right an immense castle surrounded by gardens, woods, and cultivated grounds, and with the river El N'fiss flowing just underneath the walls. Mohammed el Hosein knew the place well, and said it was called Talet el Jacub, the summer residence of the Caid el Gundaffi, the governor of the province that we were journeying through. "Please God, he is not on the look out for us," he said half laughing; and as he spoke a messenger came running to meet us, his clothes tucked into his belt, bare headed, and a long staff in one hand. We took no notice, and he overtook us and asked where we were going, and Mohammed el Hosein replied "towards God's land," an Arabic retort to an inquisitive enquiry on the road. The messenger retorted "this is no laughing matter, a man came to the Caid's house this morning and said he had heard there was a Christian on the road disguised as a Mohammedan." Luckily all this passed in Shillah, and the speaker scarcely knew as much Arabic as I myself. I called up Swani and told him to tell Mohammed el Hosein that I was going to see Basha Hamou, at Tarudant, and that I had not time to call upon the Caid, as I intended to camp that night in Sus. The man looked at me, at Swani, and at Lutaif, who spoke to him in Arabic, and he said "then you are not Christians," to which Swani replied, "No, burn their fathers;" and the messenger, after profuse apologies, returned towards the castle at a dog-trot.

Who now so certain as ourselves of our arrival at Tarudant. We agreed he will stop all passers-by and lose much time, and in five hours at most we shall be past his jurisdiction, and it is not in the Sus that he will follow us, even should he discover his mistake.

So we spurred on quite merrily, laughing and talking of the rage the Caid would fall into when he heard some day how near he had the Christians in his hand. Past walnut woods, through thickets of scrub oak, by gardens into which the water ran through trunks of hollow trees, upwards steeply ran the road passing by hedges thick with brambles and dog roses, a look in fact of Spain or Portugal, and every step we went we laughed at the discomfiture of the foolish Caid.

After an hour of steep ascent over the shoulder of a mountain called "Tisi in Test" (Hill of the Oaks), we struck a steep staircase of rocks, and Mohammed el Hosein said, "in an hour from here we shall pass a castle by the roadside, it is the guard-house of the Caid, and from thence to the N'Zala is but half an hour; and, once there, in a few hours you will see the tall towers of the mosques in Tarudant." So we determined (it was then about one o'clock) to push on without eating and sleep in Sus. The steep ascent proved steeper than any we had passed, but we cared nothing for it, knowing we were so near our goal.

At last we neared the castle by the roadside, no one seemed stirring near it, and we were just preparing to pass the gate when a loud shouting just below us made us turn our heads. To our amazement we saw our friend the messenger accompanied by several well-armed men, bounding up the steep road like an "Oudad" (moufflon), and shouting, in Shillah, in a voice to wake the dead. Men rushed out of the castle and ran for their horses, and the messenger arrived just as we were about to pass the door. We stopped, and putting on an air of quiet citizens, alarmed upon the road, asked what the matter was, although we knew. Men rushed and seized our animals, called out "Arrumin," that is, the "Chris-

tians," brandished their guns, fingered their daggers,
and for a moment things looked ugly. I sat upon my
horse hardly quite catching all that was said. Lutaif
expostulated and Swani, calling on Allah, asked the
Sheikh, who now had come out of his house, and
stood waiting till some one brought him his horse, if
he looked like a Christian. "No," said the Sheikh,
"you appear to be a cursed sailor from the coast,
accustomed to sail upon the black water, and to con-
sort no doubt with Christians." Swani looked as if he
would have liked some private conversation with the
Sheikh near Tangier, but prudently said nothing, and
the Sheikh turned to Lutaif and asked him who he
was. Lutaif replied "a Syrian and a Taleb, and
the attendant of this gentleman," pointing to me.

Then said the Sheikh, "this is the Rumi," and,
turning to me, said, "is it not so, or will you swear
you are a true believer?" Swearing is easy if you
possess a language pretty well, but difficult in "petit
negre," and so knowing we should be taken back
before the Caid and then found out, I answered "Yes,
I am the Christian," and began to feel my horse's
mouth ready for what might come.

As Allah willed it nothing occurred beyond a little
shouting, and some rather tempestuous brandishing
of guns, and threatening looks. The Sheikh, who by
this time had got upon his horse, rode up to me and
looked me in the face. I said, "Have you ever
seen a European before?" but his Arabic was at an
end, and the rest passed in Shillah between
Mohammed el Hosein and the man sent by the
governor.

It appeared the messenger had gone back to the
castle and told the Caid we were not Christians, and that
I seemed a reputable man, riding a good black horse.

On that the Caid exclaimed, "Black horse, I was told
the Christian had a black horse bought in Amsmiz,
so after them at once with four or five armed men;"
and to teach him circumspection and lightness of
foot, had him well beaten before he sent him off. A
guard of men advanced and took our bridles and
began to lead us back, as downcast a company as
you might see upon a long day's march. I felt like
Perkin Warbeck going to the Tower, and rode quite
silent, but cursing under my breath, whilst, as I take
it, the loud jokes which passed in Shillah were most
amusing to our captors, though I feel doubtful, even
had I understood them, that they would have amused
me in the least. One ragged tribesman tried to
snatch my gun, which I had borrowed from the
Consul in Mogador, but I kept hold of it and told him
that if it no longer belonged to me it was the Caid's,
and I should tell him of the theft. Nothing takes
better with the Arabs and Berbers than an answer of
this kind, and when he understood it the man grinned
like a baboon and said he was no thief. I had my
own opinion about this, but thought it wise not to
disclose it, and at that moment a heavy storm of rain
swept down from off the hills and wet us to the skin.
We now began to press our animals, and the escort
bounded like goats beside us, one of them trying to
prick my horse with a long knife to make him kick.
The headman, seeing the joke, promptly struck him
across the head with a thick stick, the blow being
enough to have stunned a European, but which did
not seem much to annoy him, and he trotted along
just like a hound who has received a cut from the
second whip for running a false scent.

In about three-quarters of an hour we did that
which had taken us two hours to come, our animals

rushing down the steep paths in the heavy storm, and
the escort shouting and cursing like demoniacs. We
plunged into a wood, crossed a flooded stream, rode
through a field of standing corn, and, crossing
the "Maidan"* before the castle, came to a horse-
shoe arch. Assembled before the entrance was a
crowd of armed retainers, loafers, herdsmen, travellers, and all the riff-raff who, in Morocco, haunt the
dwellings of rich men. Boys, and more boys, oxen,
and goats, and horses, all pressed into the gateway
and the dark winding passage to escape the storm.
Loud rose the cry of "Christians, sons of dogs." I
thought, in the dark passage, that the occasion
seemed quite favourable for some believer to strike a
quiet blow for Allah's sake.

Swani pushed forward, and placed himself beside
me on his mule ; and pushing, striving, cursing, and
dripping with the rain, we reached a second gateway,
which opened into a court; and here the travellers,
herdsmen, and the rest entered, and left us, with our
escort, standing in semi-darkness below the arch.
For a full hour we waited—I, sitting on my horse,
partly from pride and partly from the instinctive
feeling of a horseman that he is always safer on his
horse ; the others dismounted, and sat down on a
stucco bench, looking the picture of misery and
discontent. We did not talk much—though I felt
inclined to laugh—the position striking me as
comic enough in all its aspects ; and at last a fat
man, in immaculate white robes, holding a bunch
of keys, came through the rain across the inner
court, and asked my name. I told it to him, and

* A "maidan" is an open space on which to practice horsemanship,
and one is generally to be found before the gate or near to the walls of
every castle or Sheikh's house throughout Morocco.

he seemed edified, and asked what I was doing, and why I wished to go to Tarudant. This was most difficult to explain, for in Morocco few people journey out of curiosity, so I replied I had business with the Governor. The man then turned towards Lutaif, and said : " You are a Mohammedan, why do you travel with this Christian ? You are a taleb, and should know better than to connive at a Christian travelling in Moorish dress." Lutaif had to explain he was a Christian, and the fat man then turned upon Mohammed el Hosein, and said : " You are no Christian, and the Caid says he will shave your beard, give you the stick, and put you into prison with some comfortable irons on your feet." To such a speech there was no very obvious answer but " Allah Kerim," which poor Mohammed el Hosein mumbled piteously enough ; and the fat man, kilting his snow-white robes, waddled across the court, and went into the house, without another word.

And so we waited, as it seemed hours, till again across the court came the fat, snow-white-robed official, accompanied by a short, broad-shouldered man with a full black beard, who, walking up to me, held out a hand, and said, " *Bon jour.*" I answered, but his French extended no further, and he tried Turkish—of which I did not know a word. Lutaif, who spoke it well, entered into a conversation with him, when it appeared he was a Persian—a sort of wandering minstrel—who was staying with the Caid and had been sent, upon the strength of his " *Bon jour,*" to find out who we were. As I was still un- certain if the Globe Venture Syndicate's steamer was off the coast, we took good care to make it plain we were friends of Basha Hamou, for, had the vessel

arrived, we should have been thrown into prison at
once, and sent in chains up to the Sultan's camp.
However, no suspicion of this seemed to cross the
people's minds, and we sat on talking to the old
Persian in a jargon of mixed Arabic and Turkish for
some time; whilst gradually a crowd of people had
assembled, who—sitting on the ground, on stones, and
on a low divan which ran right round the arches—
glared at us silently, like men looking at wild beasts.
A boy or two threw a few stones, but they were
stopped immediately—the order having evidently
gone out to treat us well. Considering all things,
and how completely we were in their power, how
removed from any Europeans, and how strong the
spirit of dislike is to all strangers, especially amongst
the Berber tribes, the conduct of the people was quite
wonderful; and I question very much if in a European
country we should, in similar conditions, have fared
as well. Still, the uncertainty made waiting anxious
work, and we were pleased to hear from the old
Persian that the Caid was in a dilemma as to what he
should do with us—whether to send us back, let us go
on, or write for instructions to the Sultan as to what
course to take. At last the Chamberlain, wrapped
this time in one of the Atlas brown goatskin cloaks—
called by the Berber an "Achnif"—came back again,
and said the Caid had made his mind up to extend
his hospitality to us, and that he had placed a tent at
our disposal on the " Maidan." The phrase admitted
no discussion ; and so following the Chamberlain—
and preceded by an attendant with a long gun—we
rode to the " Maidan," and found a tent pitched on
the wet ground above the bank of the N'fiss, into
which all of us, with saddles and baggage, were glad
to pack, to get out of the rain. The tent was large,

and circular in shape, ornamented outside with rows
of blue cloth decanters—after the Moorish fashion—
and lined with a chintz of the most pre-Morris kind.
In addition to its beauties of form and decoration it
leaked in several places, and was so loosely pitched
that we had to turn to at once to make it safe, and
dig a trench to carry off the water, which stood about
an inch in depth upon the floor. Five men with pack-
saddles, bridles, and guns, and all the requisites for
camping, left very little room to move about. A forlorn crew we must have looked as we sat, shivering
and hungry, on the damp floor. Closing the door, I
drew from my medicine-chest a bottle of brandy
which I had in reserve for snake-bites, and adminis-
tering a dose (medicinally) to believers and infidels
alike, a better spirit soon prevailed, and we got beds
made down; and—placing some stones to keep the
blankets off the ground—a fire was lighted; and over
a cup of tea—flavoured with some mint which Ali
drew out of his bag, where it had lain for days
amongst tobacco, pieces of string, and the " menavel-
ling's " of a muleteer's profession—we set about reviewing our position, after a joke or two, as to the
enjoyment of the hospitality so generously provided
by the Caid. For myself, I was not in much trepida-
tion, knowing the worst that could occur was to be
sent under a guard to the Sultan's camp—a matter of
from five to six days' journey. As tò Mohammed el
Hosein, that was more serious. Already he had been
threatened with the stick, imprisonment, and with the
loss of beard—the greatest insult which can be put on
a Mohammedan. But the poor devil (and we ourselves) knew well that in his case the stick most
probably meant death, and that he would not live to
undergo the other punishment. Still, he was not so

much downcast as might have been expected, but sat in the wet mud—a bellows in his hand—blowing the charcoal for the tea; and said, resignedly, "We are in Allah's hand; but it is a pity I was but newly married before leaving Mogador."

Swani, as a man, so to speak, without caste, was safe, and the most he could expect was a few dozen blows with a stout stick, a matter about which he did not seem to care a halfpenny, for he knew that he could plead he came under compulsion as my servant, and the plea would almost certainly be held sufficient at least to save his life.

Ali, of course, could not be held an accessory before the fact, as he left Magador without the least idea of our intention, and I assured him if he lost his mule that I would buy him one fit for the Sultan's saddle.

As we sat talking, we perceived a group of tribesmen, all fully armed, had sat down just outside the tent, the rain having ceased for a little, and were regarding us quite motionless, but with their eyes not losing any action that we made. Of course, we were the strangest spectacle they had ever seen, and after half-an-hour, their curiosity well satisfied, they moved off silently and sat down in the same manner to watch a game of football, which was proceeding on the "Maidan," and in which all the young men, from slaves to the Caid's sons, were taking part. So we resumed deliberations, and discussed the position of Lutaif. He was perhaps, of all of us, in the most dangerous case. A Syrian and a Turkish subject, known to speak Turkish, and without a paper of protection from any European Consul, as he said himself: "If the Caid wants to kill me, he will do so as if I were a dog, and you may be certain that my Sultan will not claim compensation for the death of any Christian." I thought about Armenia, but the time was scarcely opportune for joking ; and just as all our spirits and our stomachs were at the lowest ebb, a slave came from the Caid, bringing a dish of " Couscousou,"* which we devoured at once, and could have eaten at least five times as much. The canvas door was lifted, and, with a cheerful but irrelevant *Bon jour* the Persian entered, sat down without a word and, after looking at me for a moment or two, said " Mezquin " (that is, " poor fellow "), " how far you are from home." This, though a truism, had not occurred to me, but put thus, à brûle pourpoint, it seemed to come home with great force to Lutaif, to Swani, and to Mohammed el Hosein, and for a moment they seemed about to weep, after the fashion of the two aged men who wept because they both were orphans.

The Persian promised " to stand before the Caid and speak for us," and to return to-morrow and relate his life to us. We all bid him good night with great effusion, as he had been a valued friend, and watched him walk across the " Maidan " into the castle, and perceived that round our tent, some fifty yards away, on every side, squatted a sentinel.

Whilst we sat trying to dry our clothes, from the castle mosque broke out the call to prayers, called by the Persian in a voice like the last trumpet's sound, the tower seemed to rock, and the hills gave back God's

---

* Couscousou, or cuscus as it is often called in Morocco, is something like the American hominy. It is made of wheat pounded and grated, and tea steamed, so that the result is a very dry porridge. You eat it with your hands, and the result is rather messy to the novice. Some-times mutton and pieces of pumpkin are served up on the top of the cuscus, and on grand occasions it is made with sugar and milk, and flavoured with cinnamon.

name from every crag and hollow, till the whole valley quivered with the sound, and the night air was all pervaded by the echoing cry. If God is God, surely Mohammed knew his nature when he appointed men to call by night, bidding the faithful rise to pray, and speaking as it were with Allah face to face, as standing on some tower in the night, they tell his attributes.

CHAPTER VI.

NEXT morning rain was still coming down in torrents and we awoke to find our tent, in spite of all precautions, swimming in water. Nothing to do, even without the "hospitality" of the Caid, but to cower over a charcoal brazier, and to send Swani to try and buy provisions for our breakfast. After a little he returned bringing the chamberlain, who informed us rather tartly that the Caid Si Taieb ben Si Ahmed El Hassan El Kintafi* sold no provisions, but that we and our animals would be cared for at his expense. In about-half-an hour two negro slaves appeared, bringing couscous and meat cut up and stewed with pumpkins, and so we fell to with an appetite improved by the past days spent on short commons. People arrived in bands and squatted down before the tent, and when one band had seen enough, another took its place and sat on doggedly for half-an-hour with the rain dripping down their backs. Till about midday, when the rain began to slacken, no one addressed us, though a man, shod with a kind of sandals of oxhide with the hair on, after the style of those worn in the outer Hebrides till a few years ago, and once worn by all Scotchmen, as the name "rough-footed Scot" implies, looked at us, opened his mouth,

---

* The Arabic name of the tribe is Kintafah. This in Shillah becomes Takinteft, following the Shillah etymology, which see Appendix.

but then thought better of it and passed away. Had he but spoken, it would have been in Shillah, but still I wish I knew what that poor tribesman was about to say.

After the midday prayer, a jet black negro walked into the tent, dressed all in white with a large silver earring hanging from one ear and with three stripes tatooed or scarified upon his cheek. He sat down in a friendly manner on my cloak, which I drew to me and he then sat quite as contentedly on the wet mud. He spoke good Arabic, and to my observation that it was cold, replied "Yes, but not half so cold as London." Thinking it was a joke, I said "that is extremely likely, but have you been there?" and I then learned he had been there twice, in the suite of a Sheikh from the Sahara who had been in London about some business of the Cape Juby Company. The Cape Juby Company was one of those strange ventures which when they fail, men say that their promoters were all mad, but if they prosper make their projectors founders of empires, and people think their brains effected that which was really chance. There is no really sane head either on horseback* or the Stock Exchange.

Almost in sight of Fuerteventura, the nearest in shore of the Canaries, between Wad Nun and the Cabo de Bojador, not quite within the tropics, Cape Juby lies. From the Wad Nun, almost to St. Louis Senegal, nothing but sand, a lowish coast, no settled population, and but little water; and yet a Scotchman, one Mr. Mackenzie, who in the seventies had an idea to flood the Sahara and trade direct from London to Timbuctoo, induced some lords and gentlemen to

* No hay hombre cuerdo à caballo; there is no sane man on horseback, says the proverb.

found a company and put their factory on an island off the Cape.*

The Island is a lone rock, disjoined from land by a little channel at high tide, and upon it, without much ceremony, the company erected buildings, built a wall, mounted the inevitable cannon to keep the peace, and tried to start a trade. Just opposite the island grow a few tamarisk bushes, in Arabic called Torfaia, and near these bushes is a brackish well. The tamarisks give the name, and the spot is called Torfaia up and down the coast, being remarkable as the only place where any vegetation lives. The population is nomad, and composed of wandering Arab tribes, who in remote times came from the Yemen and still speak the dialect of the Koreish in all its purity. When the wind blows, the sand moves like a sea, so that the company found their walls, built for defence, were in about three months all sanded up, and an Arab on his camel could fire right down into the fort.

Upon this likely spot Mr. Mackenzie and his company pitched to establish trade with the interior of the Sahara, pending the time their ships could sail direct to Timbuctoo. If I remember rightly, the Empire (British) was to be increased, the wandering Arabs all to acknowledge Queen Victoria's reign, and peace and plenty, with a fair modicum of profit, be the order of the day.

Below Wad Nun the Arab tribes live practically as they lived in Arabia before Mohammed. Morocco is too far away to be much feared, the negro tribes to the south and east not strong enough to fight,

* A cousin of the celebrated Abd-el-Kader, one Haj Ali Bu Taleb, was employed by them to conciliate the natives. But though a man of great parts and sanctity amongst the Arabs, he was unsuccessful.

the Touaregs not disposed to attack men like the
Arabs who can only give hard knocks; whilst in the
Senegal the French, in spite of that consuming hunger
for sand, as witness Southern Algeria, Tunis, and the
desire they are said to have to make a sandy empire
from Tripoli to Senegal, are not so foolish as to
adventure, merely for glory, to attack the desert tribes.
Thus any Sheikh, or Sherif, who has a little power
becomes a king, after the style of Cherdorlaomer in
the Bible, and rules over other kings who do him
homage, if he has power enough at his command.
Some kinglet of this kind was duly found, and a
treaty made with him. In fact, the man appeared in
London, passed by the title of King of the Sahara,
stayed at a good hotel, and no doubt did members of
the company good service by his stay. But as mis-
chance would have it, treason broke out at home
whilst the Saharan King was sojourning amongst the
infidel. On his return "patriots," that is, I fancy,
other Sheiks the company had overlooked and not
"made right," refused to ratify the treaty, and the
poor King was treated as a traitor who had sold his
fellows to the Christian dogs.

Years passsed away (sixteen I think), and managers
went out who drew their salaries; clerks not a few
contracted fever, and some died; Arabs attacked the
place with varying success; the people of the fort
went out to hunt in peace time, and in war sat drinking gin; but still no business was effected, and the
whole place began to look like a small Goa, Pondi-
cherry, or some Spanish island in the Eastern seas,
where every other man has a fine gold-laced uniform,
but has no food to eat. Then some one had a lumin-
ous idea, which was to sell the place to the Sultan of
Morocco, who, wishing to extend his empire, bought

it, and has to-day the pleasure of keeping a steamer running from the Canaries, week in week out, to keep the garrison supplied with water, for the well beneath the tamarisks has given out.

My negro visitor was from Wad Nun, had been to London twice and did not like it, in fact, remembered nothing but the cold and the striking fact the horses had short tails. And yet, intelligent after his fashion, and greatly exercised as to the reason which impelled those Argonauts to sail to such a Colchis, and glad to tell how they bought nothing but a little wool, and wondered if they knew of gold mines, or what kept them stuck for sixteen years in such a place. The manager, Mackenzie, was a Scotchman, which he interpreted to be a title of respectability, and informed us that Mackenzie's name was known far in the Sahara, and that at times natives would ride up, who had never seen him, and greet him as Sidi Mackenzie, for they all had heard of his red beard, his title (Scotchman), and the strong spirit kept in a barrel which none but he might drink. My negro tapped his head and told me it was full of news, but that, unluckily, his purse was empty, or he would long ago have left the place. I did not take the hint, and he retired wishing me patience, with a negro grin.

Patience was what I most had need of, except, perhaps, tobacco, at the time. So strolling out on to the Maidan, the rain having ceased at last, I sat down on a large stone under an olive tree to think about the situation and enjoy the view. In a magnificent amphitheatre of hills with snowy mountains towering overhead, just at the angle which the Wad el N'fiss makes after the first five miles of its course, about the middle of a valley almost ten miles in length, the

"Azib"* of El Kintafi lies; around it fifteen or twenty acres of Indian corn, a grove of olive trees and pomegranate gardens, wild and uncared for as gardens always are throughout the East. The house itself with its mosque, the various court-yards, towers, kiosques, stables, fortified passages, and a long stretch of crenelated wall, covers almost as much ground as Kenilworth or Arundel. Built all of mud, and here and there painted light yellow, it yet looks solid, and in one angle rises the tower of the mosque covered with tiles like those of the Alhambra.

The castle wall upon one side runs almost sheer down into the river which tosses on a stony bed, leaving a sort of sandy beach, on which grow oleanders, and across the stream the shoulder of Tisi Nemiri* almost reaches to the bank. Above the oleanders ran a mill stream in which the tiniest barble played or hung suspended in the slack water, aping the attitude of salmon lying suspended in the shallow water of a linn. Between the mill stream and the beach grew some Indian corn fenced in with "Suddra" bushes, looking steely-grey in the bright sun, or as if frosted, when the moon turned every twig and thorn to silver, in its cold light. Curious little round hills studded the valley in various directions, and on the west side rose Ouichidan to an apparent height of about fourteen thousand feet, or, say, six thousand feet above the bed of the N'fiss. Almost at the top of Ouichidan there is a spring held sacred by the Berbers, who have retained many Pagan customs and superstitions, although Mohammedans. It is said that from the top a view of both Morocco City and Tarudant is seen, but "Allahu Alem" God

* "Azib" is a country house or farm.
† Tisi Nemiri, in Shillah, the Hill of the Stones.

he knows, for never has the foot of unbeliever trod the
snow, nor has the pestilent surveyor, with his boiling
tubes, his aneroid, theodolite, and all his trumpery,
defiled the peak.

What is known, is that a pass leads into Sus over
a shoulder of the mountain, and a poor Jewish merchant whom I subsequently met, informed me that
whilst crossing it he had prayed more fervently than
he had done since quite a child, and said devoutly
"may Jehovah keep me from all such cursed roads."
Amongst the maize fields which, at my time of sojourning as guest of El Kintafi were all ripe, negroes
and negresses were husking the heads of maize which
had been reaped, and were all gathered up in heaps
Their flat and merry faces, red and yellow clothes,
loud cries, and air of working as for amusement,
brought back the Southern States, and as half the
men answered to Quasi, and the women all appeared
to be called Sultana, the illusion was complete. Most
of the negroes had become Mohammedans, and, of
course, the women had to follow suit; few of them
spoke Arabic or even Shillah, and a sort of ganger,
who spoke Soudanese, lay in the shade and made a
show of overseeing their pretence of work. Upon
the flat roof of the palace prisoners heavily
chained tottered about and husked the Indian corn,
each man resolved to do as little work as possible,
and spend the greatest possible amount of time in
walking to and fro. Poor devils, mostly tribesmen
from a rebellious tribe which lived upon the head
waters of the N'fiss, and which neither the Caid, his
father, or his grandfather, had ever been quite able to
subdue. The rebellious tribe is a feature of the Eastern
world. No Sultanate so small, no little caliphate
lost in the hills, no terrtitory of mountains or of

plains that is without its rebels. Throughout Morocco one comes now and then upon a tribe in open warfare, if not with the Sultan at least against its governor. They raise an army, fight in the hills, take prisoners and cut their throats, behave, in fact, as Arabs have behaved since they first came into our Western life, and at the last the Sultan or the governor prevails, and a few dozen heads of the chief tribesmen adorn the city walls, making long smears of blood down the pale yellow wash, and shrivelling by degrees into a hideous mass, like an old fly-blown shoe. Yet on the roof of the Caid's Kasbah* the prisoners gave a scriptural note, and made one think on Jeremiah,† the prisoner's prophet, who must have wandered up and down as they did, before Pashur smote him and set him in the stocks, putting him daily to derision and making everyone to mock at him. Not that the Berbers mocked at the prisoners on the castle roof, but, on the contrary, sat with the blazing sun upon their shaven pates, talking to them from the " Maidan," gave them bits of bread, and so behaved themselves that chains and famine, lice and sores discounted, the condition of the prisoners was nearer to that of men at large than that of the betracted, ticketed transgressors in a London gaol. At times, upon the roof, the prisoners lay full length and held their chains up in one hand to rest their legs, and, lying close to the parapet, chaffed the negroes as they came and went carrying as little maize as possible in small baskets holding about a peck. At night the Caid, who had a not unnatural wish to keep

* Kasbah = a castle, and from it is derived the Spanish word Alcazaba, so frequent in Spanish place names.

† In a Bible in Pentonville Prison, at the end of the Book of Jeremiah, a prisoner had written, "Cheer up, Jeremiah, old man." I used to be sorry for both prisoners when I read that Bible in my cell.

his prisoners safe, lowered them one by one into a deep dry well, a mule revolving slowly round a rude kind of capstan, as with an esparto rope hitched in a bowline below their arm-pits, one by one they were lowered underneath the ground. When all were down, four negroes placed a large flat stone over the well, and the " Muezzin " called on the faithful, all to praise God's name. What the state of the well was down below is hard to say, but in the morning when the stone was rolled aside a stench as from a Tophet rose, and early on the fourth day of our enforced "villegiatura," a starveling donkey was driven past our tent with the body of a prisoner (escaped from prison and from life) thrown over it, the head and feet dangling upon the ground, and the donkey-driver pricking his beast with a piece of sharpened cane in an old, thoroughly-established sore on which the flies buzzed, settled, flew off again and then alighted on the eyelids of the corpse.

And so the second day went past in rather greater comfort than the first, the rain having ceased, and we became aware that it was best to resign ourselves to what the Caid and Providence might have in store for us. About the evening prayer I despatched Lutaif to try and get an audience and find out why we were detained, but, after waiting more than an hour at the castle gate, he returned to say that the great man was invisible, but that his Chamberlain would come and see us after supper-time. The Chamberlain not having come by sundown, and our animals not having eaten for four-and-twenty hours, I sent Swani to "stand and cry at the gate," after the Eastern fashion, with the result that soon, the slave who had the key of the corn arrived and struck a bargain with me, I undertaking to tip him handsomely on my departure if he fed our beasts. This he declared he would do, but kept them half-starved, and totally refused to sell, either chopped straw or hay, most probably having got orders from the Caid to feed our animals well, and having sold half the corn, which he no doubt took every day out of the granary, to passing travellers. However, unjust stewards are not uncommon even in England, and he kept his key so bright (it measured nearly eighteen inches long), and dressed so charmingly in palest Eau de Nil, with a black cloak bound round with pink, and lied so easily, and with such circumstance, that I forbore to lay his case before the Caid, reserving to myself the power of not rewarding his hypothetic services at my departure if he went too far in his small villainies. Night brought the Chamberlain heading a small procession of negroes carrying our supper, composed of various dishes of meat and couscousu, piled up on earthenware dishes placed in a wooden case, shaped like an old-time stable sieve and covered with a conical shaped top of straw through which were run strips of red and black leather in a curious pattern forming a kind of check. A dish of Moorish bread fresh from the oven and made of brownish flour, well-garnished with particles of the rough stones of the bread mill in which the corn was ground, made up the banquet. We squatted on the floor, Swani went round and poured water from a tin dish upon our hands, and, after a pious Bismillah, we all dipped bits of bread in the red grease and oil of the highly seasoned dishes and began to eat, ladling the food into our mouths most painfully with the right hand, and lifting the huge dishes to our mouths to drink the soup. A loud *Bon jour* warned us the Persian was outside the tent, waiting to tell us his adventures and to impart the gossip of the place. Entering, he sat down with a sonerous " Peace be on you all," and, after one or two cups of tea and a few cigarettes, began to talk. The Caid, he said, was puzzled about us, had thought at first of sending us in chains to the Sultan's camp, again had thought of letting us proceed, and yet again of sending us under a guard of his own men to the Consul at Mogador, but at the last had not imparted his design to our informant. Still he thought that probably a messenger had been despatched to the Sultan in his camp, and if that was the case we had better make our minds up to at least a fortnight in the place, and afterwards, if the Sultan should send for us, a fortnight at the camp, for things in palaces go slowly; * but, said the Persian piously, " may God not open the door of the Sultan to you, or to any other man." By this I took it that should the Sultan send for us that we should pass an unpleasant quarter-of-an-hour, though as there were several Europeans in the camp, notably Caid M'Lean, the instructor-general to the army, and a French doctor called Linares, we might be able to get things arranged upon the peace-with-honour plan. This matter duly gone into with proper Oriental deliberation, the Persian entered on his tale. Born sometimes in Shiraz, at others in Tabriz (according to his fancy), it appeared that at an early age he had left his country as an " Ashik," † that is, a wandering singer, and gone to Turkey. There he had acquired the Turkish language as he averred, but subsequent intercourse with Arabs had

---

* Cosas de palacio van despacio.

† " Ashik " literally means " lover " in Persian, and has by degrees come to mean a minstrel, because in the climate of Persia lovers are assumed to sing to lutes and other instruments, which the climate renders unseemly in England.

mixed the tongues, in the same fashion a Spaniard,
Italian, or Portuuuese gets mixed, on learning either
of the kindred languages. Such as it was, his jargon
suited me, and I spoke Arabic more fluently to him
than I ever spoke that tongue before, or think to
speak it until I meet another "Ashik" similarly
graced. We spoke without a verb, without a particle,
like idiots or children, largely in adverbs and in
adjectives, and without shame on either side, each
thinking that the other was but little versed in
Arabic, and that he condescended to adopt a jargon
to help his weaker friend. The Persian's faithful
fiddle was out of order, owing he said, to his falling
off a donkey whilst on the "roads of hell" which led
up to Kintafi, but though without it, he sang for
hours, songs which he said treated of love in Persian,
and which I took on trust as not containing anything
subversive of morality, or fit to raise a blush upon
the cheek of those used to our western ways. Hafiz he
said he knew by heart, and much of Jami, and those
"Rubaiyat," which every weekly newspaper has
its columns full of, he knew, but found them too
materialistic for his taste.

In outward visible appearance a perfect Kurd,
squat and broad-shouldered, beard so thick that had
you dropped a pin in it it would not have touched
the skin, eyes black and piercing, face like a walnut,
and a long love-lock hanging from his shaven head
down on his shoulder, in one ear he had a silver earring, and he was gifted with a voice, perhaps the
strongest that I ever heard in man. Both a musician
and a philosopher, but yet a moralist, and a fanatic
preacher of the graces of Mohammed, but still a
sceptic at the heart, and above all a traveller, "for by
travelling, a man, although his purse grows light,

still lays up treasures on which to live when he is old.
What is a Sultan, Caid, Pasha, or Governor, compared
to he who is the Sultan of the world, when where
night catches him, he rests and looks upon the stars."

So, starting from Shiraz (occasionally Tabriz), he
had run over almost all Europe, Turkey, and a portion of the Northern States of Africa. Had been in
Serbistan, Atenas, and in Draboulis (Tripoli), Massr-
el-Kahira (Cairo), Stamboul, and Buda Pesth, and of
all lands in Europe thought most of Magyarstan; "for
there the women have eyes like almonds, though they
dr nk too much beer, the men are tall and fierce,
handsome (husnar besaf), the horses large and
elegant, they run as lightly as gazelles on stony
ground; and had the people but the blessing of the
true faith, he never would have left their land." Their
city, Buda Pesth, was larger than Stamboul, more
fine than Paris, Vienna, or than Shiraz, and in the
middle ran a river on which went steamboats, on
which he used to travel and pay his passage with a
tune, for the Magyars, he said, loved music better
than they loved their God. In this famed city he had
known one Bamborah, who by interior evidence and
after cogitation I found to be Professor Vambery.
Large hearted was this Bamborah, and speaking Persian, a Christian dervish, knowing all the East, having
read all books, explored all countries, mastered all
sciences and learning; the friend of kings, for had not
the Sultan Abdul Hamed (whom may God preserve)
sent him a ring of "diamont" worth a thousand
pounds, and Bamborah had shown it whilst they sat
discoursing in his hospitable house.

In fact of all the men, Christian or Moslem, he had
ever met, this Bamborah appeared to him the fittest
to stand before a king. But for himself even in

Buda Pesth, the travelling fever had impelled him to embark aboard a "chimin de fer," and go to Vienna, travelling all through the night and reaching Vienna about the feyzir (day break), and straying up and down the streets until at last he met a Turk who sold red slippers, and lodged with him; but after several days spent in the place, which gave him neither pleasure nor material gain, went on to Baris to find upon the journey that the customs of the East and West did not agree. The Christians know no God. With them it is all money (Kulshi flus), with them no stranger, no wayfaring man, for in that train to Baris he asked a woman for some water to wash his hands so as to address Allah after the fashion laid down in the holy books; she brought it, and after washing, and his prayers all duly said, the passengers, as he informed me, crowding about in an unseemly way to see him pray, he smiled and thanked the woman, and taking out a cigarette tendered it to her with his thanks. But she, born of a dog, knowing no God and dead to shame—for is it not set down " to strangers and to wayfarers be kind "—laughed an ill laugh and asked for half-a-franc: franc, franc, and always franc, that is the Christian's God.

Thus talking of the Alps and Alpujarras the time wore on, and after saying again most earnestly "May God not open the door of our Lord the Sultan to you," he took his leave, and as he went it seemed our only friend had gone.

Next morning found the situation still unchanged, and we began to look about us and found out that we had several companions in adversity. Camped in a tent about a hundred yards away were three Caids (*Biblicé* kings), from the province of the Sus, who had been waiting more than a month for an audience

of our captor, he having summoned them to wait
upon him to confer, as the gypsies say, about "the
affairs of Egypt." One of the "kings" turned out to
be a "saint" of some repute, a tall fine man of Arab
type and race, dressed all in spotless white, and
reading always in a little copy of some holy book
under an olive-tree, showing no trace of trouble at his
long wait, although he must have passed through
much annoyance and incurred considerable expense,
as almost all his animals had died through lack of
food and the change of climate from the warm lands
of Sus to the cold winds of the interior Atlas range.

Under the olive-tree I sat and talked to him, chiefly
through the medium of Lutaif, and asked him much
of Tarudant, from whence his house was situated but
a long day's ride. It appeared that in the main
the account of Gerhard Rohlfs,[*] the Hamburg Jew,
who visited it some thirty years ago, is applicable to
the city of to-day. The Sherif spoke of the high
walls mentioned by Rohlfs and Oskar Lenz ;[†] of the
five gates called Bab-el-Kasbah, Bab-el-Jamis, Bab-
Ouled, ben Noumas, Bab Targount, and Bab Egorgan;
of the high Kasbah, occupying, as Rohlfs says, a
space of 50,000 square metres, and cut off from the
town by a high crenelated wall. He dwelt upon the
cheapness of provisions, said that six eggs were
bought for a little copper coin called a "musonah"
(known to the Spaniards as "blanquillo") and worth
perhaps a farthing. Said that a pound of meat cost
two or three "musonahs," spoke of the trade in brass
and copper vessels, and gave us to understand, of all
the towns within the empire of his Shereifian Majesty,
that Tarudant was cheapest and pleasantest to live

---

[*] Gerhard Rohlfs's "Adventures in Morocco." London, 1874.
[†] Oskar Lenz, "Timbouctou." Paris, 1886.

in, and inferred it was because the people had no dealings with the infidel. For, said he, "the infidel are Oulad el Haram " (sons of the illegitimate), ever a-stirring, never contented with their lot, afraid to be alone, seeing no beauty in the sun, not caring for the sound of running water, and even looking at a fine horse but for his worth ; men bound to a wife, the slave of all the things they make ; then, recollecting that I too was one of the dog-descended, he gravely drew his hand across his beard, and said, " but no doubt Allah made them cunning and wise for some great purpose of his own."

No doubt, in every town throughout the East, the presence of even a small quantity of Europeans forces prices up, upsets the national life, unsettles men, and after having done so, gives them no equivalent for the mischief that it makes.

The mosques were three in number, one in the Kasbah, two in the town, of which the principal, El Djama-el-Kebir, " and the most sacred, Sidi-o-Sidi, the Saint of Saints, by which name people of a serious turn of mind call the whole town in conversation, as who should say, speaking of London, the city of St. Paul.

I questioned him about the sugar-cane plantations, of which both Luis de Marmol* and Diego de Torres† speak in their curious books written in the middle of the sixteenth century, but he had never heard of sugar-cane near Tarudant. This forms another proof of the

---

* Luis de Marmol y Carbajal was a prisoner in Fez, and wrote a curious book, called, " Descripcion General de Africa." He was born in Granada in 1520, accompanied Charles V. in his expedition to Oran, served in Africa twenty years, was made prisoner, and remained eight years in Fez. On his return he wrote his book.

† Diego de Torres (a Valencian), " Relacion del Origen, y Suceso de los Xaribes, y del Estado de los Reinos de Marruecos Fez," etc. Seville, 1584.

decadence into which all the land has fallen, for the climate and soil of Tarudant should be at least as favourable for sugar-cane as is the strip of territory in Spain which runs along the coast from Malaga into the province of Almeria, where the Moors first introduced the canes which grow there still to-day.

It appeared according to the Sherif that the town contained some 1,400 houses, and a population which he estimated at 10,000,* mostly in easy circumstances, but very ill-disposed towards all foreigners. Much information he imparted as to the mineral riches of the province; but without descending to particulars. with the exception of sulphur, which he said was found close to the town. "Romans," of course, had left their castles near the place, in the same way, the Moors have done in parts of Spain, to which they never penetrated; but who those " Romans " were remains for some more well-graced, or fortunately starred traveller than I to tell of, commentate upon, and weave a theory to content his public and himself. Caravans it seems go straight to Timbuctoo taking European goods, and bring back slaves and gold-dust, with ostrich feathers and the other desert commodities, as in the time of Mungo Park. At least they did; but I suppose the French in their consuming zeal for freedom may have stopped slaves from being bought in these degenerate days. I learned the chief fondak or caravansary was kept by one Muley Mustapha el Hamisi; but most unluckily an unkind fate deprived me of the opportunity of entering his hospitable walls. The city seemed to resemble, from the account of the Sherif, Morocco City, that is, to occupy a relatively

---

* Joachim Gatell, "Description du Sous," "Bulletin de la Société Geographique Paris," sixième série, 1871, pp. 86-89, puts it at 8,300 or thereabouts, and the houses at 1,300.

enormous space, as almost every other house had a
large garden, and several of the larger houses gardens
of many acres in extent; so that, as the Sherif
explained, "the town looks like a silver cup* dropped
in a tuft of grass." This, as I did not see it, I take
on trust, believing perhaps that Moses had died
happier had he not had the view from Pisgah's
summit over the plains of Canaan.†

And so the "Governors" waited on patiently, their
followers almost starving, and I expect themselves
not too much fed, for the Caid's servants ate or sold
all the provisions which the Chamberlain issued each
day to feed the various "guests." How the poor devils
in the prison underground fared I do not know, but
now and then a bucket with bread and "couscousu"
was let down to them, and I believe they flew on it like
half-starved jackals on a dead donkey outside a
Moorish town. Although a semi-prisoner, the Sherif
from Sus was still a holy man, and therefore I sent
Mohammed-el-Hosein to take refuge with him till
all talk of fetters, dungeons, stick and shaving beard
was past. This taking refuge (to "zoug," as it is
called) is common in Morocco. At times upon a
journey, some man will rush and seize your stirrup,
and will not let go till you promise him protection,

* The Spaniards call Cadiz "Una taza de plata," a silver cup.

† It is, however, a reproach to our travellers that this town, accessible to
travellers of all nations in the sixteenth century, is less known than Mecca
to-day, and has never been visited by an Englishman this century. Mr.
Walter Harris, the well-known traveller in Morocco, made a much more
difficult and dangerous journey to Tafilet, and if he essays Tarudant,
I wish him the success which in my case was withheld by Allah. The
inhabitants are, without doubt, the most fanatical in Morocco; but I
am certain that, had I had more time for preparation and an adequate
knowledge of Arabic, I could have both reached the place and come
safely away. As it was, I had no one to consult with, little time at my
disposal, and I knew little Arabic, and that little badly.

which, when you do (for it is not easy to refuse), you make yourself a Frankenstein, an Old Man of the Sea, an Incubus, who has proprietary rights in you, and perhaps follows you to your journey's end.

The patience of the three Sheikhs gave me an example, and I endeavoured to take our enforced detention as quietly as they did, though without success. It was truly wonderful to see them sitting all day long, half-starved, outside their tent, taking the Sun and praying regularly, yet without ostentation, telling their beads, listening to the Sherif read in a low voice from his little sacred book, and praising Allah (I have no doubt) consumedly.

And so the day went past without an incident, except that towards evening, as they drove the cattle home, that two tame moufflons came with them, as goats do in a field at home. These moufflons (Oudad) are rather larger than a large goat, almost the colour of a Scotch red deer, a tuft of hair about a span in length grows on their withers, and on their dewlap is another of the same size, the eyes are large and full, and very wild, and their chief feature is an enormous pair of curving horns. A wandering Sherif (in this case a kind of fakir) from Taserouelt, told me that " they often threw themselves off a cliff a hundred feet in height, and fall upon their horns, and then jump up at once, and run off faster than gazelles run when the hunter shouts to his horse." Just before evening we met the Caid's secretary, a quiet, handsome, literary man, who came and sat with us, and talked long about books, and grew quite friendly with Lutaif on his producing the poems of Faredi.* They read

* El Faredi, born in Cairo, 1181-1235 (Christian era). His only work which has survived is a collection of poems in praise of Allah, known as, " El Divan-el-Faredi." Little is known of him but that he was a fakir.

aloud alternately in a sort of rhythmic sing-song way, pleasing to listen to, and which is taught in Arab schools. Though I did not understand more than a word in five, the language is so fine, I enjoyed it more than all the matchless eloquence of a debate in Parliament.

To read in Arabic is a set art; to read and understand a different branch of scholarship; but these two "Talebs" both read and understood, and after an hour's intonation, strophe about, they marvelled at one another's learning, and like two doughty chieftains in an Homeric fight, stopped often to compliment and flatter one another. "By Allah, it seems impossible a Christian can read and understand el Faredi." "Strange that a Taleb of the Atlas should know the literal* language as if he were an Eastern"† and the like. The "Taleb of the Atlas" explained he had been the pilgrimage, and lived two years in Mecca, and whilst there (although a Berber) had studied deeply and perfected himself in the knowledge of the East as far as possible. Lutaif explained that though a Christian he was of Arab race, and that he worshipped God, as "Allah," in the same way as did Mohammedans. Then said the Taleb half laughing, "either you are a Moslem in disguise, or else a Taleb who has become a Christian." Seeing the conversation was becoming rather strained, I interrupted and broke it up; but when the Taleb left, Lutaif borrowed my knife and managed to haggle off his beard, though not without abrasion of the cuticle, and though without it he looked less like an Arab, still with his moustache, which he refused to

* "Literal" as opposed to the spoken or "vulgar" Arabic.
† "Eastern" carries with it something of holiness, as born near the holy places.

sacrifice, he looked so like a Turk that, as regards appearance, little was gained by all his sufferings.

The next day found us with the same postal address, still without having seen the Caid, and without a definite idea of his intentions. Most of the people seemed to be certain that a messenger had gone to the Sultan for instructions on our case, but both the Chamberlain, the Taleb, and the Captain of the Guard, denied with circumstance, and perjured themselves as cheerfully, and with as much delight in perjury for the mere sake of perjury, as any minister answering a question from the front bench of the grandmother of all parliaments. We passed the time reading el Faredi and an Arabic version of the Psalms ; writing and smoking, walking up and down the Maidan, sitting underneath the trees, and watching the Caid's horses and mules being driven to the river to bathe and drink. Although a Berber and a mountaineer, the Caid was fond of horses, and had a stud of about eighty horses and as many mules. Negroes led down the horses all "lither-fat," for our lord the Caid had "long lain in," and there had been no riding in the glen for the past month. Blacks, bays, and chestnuts, with a white or two, and a light cream colour of the kind called by the Spaniards "Huevo pato," that is duck's egg. All rather "chunky," as the Texans say, some running up to about sixteen hands, mostly all with long tails sweeping upon the ground and manes which fell quite to the point of the shoulder in the older horses. Their tails all set on low (a mark of the Barb breed), their eyes large and prominent, heads rather large, ears long and thin and intelligent, always in motion, backs rather short, round in the barrel, and well ribbed up, straight in the pastern, and feet rather small and

high, the consequence of being bred on stony
ground.

I learned the black * (el Dum) is best for show, but
bad in temper, especially if he has no white hairs
about him.   Ride him not to war, for when the sun
shines hot, and water is hard to find, he cannot suffer,
and leaves his rider in the power of his enemy. Still
the black without moon or stars (white hairs) is a
horse for kings, but he fears rocky ground. The chest-
nut† when he flies beneath the sun, it is the wind. It
was a favourite colour with the Prophet, and therefore
to be desired of all good Moslems and good horsemen.

The roan is a pool of blood, his rider will be overtaken, but will never overtake. The light chestnut
(Zfar el Jehudi, the Jews' yellow) is not for men to ride,
he brings ill luck. No wise man would ride a horse
with a white spot in front of the saddle, for such a
horse is as fatal as the most violent poison. In the
same way no prudent man would buy a horse with a
white face and stockings, for he carries his own
shroud with him.

The white is a colour for princes, but not for war.
When you advance afar off your enemy makes ready
for you.

The bay is the pearl of colours, for the bay is
hardiest and most sober of all horses. Says the Emir
Abd-el-Kader, "If they tell you a horse jumped down
a precipice without injury, ask if he was a bay, and if
they answer yes, believe them."   Lastly, the Emir
says with reason, "Speak to your horses as a man
speaks to his child, and they will correct their faults
which have incurred your anger, for they understand
the mouth of man."

---

* The Spaniards also say a jet-black horse (zaino) is bad tempered.
† " Remarks on Horsemanship," by the Emir, Abd-el-Kader.

Armed with these maxims and on the look-out for others, I was not dull as long as the horses were in sight. Sometimes a boy would ride them in to swim in the swift current, snorting and plunging till they lost their feet, and then their heads appeared out of the water, their backs almost awash, the boys clinging to them like monkeys as they struck out for the bank, raising a wave like small torpedo boats. At other times two would break loose and fight, screaming and standing up, or rushing in, seize one another by the necks like bulldogs, when their respective negroes dodged outside, like forward players in a football scrimmage waiting for the ball, trying to catch their ropes, but afraid to venture in between them. Generally the fight was ended by an Arab or a Berber rushing up armed with a thick stick and a handful of round stones, with which he beat and pelted them till they let go their hold. Others again would break loose all alone, and career about the sandy beach, head and tail up, or gallop through the corn, their attendant running after them in agony till they were captured. The most sedate walked delicately as they were Agags down to the water, plunged their muzzles deep into the stream and drank as if they wished to drain the river dry, looked up and drank again three times, then turned, and after executing several perfunctory bounds, lay down and rolled in the wet sand and quietly walked home beside their negro, not deigning even to look at any other horse, then disappeared under the horseshoe gateway to the inner courtyard where they lived. The mules were not so interesting, though valuable, fetching more money than the best horse, and if accomplished " pacers," often bringing two or three hundred dollars, whereas a horse rarely exceeds a hundred and fifty at the most ;

but still they have an air as of a donkey, which makes them quite uninteresting, for they are lacking in the donkey's inner grace.

In districts like the Atlas mules are more service-able than any horse, and on the mountain roads will perform almost a third longer journey in a day. Where the horse beats them is on the plain, for no mule can live beside a horse at the horse's pace, though on a rough road the mule's pace is much the faster of the two. Sometimes five or six mules would break loose and follow one another in a string, jump-ing the thorny fences heavily, their ears flapping about ridiculously, and their thin tails stuck high up in the air. They never swam, and, on the whole, had I been limited to mules exclusively, I could not have passed my time so well. One horse especially in-terested me, a large creamy-white animal with an immense and curly mane, he always came alone, led by two negroes, and had an open wound upon his head and two upon his chest. I learned he was the Caid's special favourite, and that about a month ago, during an expedition to the Sus to aid the Sultan against a refractory tribe, the Caid had received a bullet in the leg, and the horse had got his wounds at the same time. None of the horses that I saw would be of any value, except to an artist, in the European market; but for the country where they were bred they were most serviceable, hardy, and indefati-gable, sober beyond belief, eating their corn but once a day, drinking but once, and up to any weight, and if not quite so fast as might be wished for, still a glory to the eye.

The horses gone, the entertainment of the day was over, and I got quite accustomed to expect them at a certain hour, and to be quite annoyed if they were late.

Thus did one day tell and certify another, leaving us quite cut off from all the world, as far removed from European influence as we had been in the centre of the Sahara; well treated, but uncertain of how long we should be kept in honourable captivity, growing more anxious every moment, and yet with something comic in the situation; nothing to do but make the best of it, eat, drink, and sleep, and stroll about, talk with the natives, sit in our tent, and read el Faredi, and giving ourselves up with the best grace we could, to watch and pray.

CHAPTER VII.

THE 24th still found us, so to speak, in Poste Restante at Kintafi, the Caid invisible, tobacco running low, food not too regular, and our animals becoming thinner every day. But still the example of the prisoners, the Sheikhs from Sus, and a tent full of miserable tribesmen, all almost without food, and glad to eat our scraps, kept us for shame's sake patient. So we talked much to everyone, especially with the negro who had been in London, and found he was a man of much and varied travel, some experience, no little observation, and ready to talk all day on all that he had seen. London had not impressed him, or else impressed him to such purpose that he was dumb about it, but of the Fetish worshippers below the Senegal he could tell much. In speaking of them, though a negro of the blackest dye, he treated them as savages, being a Mohammedan, and laughed at their religion, although the most foolish portions of it seemed to appeal to his imagination, in the same way that negroes in America (all Christians, of course), are seldom pleased with moderate Christianity, but usually are Ranters, Bush Baptists, or members of some saltatory sect, which gives them opportunity to enter more fully into communion with the spirit of the thing than if they sat and listened to a prayer, slept at a sermon, or dropped their money in the plate, merely conforming in a perfunctory way, as their less animistic lower-toned brethren in the Lord seem quite content to do.

Fetish, our friend explained, is good, and works great deeds; sometimes a man will die, and then the Fetish man appears and cuts off a cow's tail, fastens it on the dead man's forehead, who at once gets up and walks to where he wishes to be buried, and dies again. Why he does this the speaker did not know, or why, before he dies, the man does not explain in the usual way to his friends where he wants them to lay him after death. Nor did he know what good the fetish man receives by his operation, or if the tail should be taken from a dead or living cow, but he was certain that he had seen a miracle, and told us plainly that he never was so certain of anything before. Fetish to him seemed rather an incident than a religion, for he went on to say the heathen negroes have no God, just like the Christians; and then turned grey, which, I think, is the negro way to blush, and said, he did not point his observation at ourselves, for he had heard in London that we worshipped several Gods, and that the Christians he referred to were the people in the Canaries, who, he was positive, worshipped a goddess, for he had seen them do so in a Mosque. Again he said his head was full of news, but his purse still continued light, and so he drew it out and showed it to us, and it was empty certainly, but beautifully made, of a most curious pattern and workmanship, and cunningly contrived of pieces of thin leather which all fitted into one another and drew out, after the fashion of those painted boxes which used to come from India, which in one's childhood when one opened them, one always found another underneath. It appears he has been often in the

Canaries, and knows the islands, as Lanzarote which he denominates "Charuta," Fuerteventura which becomes "Fortinvantora," and Grand Canary, where he saw one Christian kill another with a knife.

In form he was almost perfect as a type of race; blacker than shale, with yellowish teeth like fangs, nostrils as wide as a small donkey's, huge ears like a young elephant's, and bloodshot eyes, thin, spindle legs, and all his body covered with old scars; for he had been in many wars, shoots, as he said; "plum center" rides well, and to crown all had feet about the size and shape of a cigar box, stuck at right angles to his legs, so when he walked he looked like a flamingo, or a heron in a swamp. Knowing by actual handling the exiguity of his purse, I approached the negro to try if he would carry letters for me to the outside world. But after having bargained for five dollars, a sudden panic took him, and he refused, and ever after during our stay avoided us, although I did not hear that he informed the Caid or any of his men.

All the day long a constant string of people kept arriving at the Castle gate. Little brown sturdy-legged Berber tribesmen, armed with long quarter-staffs, dressed in their dark "achnifs," barefooted and bareheaded, save for a string of camel's hair bound round the forehead; small-eyed, and strangely autochthonous in type, as if they and the stones upon the hills had sprung into existence long before history. Small caravans of donkeys carrying Indian corn, with fruit, with almonds, and with meat entered the gate full laden, and came out empty. Negresses walked down the hill tracks, bending beneath the weight of immense loads of brushwood, or of grass, or the green leaves of Indian corn or sorgum,* to feed the horses, and to heat the ovens of the Caid.

I found that, though the Caid oppressed and plundered all the district, his oppression was in a measure balanced by his charity, for he fed all the poor people of the valley, and dispensed his hospitality to all and sundry who passed his gates. So that, take it for all in all, his tyranny was only different in degree from that of the manufacturer in the manufacturing towns of England, who lives upon the toil of several thousand workmen, discharges no one useful function to the State, his works being run by paid officials, and he himself doing nothing but sign his letters, whilst he uses the money wrung from his workmen to engage in foreign speculations, to swindle the inhabitants of distant countries ; and for all charity subscribes to missions to convert the Jews, or to send meddling praters to insult good Catholics in Spain.

The Caid, Si Taib el Kintafi, lives like a veritable prince, is almost independent of the Sultan, and reminds me of a Mohammedan Emir in Spain after the Caliphate of Cordoba broke up. These Emirs were called by the Spaniards Reyezuelos de Taifas,† that is, Kings of a Section, or Hedge Kings ; they had their courts in Jaen, in Malaga, in Almeria,‡ and in the South of Portugal. But in especial it recalled Jaen, being situated amongst the mountains, as that kingdom was with towering Atalayas (watch-towers) on every hill, and the Caid's palace in the centre of the land. Guards were on every road patrolling

* Sorgum is the Sesame of the Arabian Nights.   In Spanish it is known as Ajonjoli, a corruption of a word of similar sound in Arabic.

† Taifa means a Band or Company.   The word is more used in the East than in Morocco, in the Arabic of to-day.

‡ Almeria was one of the few cities is Spain founded by the Moors.   Its name in Arabic is El Merayeh, the Looking Glass.

within sight of one another. About five hundred negro
slaves were scattered in the various castles. The
Caid kept all his money in iron boxes underground,
and all his wives were guarded by gentlemen of the
third sex,* so that the parallel between Kintafi and
Jaen was almost perfect. For enemies he had the
Sultan and every other Caid of equal strength, but the
impenetrable nature of his territory made him almost
impregnable, and the armed soldiery, who lounged
about in numbers round the Castle and at every fort,
made him secure as long as he could pay their
services. The difference between a Spanish Moorish
mountain state and the "Taifa" of Kintafi was
(though not apparent in externals, in policy, and in
ideals of government), in other matters, very striking,
for in the smallest Moorish Courts of Spain, arts,
sciences, literature, and general culture, all flourished,
and were encouraged by the kings.

Poets, musicians, doctors, and men of science
flocked to the capitals; both Almeria and Malaga
were centres of culture, and many writers who
flourished in those cities still survive. But in Kintafi
all was in decadence; for music, only a little thrumming
on the Gimbri,† beating of tom-toms, an occcasional
song sung to the lute, and the shrill music of the
Moorish pipe known as the "Ghaita," and which
survives in parts of Spain under the name of "Dul-
zaina," and which, in both countries, is always accompanied by a small hand-drum.

Literature, in the modern Moorish state, is confined
but to the Koran, the sacred books, an occasional

* Someone, I think, has called Journalists "Gentlemen of the third
sex," but these guardians were connected with no newspaper.

† The Gimbri is a diminutive mandoline, the front of which is of parchment. It has only three strings, and yet its sound is less unpleasant than
that of more pretentious instruments I have heard.

Arab poet, and the study of the one book known to
be written in the Berber tongue, and called El Maziri,
which deals exclusively with the ceremonial of the
faith.   Strange that a people like the Moors, still
brave, so fine in type, ardent in faith, sober in habit,
and apparently (if history lie not more than usually),
so like to what they were externally, when they shook
Europe, should have fallen into such absolute decay.
Literature, art, science, everything forgotten; architecture but a base copy of their older styles, though still
not so degraded as our own ; bad government crying
aloud in every town, on every road corruption rampant, and still the people, as mere men, infinitely
superior to any race in Europe I have seen; patient,
and bearing hunger and oppression with a patience
to put a saint to shame, and yet incapable to strike a
blow to free itself from the base tyranny which all
must see and feel.   Apparently no outlook but to
become the slaves of one and another peddling buc-
caneering European race, to lose all individuality as
the Algerian Arabs have done, or be reduced to
bankruptcy like the natives of our glorious Empire
in the East.

No man in all Morocco to rise and say, as the Sheikhs
said to Omar when he asked if any one had a complaint against him : " By Allah, if we had had cause
of complaint against thee, we had redressed it with
our swords."   And still, in spite of decadence, I never
met a Moor who knew anything of our European
life and institutions, except, of course, the servant class
and a few men in place, and money-lenders who
wished to change their decadence for our prosperity
upon the terms of bowing to a foreign race.   They
know that to the individual man, with all its faults,
their life is happier than ours—somehow they feel

instinctively that when we talk ot freedom, liberty, and of good government, that these mean freedom, good government and liberty for ourselves, and that they, by submitting, would become slaves, receiving nothing in return. Still they accept our gin, our teas, our powder, and in general, all the good things which Europe sends them, with civility, but decline to see that we, for all our talk, are any better than themselves. Baulked of our negro, I cast about to find some other stranger willing to earn a dishonest penny by carrying letters for the prisoners of the Caid. After much talking and long negotiation over night, a man made up his mind to venture to Morocco city, a journey of about three days, for the magnificent guerdon of four dollars, one dollar to be paid at once, and the other three upon arrival, either at Mr. Nairn's, the missionary's house, or that of Si Bu Bekr, a well-known merchant, and for a long time " British Agent " in the town, or at the house of the Sherif of Tamasluoght, a protected British subject, whose Zowia is about ten miles outside the town.

The letters duly written, with much care and secrecy, some to our friends, others to Consuls, one to the British Minister in Tangier, and two* to newspapers, were wrapped up carefully in a piece of strong French packing paper, tied round with a palmetto cord, and given to the man, who crawled up to the tent door at dead of night, whilst we sat waiting for him like conspiritors. At the last moment, he demanded "one more dollar in the hand," dwelling upon the risks he ran, and which, indeed, were great. Not being prepared to bargain at such a time, I put the dollar in his hand, and bade him go with God, telling Mohammed-el-Hosein to explain in Berber all that he should do.

---

* These two are to be found in the notes, in extenso.

They seemed to talk for hours, though I suppose it was not really long, and after having received instructions, minute enough to confuse a lawyer, he slipped away, crawling along the ground (his single long white garment looking like a shroud), until he reached a bank beside the mill stream, over which he dropped.

We sat late, talking over our tea, smoked the last of our tobacco, and calculated how long it would take to get an answer, if all went well, and if our messenger escaped the perils of the road. Mohammed-el-Hosein, thought in five days, if in the interim it did not rain, and the rivers rise, we might have word, for he said when the man arrives, either the missionary or Bu Bekr, or both, will send off messengers both to the Consul, to the Sultan, and another to the Caid to tell him where we are. The messengers, he said, having their own spurs and other people's horses, will not spare either, so that upon the evening of the fifth day, we shall hear, Inshallah, if all goes well. All the night long we slept but little, fearing to hear shots and see our guide brought back escorted by a guard, but all passed quietly, and we congratulated ourselves on his escape, as we knew well the first ten miles of the road would be most difficult for him to pass.

Next morning we kept wondering, like children, how far our messenger had got upon the road, and trying to encourage one another by talking of the tremendous distance an Arab " rekass " could go when pushed to exert himself by fear or gain. The stories grew as the morning passed, until at last from eighty to a hundred miles seemed quite an ordinary trot. Privately, I thought the thick-legged mountaineer did not look like a record breaker, but I kept my opinion to myself, and let my followers' yarn, seeing that it relieved their hearts. By this time, Mohammed-el-Hosein had

ventured back from his refuge with the Sherif from
Sus, and was quite sure that the Caid had sent a messenger off to the Sultan, for, on the morning after we
were captured, a "rekass" was seen to strike across
the hills. The Chamberlain, Si Mohammed, honoured
us with a visit, wrapped up in fleecy, voluminous
white clothes, new yellow shoes, beard dyed with
henna, finger nails turned orange with the same substance, and followed by two stalwart, well-armed
mountaineers, who strode behind him as he waddled
to our tent.   After due compliments and salutations,
he officially informed us that the Caid was wounded,
and could not see us for a day or two.   Though we
knew this before, to show good manners, we pretended
great astonishment, asked who could have dared to
wound so good a prince, where it had happened, and as
to seeing us, begged he would use his pleasure in the
matter, though, of course, we counted every minute,
till we should see his face.   The Chamberlain, as
excellent a diplomatist as could be wished for, said he
was glad to see us in such spirits, for he had thought
by my expression on the first day, that I was irritated
with his lord, the Caid, who had detained us (as he
now said) merely to save our lives, as, had we crossed
into the Sus, the "Illegitimate Ones" (Oulad el
Haram) would have slain us, not for Christians, for,
said the Chamberlain, looking at me with a slight
smile, you wear our clothes as if you had been born
amongst the Arabs, but as strangers, for God had
made their hearts like stone to all they did not know.
The conversation languished till he startled me by
asking if I was a "Moskou," which at first I did not

---

* I render the Arabic word " Hajib," by Chamberlain, though I am not
quite sure whether Chamberlain does not better correspond to the Moorish
dignity of Kaid-el-Mesouar.

comprehend, and thought he meant to ask me of what
sect I was. Just as I had instructed Lutaif to inform
him I was a member of the U.P.* Church, and was as
orthodox† a Christian as he was a Mohammedan, it
dawned upon me that he meant to ask me if I was a
Russian, and might have said I was one, had I not
feared to bring about a diplomatic question of some
sort. Our guns against the tent-pole next struck his
eye. Mine was a double-barrelled gun lent by the
British Consul in Magador. Lutaif's, a single bar-
relled, Spanish gun, made in Barcelona, and so light
upon the trigger, that on the only occasion he tried to
fire with it, it started before he was expecting it, and
the whole charge passed close to the head of an old
negro on a donkey passing along the road. The
negro did not turn a hair, but was just starting to
abuse Lutaif, when, in my capacity of a Sherif, I rode
up and cursed him for a dog for getting between the
gun and the partridge Lutaif was firing at. This
made things right, and the poor man rode on with
many apologies for having frightened us. The
Chamberlain examined the two weapons, and asked
leave to show them to the Caid, and, before we had
time to answer, motioned to one of his attendants to
take them off. I sat as solid as a rock, and said it
was not usual to deprive a guest of his gun without
consent, whereupon the Chamberlain poured out a

* U.P. in N.B. stands for United Presbyterian. Stevenson refers to this
sect, in one of his ballads in the Scottish dialect. This sect is little known
amongst well-informed people, and its tenets have been greatly misunderstood.

† In Morocco the people belong to the sect of Malekiayahs, one of the
four sects into which orthodox Mohammedans are divided, the other then
being the Hannafiyahs, Shafiyahs and Hambaliyahs. Thus, had I declared
myself a member of the N.P. church, I fear I should still have been less
orthodox than the Chamberlain.

torrent of excuses, and said the Caid had now determined not to hurt a hair of any of our heads, and only
wanted to see the guns from curiosity.   Seeing the
turn events were taking, I tried to get the Chamberlain to say if a "rekass" had been sent off to the
Sultan or not, and if it was not possible for him to use
his influence (for a consideration) to enable us to go
on to the Sus.

Tipping throughout the East is understood to the
full as well as it is understood in England, and his
eyes glistened at the word "consideration," but with
an effort he replied, as far as he knew no messenger
had gone, and, as to going to the Sus, had he not told
us of the Sons of Belial who in that land cared for
men's lives as little as an ordinary man cared about
killing lice.   After some tea and a surreptitious
cigarette which I found in the corner of my saddle-
bag, and which to make him smoke we had to close
the tent, so that no one should see him "drink the
shameful," he departed, telling us to be of good cheer
and we should soon be honoured by an interview with
his liege lord the Caid.   As he departed I responded
to his compliments ceremoniously in English, devoting
his liege lord to all the devils mentioned in the Tal-
mud, Cabala, Apocalypse, and other works upon
theology which treat of angels, devils, and like works
of human ingenuity. Lutaif almost exploded, and
even Swani, who knew a little expletive English,
seemed amused.

After the interview we walked up the river and
sat down underneath an algaroba tree, to watch
thirty or forty people, men, children, and women,
more or less carelessly veiled (for in this matter Berbers are much less strict than Arabs), all cracking
almonds in a long open shed.

Almonds are one of the staple articles of trade in the Atlas Mountains, long trains of mules, during the autumn, convey them to Morocco city, from thence they go to Mogador and are shipped off to Europe, "though what you Christians do with such a quantity of almonds we do not know." I took especial care not to enquire the price per bag, or ton, or box, they sell at; how many qualities there are; when they are ripe; how they are picked, sorted, or anything of that fatiguing nature, knowing how much I had disliked that kind of thing in books of travel I have read. Is not all that set forth in Consular Reports, in Blue Books, and the like, and who am I, by means of information got meanly at first hand, to "blackleg," so to speak, upon a British Consul, or to "springe cockle in his cleene corne" with unofficial and uncalled details which would not bring me in a cent.

Lutaif, and I, the Sherif from Sus, and the Persian, sat under a walnut grove for several hours, reading el Faredi, trying to learn the Berber tongue, talking of other things, and I began at last to understand the lives passed by the Greek philosophers, who no doubt wandered up and down talking of things they did not understand, dozing beneath the trees, and weaving theories about First Causes, Atoms, Evolution, the Nature of the Gods, Schemes of Creation, and other mental exercises, at least as interesting as essays upon View of Frank Pledge (Visus de Francopledgii), Courts of Attachment, Swanimote, or any of the Judgments or the Entries of the Assizes of the Forest, either of Pickering or Lancaster.

Much did the Sherif enquire about the "Chimin di fer"—how it was made, how fast it went and why, and if men sat upon it (as he had heard) and worked it with their legs. I told him all I knew (and more),

and about bicycles and women's rights; gave a brief
digest of our common law and current theology, tried
to explain our parliamentary system, the Stock Exchange, our commerce, glory, whisky, and the like;
told him of London's streets at night, our churches,
chapels, underground railways, tramways, telephones,
electric light, and other trifles of our pomp and state
which might be interesting. His observations were
few but pertinent, and certainly, upon occasions, hard
to answer out of hand. The bicycle, the Persian kindly
corroborated: the telephone, Lutaif explained; a railway underground was no more wonderful than one
upon the surface of the earth; our parliament seemed
foolish to him, and he could not understand how one
man could represent another, still less ten thousand
men; the Stock Exchange he summed up briefly as a
fraud, remarking, "How can they sell that which they
have not got"; but he reserved his chiefest comment
for more simple things. "Whose are those wives,"
he said, "who walk your streets; I thought you Christians were monogamists? Do you not keep the law
you follow then, or are there not sufficient husbands
for the women, or are your women bad by nature;
and how is it your Cadis tolerate such things?" I
told him, courteous reader, just what you would have
said in my position: confessed our faith in strict
monogamy, but said the flesh was weak; that even
amongst ourselves the Oulad-el-Haram were a large
tribe; that all worked towards perfection, and no
doubt, some day, things would improve. And he quite
courteously rejoined, "Yes, yes, I see, you Christians
are like us, that is your faith is stronger than your
deeds; well, even with us there are some men who
read the Koran, and yet forget to follow all it says."

I dropped the conversation and urged the old Persian on to talk about himself; to tell of Persia, Turkey, the Sahara, and the Oasis of Tindoof, which he described by smoothing his hand upon the sand to show the flatness of it, and then said "Tindoof walou," that is, in Tindoof, nothing ; though he confessed it is the mouth of Timbuctoo. In the same way Canada is said to have got its name from the two Spanish words "Aca" and "Nada," as signifying "there is nothing here." "Baris,"* he said was beautiful, the houris as the houris in paradise, but more expensive; and he detailed to his astonishment that once on entering a "cabinet" (presumably inodore) he had to pay a franc on coming out. And still he dwelt upon our hardness towards our co-religionists, and said, "Amongst you, look how many starve; here they may kill us, or throw us into prison, mutilate us, put out our eyes (these things are all against the Koran, as your women on the streets are clean against the teachings of your Book), but who can say a poor Mohammedan was ever known to starve. Look at me here," he said, "I came walking along the road carrying my broken fiddle, not cursing God, after the fashion of the Christians, for my bad luck, but praying at the Saint's tomb, leading the prayer in wayside mosques, calling to prayers when asked, maintained by all, till I arrived at this place and was received by the great Caid with favour, given food and clothes and twenty dollars,† and fell into the disgrace in which you see me by my own act." Though I knew of the Caid's face being averted from

---

* Paris is always pronounced "Baris" by Arabs. Vapor a steamer "Babor" and so on.

† Read perhaps "two dollars," for it is politic to exaggerate the munificence of the great. The politic man shall stand before kings, and they shall honour him.

him, and that he was about once more to take his fiddle up and walk, I had, out of politeness, to pretend my ignorance, and then he spoke.

"Yes, I was well received, and nightly the Caid would send for me, and I discoursed to him of Persia, Turkey, and other countries which I had seen, and also of El Hind and China which I have not visited, but trust to visit before I call myself a traveller, and all went well and others envied me. Till, on a night, puffed up with pride, I let my tongue escape. Unruly member! (Here he drew it out and held it, like a slippery fish, between his finger and his thumb). With it I told the Caid that he might be as a great Sultan, but that I was greater, for was not I a Sultan of the mind. and since that time I have not stood once in the presence, and shortly I shall leave this place without a friend unless it be that you and this same noble Syrian, who speaks for you, can be counted in the number of the men who wish me well."

He ceased, and I determined later on to take the hint, and fell awatching a small brown tree-creeper, not larger than a wren, which ran along the branches of a walnut-tree, and put its head upon one side and looked at us as it had been a fashionable philosopher, and no doubt just as wise. The grove of walnuts, sound of the running stream, at which a large grey squirrel sat and drank, noise of the wind amongst the leaves, the distant glimpses of the snow-capped hills, the long sustained notes of the negroes singing in the fields, set me athinking upon some not impossible Almighty Power, a harmony in things, a not altogether improbable design in nature, and, in fact, embarked me on the train of thought, which the deep-thinking author of the libretto of " Giroflee et Girofla " has typified as thoughts about " de l'eau de l'amour

des roses," when the irruption of a scabby-headed boy
summoned me back to earth.

He (the scabby-headed one) had heard I was a
doctor of some repute, and had cured divers folks, as,
indeed, I think I had, or at least medicined them out
of self-conceit, and came to ask my help for the afflic-
tion which had come upon his head. Taking rather a
hasty look, I almost had prescribed washing and an
ointment with some butter mixed with sulphur, when
I bethought me, what was expected of a doctor in the
country where we lived. So, after thinking carefully
for a little space, I said, " This requires thought,
come to the tent in two hours' time (three hours were
better), and I hope by then to have thought out,
Inshallah, a fit medicine for your case." Duly interpreted into Berber this satisfied him, and he promised
to comply. Our *tertulia** then dispersed, and we
went back to sleep inside the tent, or resting on our
rugs, to watch the constant passing stream of white or
brown-dressed, bare-footed figures, which, in Morocco,
is always to be seen passing upon every road.

Considering that, in the Roman times, Pliny, quoting from the lost journal of Suetonius Paulinus,
informs us that the Atlas Mountains were full of
elephants, and swarmed with wild beasts of every
kind, who took refuge in the impenetrable forests with
which those mountains then were clad, it is strange
to find the Atlas of to-day so largely a treeless and a
gameless land. True, that much later than the Roman

---

* *Tertulia* is the Spanish word for a gathering of people sitting talking
about nothing, or important matters, for amusement. Thus after an hotel
dinner at a watering place, there is always the " Rato de tertulia," *i.e.* the
half hour of conversation in which the affairs of the world and one's
acquaintances are discussed and settled. The word is also used for an
evening party.

times, the white wild cattle, to-day confined to Cad-
zow, Chillingham, and Lyme, roamed through the
glades of Epping Forest, where to-day nothing more
fearful than sandwich paper, or a broken bottle, makes
afraid the explorer, and that wolves and wild boars
were common till almost modern times with us.   The
destruction of the forests can be accounted for by the
constant burning for pasturage, and with the forests
much of the game would go, but why, besides large
animals, there should be a dearth of birds, I do not
know? With the exception of a hawk or two, pigeons
and partridges, the lesser bustard, the little tree-
creeper before referred to, a species of grey wagtails,
and a reddish-brown sparrow, I hardly saw a bird.
The ibises that follow cattle, the wild ducks, water
birds, the greater bustard, herons and large hawks,
all so common in the plains, are here conspicuous by
their absence.   I saw no storks,† and I believe they
rarely come so high into the mountains as Kintafi,
though in the plains no Arab hut so small as not to
have its nest, with its two storks chattering all day,
quite as persistently, and as far as I can see, to quite
as little purpose as do members of the Imperial
Parliament.

As regards animals—hyenas, foxes, jackals, wild
boars, moufflons, porcupines, grey squirrels, small
hares, and rabbits in considerable numbers, are to
be found, with a few wild cats, and now and then
a panther; lions are unknown, except in the great
cedar forests of the Beni M'Gild to the north of Fez.
In many parts of the plain country of Morocco the

---

* Much offence has often been given in Morocco by " sportsmen " firing
at storks.   The Arabs who are not civilized people, cannot understand
killing anything you cannot eat.   Besides, the stork, amongst birds, is
the friend of man, as the porpoise is amongst fish.

animals above referred to (except the lion), but with the addition of the gazelle, are numerous, but in the Atlas Mountains, at least about Kintafi, they are scarce and hard to find. In the plains sand grouse and several kinds of plovers are frequent, but I never saw them in the hills. Certainly both in the mountains and the plains all men have guns, and some of them shoot well; but though they shoot partridges, ducks, and pigeons in the plains, and in the mountains hunt the "moufflon," and the wild boar and porcupine, I never saw an Arab or a Berber fire at a small bird; so that they cannot have been all destroyed, as is the case in certain parts of Europe, by the efforts of the "Sontags Jaeger" and his twenty-five mark gun. Curious idea that known as "sport," and perhaps liable, as much as anything, for the degradation of mankind. Witness the Roman show of gladiators, the Spanish bull fight, and the English pheasant butchery, where keepers wring the necks of dozens of tame birds to swell the bag which has to figure in the newspapers, so that the astonished public recollect Lord A. or Mr. B. is still alive.

One thing is certain in Morocco, and that is, that the domestic animals and man understand one another better than they do in any other country I have seen. It may be that it is because in the East the animals, now become so terribly mechanical in Europe, were first domesticated. It may be that the peaceful life gives time for men and animals to make each other out. It may be that the monstrous cart horses, greyhound-like thoroughbreds, ridiculously cropped and docked hunters, and capitalistic looking carriage horses, with the whole Noah's Ark of beef producing, milk secreting, wool growing missing link between the animal creation and the machine world, which

we see in the fat "streaky bacon" pigs, disgusting
short horns, and improved sheep with backs like
boxes, feel their degradation, and hate us for imposing it upon them and their race. No one can say
it is because the intellect of biped and of quadruped
is nearer in degree than it is in Europe, for between the
Arab tribesmen and the English or Scottish country-
men, the balance certainly is not in favour of the
northerner, if abstract power of mind apart from education is to be the test. What makes a flock of sheep
follow an Arab, and have to be driven by a European,
I do not know. Why, if an Arab buys a kid, in a few
days it follows him about, I cannot tell, but there is
nothing commoner than to see Arabs walking on the
roads with curly black-woolled lambs and goats
walking along beside them, as only dogs, of all the
animals, will do with us.

Curiously enough, in South America, where animals
of every kind are much more plentiful than in the
East, they are not on the same familar terms with
man.

Who ever saw a lamb follow a Gaucho, Texan,
Mexican, or any man of any of the countries where
sheep abound in millions, such as Australia or New
Zealand? I do not say that in Morocco animals are
greatly better treated than with us, though on the whole
I think, perhaps the scale inclines against ourselves,
but still there is community of feeling which I have
never seen in any other land. Sometimes this same
community makes the tragedy of animal life even
more hard to understand, as when a man is followed
by a lamb or kid up to the butcher, and stands and
sees the thing which followed him so happily have its
throat cut before his face, sees its eyes glaze, and its
hot blood pour out upon the sand, pockets his half-a-

dollar, and walks serenely home, after a pious ex-
clamation about "One God"; as if God, either in one
or three, could possibly be pleased to see one of his
own created creatures so betray another only because
it walked upon four legs. However, let "the One"
(El Uahed) be pleased or not, no section of his clergy
throughout Europe have said one word in favour of
good treatment of their brother animals. Popes and
Archbishops of Canterbury, of Paris, York, Toledo,
and the rest, are dumber than dumb dogs, fearing
to offend, fearing, it may be said the animals have
souls, or daring not to speak for fear of the stronger
brethren; for when did priest, tub-thumper, bishop,
Pope, or minister of any sect, take thought about the
feelings of the brethren who are weak.

My scabby-headed patient turned up towards evening, and sat expectant in the door of the tent. After
some thought, I told him to rise exactly one hour
before the "Feyyer," and get water from a stream
(not from a well on any account), then put it in a
vessel and pray exactly as the " Muzzin " called to
prayer, then to walk backwards round an olive tree
three times ; every third day for twice nine days, to
avoid all food cooked with Argan oil, finally, to wash
his head well every day with soap, then to rub in
butter mixed with sulphur, and then, if God so willed
it, he would be well. A Seidlitz powder which he
drank at once, and said there was " a spirit in the
water," and nine Beecham's Pills to be taken alternately upon the third, the seventh, and the ninth day,
till they were finished, sent him away rejoicing, and
laid my fame for ever as a first-class " tabib."

We now began to think how far our messenger had

---

* Literally a Djin. The belief in the Djinûn, seems to be a relic of
Pantheism, or some older faith than that of Mohammed.

got, and were discussing how great the astonishment of the few Europeans in Morocco city would be on hearing of our fate, when the tent door was lifted and our messenger walked in, and silently laid the packet and the two dollars at my feet. Had a volcano opened upon the neighbouring hill I could not have been more surprised, and for a moment no one spoke, so much had we counted on the letters being well upon their way.

Swani first broke the silence with a string of imprecations on the unlucky messenger's female relations whom he defiled, gave up to Kaffirs, compared to hens, cows, goats, and finished up by telling the poor man he evidently was born of a family the women of which were shameless, veilless, and as hideous in their persons as their characters were vile. The poor man sat quite patiently, and then replied it was no use to curse him, his heart had failed, and that he feared if he were found out the Caid would kill him, burn his house, and throw his children into prison to rot and die. Though I was much annoyed, I was sorry for him, as one is always sorry for all those whose hearts fail at the wrong minute, and I was touched that he had brought me the two dollars back. Most likely in his life he had never seen himself at the head of so much capital, and it would have been easy for him to throw away the packet and not return. Therefore I handed him a dollar, and remarked, those who have families should not engage in enterprises such as these; God loves stout-hearted men, but perhaps loves quite as much fathers who love their children, but, children or no children, we are all in his hand. This, though they had heard it a million times, seemed to console all present, and the messenger slunk from the tent ashamed, but happy, having been paid on a scale he thought was lavish for a mere twenty-two hours' walk.* Certainly when he went we were cast down, for it appeared impossible to get a letter safely conveyed, and we agreed next morning to saddle up our animals and see if the Caid would allow us to return, thinking, perhaps, his injunctions only lay upon the road towards the Sus. This settled, Lutaif and I walked long backwards and forwards on the " Maidan," in the clear moonlight, and heard the long-drawn, quavering notes of a wild song like a Malagueña rise in the still night air, wayward and strange in interval, sung in a high falsetto voice, and yet enthralling and penetrating to the marrow of the bones, once heard, haunting one's memory for ever afterwards, and still almost impossible to catch, but which recalls Kintafi to me as I write, just as the scent of fresh-cut oranges brings me back Paraguay, so that perhaps perfumes and sounds are after all the most stable of the illusions amongst which we live.

* After he had gone a doubt occurred to me whether he had left the place at all, and had not merely hidden himself, and came back to amuse us with a comedy. But I consoled myself by thinking that even if this were so, I had paid more money to see worse acting in a theatre.

CHAPTER VIII.

JUST about daylight we began to load our beasts, looking anxiously the while to see if any notice of our proceedings was taken from the castle walls. But no one stirred, and hungry, without provisions for the road, our animals half-starved but lightly laden—for the greatest weight we had in coming had been food and barley—we prepared to start.

In the other tents the people made no sign, it was so early that neither the slaves were in the fields, nor yet the prisoners come up out of their living tomb, and still I thought it would be prudent before leaving to send Mohammed-el-Hosein to say that we were going, for to escape unseen was quite impossible, and even if we had slipped off unseen, once the alarm was given we should have been overtaken and brought back at once. We had not long to wait; Mohammed-el-Hosein soon came back crestfallen, and the postern door was swung wide open and the Chamberlain emerged, followed by several tribesmen all ostentatiously carrying long guns. Although it was so early he was dressed, as at all times, in most spotless clothes, and walked across the Maidan with as near an approach to haste as I had ever seen him make. Arrived at where we stood, he saluted us quite ceremoniously, and asked where we were going, to which I answered " back to Mogador." On this

he said "the Caid bids me to tell you not to go to-
day as he could never think of letting Europeans go
without an audience, but most unfortunately his
wound pains him this morning, and besides that, now
you are known as Christians, he would not let you
wander through the hill passes without an escort,
therefore, he bids me tell you to unload and wait."
For a moment I thought if we go on he will not dare
to stop us, and taking my bridle in my hand, prepared to mount, when the armed followers drew near,
handling their guns, as if to shoot a Christian would
have been great sport.

The Chamberlain said a few words in Shillah, which
having been interpreted, said if we insisted upon going
he must see his master's orders carried out. Seeing
that the Caid was resolved we should not go, I gave
my horse to Swani and went into the tent. The
Chamberlain came after me, and standing in the door
told me most civilly that he had done what he was
told to do; as he had done it in the most well-bred
way, with every consideration for my feelings and
without a trace of swagger, I thought the moment
had arrived to talk and understand each other if we
could. The Chamberlain, Sidi * Mohammed, was a
well-favoured, "coffee and skim-milk" coloured man;
portly, of course, as became his office, honest as
officers of great men go, well-dressed and courteous;
in fact, a sort of Eastern Malvolio, with the addition
of some sense.

I laid before him my two chief complaints, which I

* "Sidi" originally meant "Lord" in Arabic. To-day, in Morocco at
anyrate, it has, like "Esquire" fallen from its proud estate, and now about
answers to "Mr." It is used in addressing anyone who has good clothes,
the chief class distinction in Morocco, where all are socially equal to an
extent unknown in Europe, except in Spain. "Sidi" was the word from
which the "Cid" took his title.

said I had no wish to bother him about, but that it
seemed the best thing I could do was to marry a
maiden or two belonging to the tribe and set up
house, as there seemed little chance of ever moving
from the place. However, in the meantime, should
the Caid consent to let us go, I did not want to walk
back to the coast, and my horse and the other animals
were growing weaker every day for want of food.
Without preamble, therefore, I promised Sidi Mohammed a handsome present when I went if he
would see the man who kept the corn gave a sufficient quantity every day and did not sell it or keep it
back as he had done for the past week. Sidi Mohammed expressed astonishment at such behaviour, and
perhaps felt it, as no doubt the Caid had ordered
our horses to be fed, and promised to see about the
matter instantly and put things right.

My next complaint was that there were five of us
all in one small tent, and that such crowding was
neither comfortable nor seemly, either for a Christian
"caballer" or for a Moorish gentleman, which rank
my clothes and following entitled me to take.
The promise of the present smoothed the way, and
Sidi Mohammed said he would take upon himself to
give permission to pitch another tent. This being
done, and the men, the saddles, harness, and saddle-
cloths transferred to a smaller tent, we had our own
swept out and aired ; a new drain cut to carry
off the water, and stones arranged (which looked
exactly like an Arab grave), to place our rugs upon,
and keep them off the damp. For the first time for a
week Lutaif and I were comfortable, washed in a tin
basin, changed our clothes, and sitting in the sun at
the open door of the tent drank tea and smoked,
planning the while to get another man to take the

letters which the faithless or heartless messenger
had brought back the night before. Swani and
Mohammed-el-Hosein went to the river and washed
their clothes, and even Ali, who had nothing except
what he wore, borrowed an old "Djelab" and, standing in the river, stamped upon his rags.

Our friend the Persian came and sat with us, con-
doling on our having been prevented starting, but
saying I had taken the right way with Si-Moham-
med, and that he was glad we had got another tent.

As we sat talking, a Jew peddlar arrived bringing
two laden mules. The Persian said he might by
chance have some tobacco, and being out of it
I sent and asked the Jew to come and talk. He
came, and thinking I was a Moor began to offer all
his goods, henna, and looking-glasses, needles and
cotton, scissors from Germany, knives made in Spain,
and cotton cloths (well-sized) from Manchester. I
let him talk, but when he saw that every now and
then I missed some words and had to ask an explanation from Lutaif, who answered me in English, he
began to stare, and at last said in stumbling Spanish,
"Are you not a Moor?" "No," I replied. He said,
"What, then, you cannot be a Jew?" On hearing
that I was a Christian,* his amazement knew no
bounds. "Christian," he said, "and dressed like a
Moor, camped in the middle of the Atlas, however
came you here?" When I informed him I had
passed a as Sherif, he roared with laughter, and said he
would have given all his mules' load to see the people
come and kiss my clothes.

It seemed he lived in Agadhir-Ighir,† and traded

* Christian is official in Morocco. If you are not a Mohammedan or a
Jew, you are a Christian.

† Ighir means a castle or fortified place, in Shillah.

through the Atlas, as he informed me many of the poorer Jews do, selling their goods, and buying wool and goat-skins to take back. He had tobacco from Algeria of a villainous quality, strong, black and common, and done up in gaudy-coloured packets, adorned, one with a picture of a lady dancing "le chahut," another of apocryphal-looking Arabs resting in an Oasis, and the third displayed a little French soldier running his bayonet through a picture of Bismarck, and underneath the legend, in Italian, "Furia Francese," and to make all sure the "Regie" mark. I bought all three, which sold him out, and all my men were gratified with about half-a-pound apiece. They said it was the best tobacco they had ever smoked, but I think that tobacco was to them as it was to a Scotch gamekeeper to whom I gave, when a boy fresh from school, a packet of "Honey Dew" which I had bought in London, and who said upon my asking him if it was good, "Ye ken, Sir, if she burns she is good tobacco, and if she willna burn, then she's nae good." The Persian too, participated in the tobacco, being reduced to smoking "Kief."* Under the influence of the Algerian tobacco, which, to make himself intelligible to me, he characterised as being "bon besaf," he got back to his wanderings up and down the world.

Ifrikia, as he called Africa, he thought the most savage and abominable portion of the earth. Even

---

* "Kief" is hemp mixed with some other herbs and cut up fine and smoked in little pipes about the size of those used for smoking opium. It does not produce torpor as the Turkish "Hashish" does, but if too much indulged in destroys the health and gives a curious livid look and glaziness of the eyes to the habitual smoker. Taken in moderation it has the sustaining qualities of the "Coca" of the Andes and the "Beetel Root" of Java and the Far East. A slight headache is all that I have ever experienced on smoking it.

the Kurds, whom he knew well, he thought were not
so fierce as were the Arabs of the Wad-Nun. The
poor man, an ardent believer in Mohammedanism,
though not a bigot, and at times gaining his livelihood by discoursing on Mohammed and the Koran,
whilst travelling in Wad-Nun upon the road to Timbuctoo, which as he said he did not reach, there being
"too much powder on the road," was frequently in
peril of his life, being taken for an unbeliever, being
himself a Sufi, and the Moors all members of the sect
into which orthodox Mohammedans are grouped. The
poor old Ajemi* it appeared on one occasion was
surrounded by a band of Arabs who held their daggers
to his throat, and put their guns up to his head until he,
losing patience, knelt upon the sand, said " Bismillah, kill me in God's name," reciting the confession
of his faith in a loud voice. However, Allah, he said,
had spared him, for after taking all his money, and
almost all his clothes, the Arabs had let him go, and
cautioned him to walk with God and not return to the
Wad-Nun again. This he was confident he would not
do, preferring even Franguestan and its peculiar ways
to the companionship of such evil-begotten men as
those. I like to think of him, friendless and all alone,
kneeling upon the sand, surrounded by a crowd of
horsemen, ready, although not wishing, to be killed,
and wonder if he thought about the irony of things,
that he, an ardent votary of his religion, was to be put
to death for heresy. At times when thinking upon other
people's travels (always so much more interesting
than any of my own), it comes before me how that,

* "Ajemir" is the Arab term applied to any foreigner as distinct from
themselves. As at the inception of Islam the Persians were almost the
first foreign nation they met, the term has become used exclusively to
designate them.

in desert places, mountain passes and the like, so
many men must have been killed, and met their fate
heroically, the situation so to speak thrown away,
with no one there to see, record, to write about, as
if the poor, forlorn and wasted heroes were no more
worth a thought than the fat man of business who
snorts his life out on a feather-bed between a medicine
bottle and a mumbling priest. So the old Persian
left us to make his preparations for an early start
next day, hoping to reach a Saint's tomb of great
sanctity on the hill path which leads from Kintafi
to Tamasluocht, but is only to be passed on foot. He
said he was tired of this wild part of Africa, and would
make his way to Mogador, thence to Tangier, return
to Persia and push on to China, which he hoped to
visit ere he died. Considering that he had little
money, for I expect the twenty dollars of the Caid
were for the most part quite apocryphal, and that the
journey, made as he would make it, would probably
take years, he did not seem too excited, or as much
so, as a man who thinks his things have been put into
the wrong luggage van at Charing Cross.

People who write about the progress of the world,
the wealth of nations, of economic laws, and subjects
of that kind, requiring rather stronger imaginative
powers than reason, logic, or than common-sense,
are apt to take it as a well-established fact that before
railways were invented people, especially poor people,
travelled but little, and generally never moved far
from the places were they were born. This may have
been so in the last two hundred years, although I
doubt it, but certainly during the Middle Ages they
must have travelled much. Leaving the pilgrimages
out of account (and they, of course, brought every
European nation into contact), I take it that many

roved about, as they still do in Eastern lands. People, no doubt, had no facilities for travelling for mere amusement's sake; but if we read any old book of travels, how often does the writer meet a countryman, a student, minstrel, soldier, or wandering artisan in countries far away?

So, when the Persian went, we strolled out for a walk, followed the river for a mile or two, and found it full of fish; but the whole time we sojourned at Kintafi we saw no one fishing either with rod or net. The people whom we met were all well armed; and when they met us, kissed our clothes, taking us for Arabs of rank upon a visit to the Caid.

It always pleased me to see two Arabs or two Berbers meet, embrace each other, kiss each other's shoulder, ask respectively, How is your house? (Dar-de-alic), for to enquire after the health of even a brother's wife would be indecent; and then, the ceremony over, sit down to talk and strive with might and main to cheat each other, after the fashion in which Englishmen proceed in the same case.

Seated beneath a cliff, our feet just dangling in the stream to cool, smoking the vile Algerian tobacco, Lutaif began to tell me of his life in Syria, described his father's house, a great, gaunt place with a long chamber in the middle, given up to winding silk; spoke of the undying enmity between the Turk, the Druse, the Maronite, and the Old Catholics, of which sect he was a member; leaving on my mind the feeling that the Lebanon for a residence must be as undesirable as was Scotland in the old wicked days, when they burnt witches, and the narrow-minded clergy made the land a hell. One thing particularly struck me when he said, upon a walk, if we had been in Syria, dressed as we were in clothes which marked us for Mohammedans, and had we met four or five Christians, they would have either insulted or attacked us; and, of course, the same held good for Christians who on a walk met Turks. Remembering this happy state of things, and having from his youth looked upon every Mohammedan as a sworn enemy, when he first came to Morocco, knowing the people were fanatical Mohammedans, he passed his life in dread. Once in Tangier, not thinking what he did, or of the peril that he naturally incurred, he took a country walk. He started from the town dressed as a European, carrying a silver-headed stick, and several oranges in a brown paper bag to eat upon the way. After a mile or two, he took an orange out of his bag and, sitting down, was just about to eat when to his horror, on the sandy road, what did he see but five or six well-armed young men come, as he said, dancing like devils up the road and brandishing their knives. He called upon his God and closed his eyes, being quite sure that his last hour was come. Then to his great surprise the men stopped dancing, sheathed their knives, and after saluting him respectfully sat down, several yards away without a word. At last one asked him humbly for an orange, and Lutaif took the whole bag, and was about to entreat them to take all his oranges, his clothes, his money, everything, but to spare his life. To his amazement, the man took an orange from the bag, divided it into five portions, one of which he handed to each of the young men, and handed back the bag. The exiguous portions of the orange discussed, the spokesman asked him not to point the silver-headed stick their way, for it appeared they had got into their minds it was some kind of gun, which, if Lutaif discharged it, would destroy them all. He promised faithfully, and the wayfarers went upon

their way, leaving Lutaif as frightened as themselves. No doubt when first he saw them they were
exercising, skipping about like fawns, in the sheer
joy of life, but as they came upon him suddenly,
their sandalled feet making no noise upon the sandy
road, for a Syrian the vision must have been horrible
enough.

When he wrote home and told his friends what had
occurred to him, and how a Christian was regarded
(near Tangier) with respect and awe, the answer that
he got was curious. Of course they thought he was
telling lies, but his best friend admonished him it was
bad taste to jest about Mohammedans; for, though
no doubt they were bad neighbours, no one in Syria
could call them cowards. In fact, the friend appeared
to me to be like every Eastern Christian I have met,
quick to run down the Turks, to fight with them,
hating them bitterly at home; but yet if a stranger
slighted them abroad, quick to resent the slight, say
they were brave, and that they erred through wicked
councillors and not from lack of heart.

All the above he told me, and plenty more, with
the inimitable charm that Easterns have in story-
telling, compared to which even Guy de Maupassant,
Chaucer, Boccaccio, Balzac, or Fielding fall immeasur-
ably behind. The doubtful author of the " Celestina "*
and Cervantes, perhaps, come nearer; but then they,
being Spaniards, were more nearly in communion
with the East.

As we returned, tired and half hoping that there
might be news, we learned a " rekass " had just arrived

---

* Mr. Fitmaurice Kelly is confidant that Rojas threw off the Celestina
in a fortnight's holiday, but if so, I cannot help wondering why he threw
off no more, as writers, ancient or modern, seldom knew the force of
the American adage, "when you strike ile, stop boring."

bringing despatches from the Sultan to the Caid.
Though we knew well there had not been time for the
Caid to get an answer to the letter he had sent about
ourselves, yet outside news was valuable, and, in fact,
had I chanced to come upon a copy of the "Rock,"
I think I could have read it, advertisements and all.
In half an hour or so the "rekass" strolled past our
tent, and I invited him to come and have some tea.
Out of respect he sat outside the tent, saluted us, and
remained waiting to be interrogated: A tall, lean,
teak-complexioned man, in face resembling a Maori
god stuck up outside a Pah; vacant and glassy eyed
and at first sight a "Kieffi," that is a "kief" smoker,
thick lipped and with uncertain speech as if the
tongue was (like the tongues of Bourbons) too large
for his mouth, also a symptom of too much kief smoking; legs like a "bronco's" from the Bad Lands,
a mule's, or a "bagual's" from the stony deserts of
Patagonia; feet rather large, with the toes so flexible
that the whole member seemed to quiver as he walked.
For clothes, a single white garment like a night-shirt
(long freed from all the tyranny of soap), hanging
down almost to the ankles; girt round the waist with
a string of camel's hair; bare headed and a cord of
camel's hair bound round his temples, with a long
lock, at least eight inches long, hanging from the top
of his bare shaven head beside his ear. Though he
had walked incessantly for the last seven days, sleeping an hour or two with a piece of burning match tied
to his toe to wake him as it burned away, he strolled
about, or sitting drank his tea, taking a cup now and
again, which Ali or Swani passed to him out of the
tent. He said as long as he had "kief" he never
wanted food, but munched a bit of bread occasionally,
drank at every stream, and trotted on day after day,

just like a camel, for, as he told us, he was born to run.
Withal no fool, and pious, praying now and then
whenever he passed a Saint's tomb and felt wearied
with the way. Just such a man as you may see
amongst the " cholos " of the sierras of Peru, with the
difference that the " cholo " takes coca instead of
kief, and is in general a short, squat, ugly fellow,
whereas our " kieffi " stood over six feet high, straight
as a pikestaff, and was intelligent after his fashion,
could read and write, and no doubt knew as much
theology as was required from a right-thinking man.

For impedimenta he had a little bag in which he
kept his kief, his matches, pipe, and the small store
of money which it was possible he had, and in one
hand he carried a stout quarter-staff full five feet long,
which all " rekasses " use to walk with, try the depth
of water in crossing streams, defend themselves, and
ease their backs by passing it behind them through
their two arms, and resting on it as they trot along.

His news was brief but bloody. " Our Lord the
Sultan is camped in Tedla.* He is indeed a king,
fifty-one heads cut off, two tribes quite eaten up, three
hundred of the " Kaffirs " wounded ! O what a joy it
was to see the " maquina," the Christian devil gun,
which fires all day, play on the enemies of our Lord
the king. Praise be to Allah who alone giveth
victory." Which being interpreted meant that the
Sultan had gone under pretence of peace to Tedla ;
had by the advice of the grand vizier Ab' Ahmed
attacked them ; butchered as many as he could, and
probably sent a few hundred to die in gaol. The
self same fate overtook the Rahamna tribe close to
Morocco City. They fought a year with varying

* A district a little north-east of Morocco city in which the tribes are in
constant rebellion.

success, but at the last were decimated, butchered in hundreds, and their power destroyed.

The Grand Vizier Ab'Ahmed, if all reports be true, is a bad councillor for the young Sultan, Mulai Abdul Assiz. But be this as it may—for some who know the country say that the Grand Vizier, being a Moor, knows how to rule his countryman—Sidi Ahmed ben Musa, usually called Ab'Ahmed (Father Ahmed), is an ambitious and most powerful man, holding the Sultan in a sort of tutelage, and piling up a fortune by his exactions, which report says he has invested in safe securities abroad.

The father of the Sultan, Mulai el Hassan, who died or was poisoned some four years ago, was a remarkable personality, and perhaps one of the last Oriental potentates of the old school. Standing about six feet three inches in his slippers, he was dark in face, having through a descendant of Mohammed some negro blood: a perfect horseman, shot, and skilled in swordsmanship; though educated in all the learning of the Moors, he yet was tolerant of Christians, kind to Jews, and much more liberal in regard to new ideas than is his son, that is to say, if it is not Ab' Ahmed who directs his policy. Mulai el Hassan was what is called a "riding Sultan," that is a warrior, always on horseback, and passing all his life either in journeys between his various capitals, or on long expeditions to reduce refractory tribes. His fine white horse has been described by almost every embassy for the past ten years that went to Fez, for from his back the Sultan used to receive ambassadors, who bound in their hats, hosen, coats, swords, tight boots, and dignity, and forced to stand in a hot sun, on foot, must have presented a very lamentable sight.

On the white horse's back the Sultan almost died,

for one who saw him shortly before his death was standing in a street in the outskirts of Marakesh when the Sultan passed, having been sixteen hours on horseback in the rain, and looking like a corpse. Next day he died so suddenly that some thought he had been poisoned, but others think worn out with care and trouble, long journeys, and all the burden of a ruler's life. All those who knew him say that his manners were most courteous, kind, and dignified, and that through all his life none of his servants ever heard him raise his voice, even in battle or when he ordered some unlucky man to death, above its ordinary pitch.

His clothes were spotless white, but made in the fashion of those worn by an ordinary tribesman, only of finer stuff. Colours he never wore, or jewellery, except a silver ring with a large diamond, and which when once an individual, whose name I forbear to mention, asked him for it for a keepsake, he half drew off (for usually he gave all he was asked for), but replaced and said with a quiet smile, " No, I will keep it, but you can have its value in money if you choose." His clothes he never wore more than a day, and then his servants claimed them as perquisites ; so that his wardrobe must have been pretty extensive even for a king. Upon a journey he carried almost all he had, packed upon camels, and, being troubled with insomnia at times, would say, " Bring me the telescope the Belgian Minister gave me ten years ago," or " the watch the Queen of England sent me," and the unlucky man to whom he spoke had to produce the thing, if he unpacked a hundred camels in the search.

The taxes he used to collect in person with an army, so that his camp was like a town of canvas, and yet the order of his own tents so great and his men so skilled in pitching them, that at a halt they used to rise like magic from the ground.

Wives, and that sort of thing, he had about three hundred, and was much addicted to their company, and some of them accompanied him on all the journeys which he made. His son, the present Sultan, was born of a Circassian, white, and report said beautiful and educated; but she transmitted little beauty and less education to her son, who is a rather heavy youth of about twenty, not well instructed, and completely in the hands of his Vizier, Ab' Ahmed, who, by exactions, cruelties, and bloodshed, has made his master's name detested all through the land. Still a strong man, and no doubt in such countries as Morocco, when a Sultan dies a strong man is required, for the tribes usually rise in rebellion, kill their Caids, burn down their castles, and a recognised period of anarchy takes place, known as "El Siba" by the natives, and of which they all take full advantage.

That the Vizier was a man of readiness and resource is shown by the way he foiled the expedition of the yacht *Tourmaline*,* by means of which a Syndicate in London endeavoured to procure a footing in the Sus. Thinking the "kieffi" would be an excellent man to take our letters, we sounded him, but in a moment he became mysterious, said he must sleep, would think about it, and though we often saw him subsequently strolling about, he never visited our tent again.

After the "kieffi" went, the Persian came to say good-bye, and sat long talking about Montenegro, where the people are all brave, and to his astonishment, for they are Franks, the women virtuous. He tells us that their enmity with the Arnauts is constant, and this he illustrated by linking his two fore-

* For the yacht *Tourmaline* see Appendix.

fingers to indicate a fight. "Brave men," he said,
"who, when they draw the sword, never go back, and
a fine country, but lacking the true faith." Then
came the leave-taking, and I presented him with a
dollar, which he has magnified in talking of it to at
least twenty, and he, after a few well-chosen, dignified
sentences of thanks, pressed his open palm against
my hand, and then pressed it upon his heart, saying
again, "Mesquin, may you have patience, and may
Allah not open to you the Sultan's gate!" And so
he took the road, shouldering his sack of "possibles,"
and in his hand a staff, and carrying, God knows
why, a wooden board, and in a little faded away on
the hill track, out of my sight and life. Vaya con
Dios, I never knew his name, for he was not a man
given to descending to particulars of such a kind, and
it is rank ill manners to ask an Oriental what his
name is, the fiction being that he is so well known,
to ask would be impertinent. It may be that he may
cast up some day across my path, for he is always on
the march, but if he does not, in many an Eastern
khan and fondak men will know of me, not by my name,
for that he never knew, but as the Frankish stranger
whom he met a prisoner in the Atlas, and who gave
him gold and more gold, so that he had to buy a sack
to carry it away. And at the Saints' tombs, and in
mosques, there he will pray for me (at least he said
so), and I shall know that what he says will not be
said in vain, for has not Sidna Mohammed himself
averred that "the prayers of a stranger are always
heard by God." *

---

* Swani, so that the *odium theologium* might not be wanting, hoped
that the Persian would be killed on the road, for, said he, these Persian
heretics are worse than Christians. The Persians are, as is well known,
unorthodox, and who does not prefer an infidel to an unorthodox believer?

So, sadly, as if we had lost one we had known from youth, Lutaif and I wandered along the river; and by a stony beach, under some oleander bushes, came on a little tea-party, all seated on the ground. A little pleases Arabs, who in a measure are like children, easily pleased, and passing easily from good temper into rage, and nothing gives them greater satisfaction than when a stranger comes and joins their pleasure or their meals. So we advanced, and found they were three Sherifs from Taseroault : Sherifs, but practically beggars, though white men of pure Arab blood and race. One was a little thin and wizened man, with hardly any beard, his clothes quite clean, but washed into holes by frequent soaping and thumping against the stones of streams. Quick, taciturn, and most intelligent, a hunter and, I think, an acrobat, and wearing round his head a yellow cloth gun-case twisted like a turban, which, with his meagre features and pale face, gave him an air as of a dwarf ghost or spectre, as he sat smoking "kief." The other two were fine young men, but poorly dressed, and perhaps got their living by praying, or by writing charms, for all could read and write, and neither of the three seemed ever to have done any of that same honest toil which so much ennobles man. Placed on the sand before them stood a small brass tray, and on it three small glass tumblers and a tin teapot of the conical pattern which Germany supplies. Dried figs and walnuts were on another tray, and all were smoking "kief." Close to them, on a little patch of grass, fed a black curly lamb, which I supposed they had reared and brought with them from Taseroault, but they assured me it was given to them only two days ago, and now followed them like a dog. I asked if they intended to dispose of it, and they said no, they

would teach it to do tricks, and gain much money by
its antics, and as we spoke it walked up to the tray,
took up a fig, smelt at it, but thought it unfit to eat,
and then, after skipping about a bit, came back and
went to sleep with its head resting upon its special
owner's feet.

We squatted down beside the three Sherifs and
became friends at once, drank endless cups of tea as
sweet as syrup, ate figs and walnuts, talked of Europe
and of Taseroault, and, I think, never in my life did
I enjoy an afternoon so thoroughly. They asked no
questions, thinking it apparently not strange we
should be there dressed as Mohammedans, and I
almost unable to speak Arabic, as if, for example, a
Chinese dressed as an English country gentleman
should stumble in upon a gang of haymakers in Rut·
landshire, and sit down and drink beer. Much did
they tell of the Wad Nun, and of the desert horses,
known as "wind drinkers," on which men hunt the
ostrich, feeding them well on dates and camel's milk,
and flying through the sands after the ostriches in the
same manner that the Pehuelches hunt their ostriches
in Patagonia, save that the Arabs throw a club instead
of the ostrich "bolas" which the Pehuelches use. But
in both countries the tactics are the same, the hunts-
men spreading out like a fan, striving to join their
ranks and get the birds into a circle, or to drive them
into a marsh, edge of a stream, or some place out of
which they cannot run.

The little dwarf Sherif got up and showed me how
an ostrich ran, waving his arms and craning out his
neck in a way which would have made his fortune on
the stage. It then appeared he had been a "moufflon" hunter, and he told how they can jump down
precipices alighting on their horns, how shy they are

and here he worked his nose about to show the way they snuffed the wind when danger was about, so that he looked more like a " moufflon " than the very beast itself. His friends smiled gravely, and said Allah had given their comrade excellent gifts, and one was to be able to imitate all beasts, and another was to run all day and never feel fatigue.

On hearing this I mentally resolved he should run to Morocco City with our letters, starting that very night, but mentioned nothing of my purpose, intending to leave Swani to arrange it by himself. We thanked our entertainers, gave them some of our Algerian tobacco, which they prized highly, and the deputation then withdrew. As I looked back they had not moved, but the black curly lamb had gone back to the grass, and they, beneath the oleanders, seated on the stones, still sitting happily, smoking before their little tray, as if the world belonged to them, as after all it did.

Just before nightfall Swani brought the small Sherif ostensibly for medicine to our tent. When asked to carry letters he said yes, that he was poor and wanted to buy clothes for winter, and would go at once, and his companions and the lamb could meet him somewhere near the coast. I asked if he could run, and he replied " like an Oudad,"* and by that name we knew him ever since. Five dollars was our bargain, two in the hand and three upon arriving at the missionary's house. He asked no questions save the position of the missionary's house, took the two dollars and the packet and a note asking the missionary to pay him three dollars when the letters came to hand, thanked us, and said " Your letters shall arrive," walked quickly off, and disappeared into the night.

* " Oudad," the Moufflon.

But on the evening of the third day from that on which he went, a dusty little man knocked at the missionary's door more than a hundred miles away, handed a packet in, and waited whilst the note he brought was read, got his three dollars and an extra one for speed, and when the missionary, who went for a moment into his house to read the letters returned to question him, he was already gone. So the "Oudad," after the "Persian" flashed across my path, or I intruded upon theirs, we talked, made friends, and separated, and shall never meet, but the impression that they made was much more vivid than that caused by worthy friends whom one meets every day and differentiates but by the checks upon their shooting jackets.

Determining to leave no stone untried, Lutaif, who fancied himself on his epistolary style, said he would write a letter to the Caid to ask for an interview About an hour he spent upon the task, lying upon his stomach in the tent, and writing on a large flimsy sheet of Spanish note paper with a small pencil end ; but after so much trouble he produced a gem, crammed full of compliments, in such high Arabic that he thought none but the "taleb" would decipher it, and uritten as beautifully clear as Arab copper-plate.

"To the most happy and exemplary, the most fortunate and honourable, the Caid Si Taieb Mchammed el Kintafi.

"May God's peace and blessing be upon you whilst day lasts and time endures. Oh, Caid, thou art the wielder of the sword and pen. Fate and a love of travel have led us to your happy and well-governed land, and you have generously received and entertained us, extending to us all the hospitality of your thrice blessed house. May God establish it for ever, and may the hand of no man be ever higher than your hand. But, mighty prince, we fear to trespass too long upon your kindness, though we know your hand is never tired of shedding blessings upon all. Therefore, we wish to see your face and thank you for your hospitality, so that on our return on talking of you we can say this was a man. May Allah bless and keep you, and at the last may Sidna Mohammed welcome you upon your entrance into Paradise. Deign, therefore, to accord an hour to-morrow on which to speak with you."

This missive read aloud, evoked great admiration both from Swani and Mohammed el Hosein, and they declared it certainly would have a good effect. So Swani, dressed in a clean white burnous, which Lutaif had with him in his saddle bags, and with a pair of my new yellow slippers, went off, and with much ceremony handed the letter to the keeper of the gate. Knowing the respect the Moors attach to letters, and the astonishment they show if any Christian can write their characters, I thought perhaps the letter might bring an interview; but thinking of the happy afternoon I had spent with the simple fakirs upon the stony beach did not care much, knowing the happy hours that a man passes in his life are few, and of more value than much gold or all the jewels of the Apocalypse.

CHAPTER IX.

THOUGH not so sanguine as Lutaif, as to the emollient powers of his epistle, I was pleased to find that for the first time, next morning, we received ample supplies of food, baskets of grapes and oranges, and for the first time people spoke to us without an air of breaking some command.

During the morning a miserable bundle of rags arrived and stood before our tent, asking in broken Arabic if we were the Christians, and on being answered in the affirmative broke out into French. It appeared he was a French deserter from Algeria, having deserted in Ain Sefra,* walked to Figig, and pretended to turn Mohammedan, he came by Tafilet, and was about to make his way down to the coast. This, as he said, was his itinerary, but why he should have come round by Tafilet, he did not explain. He certainly was not a personable man ; a weasel-faced, pale, and fair-haired Parisian " voyou," thin, active, and half-starved, foot-sore and weary, dressed in rags, and speaking a jargon of bad Arabic, compared to which that spoken by the Persian and myself became as the language of the " Khoreish " ; or the best

---

* Ain Sefra is, or was a few months ago, the terminus of the French Railway system in the Western Sahara. I should not be surprised that it was pushed on close to Figig by now, for the French in matters of this kind are not hampered with conscience, nonconformist or otherwise.

literal Arabic which Cairo boasts. He told us that he slept in the mosques, making the profession of his faith if there was any doubt about him before going in, this with a wink, and " Sont-ils bêtes, ces Arabes, à la fin ! " After he had eaten and smoked, he said that it was common in Algeria for soldiers to desert, adopt the Arab dress, and make their way into Morocco; some reached the coast, but many disappeared, murdered by the tribesmen or the villagers upon the way. Withal a merry knave, relating how he had served in a Spabi regiment during the war in Madagascar, and that the Arab troopers, when the war broke out, talked of the war with " Madame Casba,"* and thought she was Sultana of some island, who was fighting with the French. Although he had no arms or money, he did not seem afraid, but trusted to arrive in Mogador or Saffi in a few weeks' time. We went to bathe and left him smoking under a tree with Swani, talking a mixture of Arabic and French: on our return in half-an-hour, thinking to see him still before the tent, and make him tell us what he had seen in his long tramp, we found, without a word to anyone, that he had slunk mysteriously away.

Once in Morocco city I met three Englishmen dressed in the red baize rags which form the uniform of the Sherifian troops. Where they came from they did not say, but wanted money to buy " magia "† and tobacco; I gave them something, and on receiving it with not too laboured thanks, they too mixed with the crowd in one of the bazaars and disappeared.

* " Uaheda Sultana Madam Casba."

† Magia is a spirit made by the Jews in Morocco; it is sometimes made of grapes, sometimes of figs, and again of dates. The magia made of dates is less lethal, than that from figs or grapes. It is of a milky colour and very strong.

In the crowded " Kaisariehs " of the towns, and in the endless processions of noiseless-footed people on the roads, nothing is more surprising than the way in which odd characters come to the surface for a moment (like a fish rising), and then sink back again into the depths from which they rose.

On mules and donkeys, on horseback and on foot, beggars, or travelling well attended, Berbers and Arabs, Jews, Negroes, Haratin, men from the Sahara, and from the mountains of the Riff, Syrians, and Levantines, outcast Europeans, and an occasional Hindu, with Turks and Greeks, and people from the utmost regions of the Oriental world, they all are there, and always on the move, travelling about as if some not too swiftly circulating quicksilver ran in their veins; whither they go or why, whence come from, and what urges them to wander up and down, is to me inexplicable, and forms one of the many of the unfathomed and unfathomable problems of the East. Not that I mean the various passengers whom I have named bulk largely in the population of Morocco, but they are there, and every now and then one feels how all the Oriental world is linked together by nomadic habits, from Bagdad to Wad Nun, and from Shiraz to the oases of the Sahara.

In Morocco the prevailing tone is greyish white, men's clothes, and houses, towns, bushes, tall umbelliferæ, nodding like ghosts in autumn, all are white; white sands upon the shore, and in the Sahara, and over all a white and saddening light, as if the sun was tired with shining down for ever on the unchanging life. In no part of Morocco I have visited does the phrase " gorgeous east " have the least meaning, and this is always noted by the wandering easterns, who find the country dull and lacking colour compared to Asia, or as the Arabs call it, "Blad Es Schark."*

Almost all day on the Maidan behind our tent football went on (called in Arabic "El Cora"), and every one joined in, middle-aged men, slaves, and the various hangers-on about the place, the Caid's sons playing furiously, and whilst the game went on they were not more respected, and received as full a share of kicks, shoves, trips, and pushes, as did all the rest. The ball they used was little larger than a pomegranate, no rules seemed to be observed, for everybody pushed, shoved, bit, scratched, and kicked as it seemed best to him, and as they had no goals, but played simply to drive the other players back, the play was wild, and now and then extremely savage, and I saw a man get his shoulder dislocated after a violent fall. Still I sat watching it with great delight, sometimes for hours, as certainly they played it with their whole souls, shouting and yelling, leaping like roe, and everybody playing "off side" when it seemed good to him, and glorying in his crime.

Towards midday came the Chamberlain bringing back our guns with many thanks and offers of purchase, which we had to decline, as neither of the guns belonged to us. With him he brought a double-barrelled hammerless gun in good condition, and with the maker's name (Green, Haymarket, London,) engraved upon it. He said it was the Caid's, who set great store by it, having received it as a present from a merchant on the coast, and specially he wished to know if the gun was what would be called of first-

---

* Es Schark, the East. It is possible that the word Asia was derived from it when it is remembered that the Greeks and Romans must have had great difficulty in pronouncing both the Arabic gutturals, and semi-gutturals.

rate workmanship in England. I told him that it was and probably cost about twenty pounds, and that the son of our Sultana could buy no better or more expensive weapon, unless, which I said did not seem probable to me, he had his guns adorned with gold or precious stones.

But better than the guns, or talk of guns, was the invitation which he brought from the Caid, saying he would like to see us in the afternoon. As such an invitation was, in our position, really a command, I hesitated some time before accepting it. The Chamberlain saw what was passing in my mind, and to gild the pill, remarked that had the Governor not been suffering from his wound, he would have got upon his horse and ridden to our tent. Though I felt sure that what he said was quite untrue, still mankind is so constituted that humbug flatters us, even although we think we see through it. So I accepted, and Si Mohammed departed after many compliments and with a promise to come and fetch us, and usher us into the Presence, in the afternoon. Lutaif lamented bitterly that we had no European clothes with which to endue ourselves, and properly impress the Caid.

It must not be forgotten that in the East (and Mogreb-el-Acksa, though it means Far West, is perhaps as eastern as any country in the world) European clothes, hard hats, elastic-sided boots, grey flannel shirts, with braces, mother-of-pearl studs, two-carat watch-chains, and all the beauty of our meanly contrived apparel, are to Mohammedans the outward visible sign of the inward spiritual Maxim gun, torpedo boat, and arms of precision, on which our civilisation, power, might, dominion, and morality really repose. A shoddy-clad and cheating European pedlar, in his national dress, always suggests to Easterns the might of England somewhere in the offing, and though they laugh at the wearer of the grey shoddy rags behind his back, they yet respect him more than if he were attired in the most beautiful of their own time-hallowed garments, which they know no European puts on but for some purpose of his own. But if a European loses respect in wearing Moorish clothes, he gains in another way, for the Moors are constituted like other men, and, seeing a man dressed in the clothes they wear themselves, converse with him more freely, even if, as was my case, his knowledge of the language is so slight as to make conversation through an interpreter a necessity.

So we put on the best we had all cleanly washed, and Lutaif arrayed himself in a brand new white "Selham" (burnouse), and looked more Biblical than ever as he stood forth to be my Aaron, I having resolved, in order not to make myself ridiculous, to refrain from saying anything in Arabic, unless I saw a chance to get some phrase in pertinently, and with effect.

Punctually at half-past two the Chamberlain, accompanied by a single follower, came for us, and we —that is, Lutaif, myself, Mohammed-el-Hosein, and Swani—walked as majestically as we could across the deserted Maidan, baking in the sun. We passed through several courts in which our friends the horses and the mules were tied, and I observed the wounded cream-coloured stallion of the Caid tethered alone and guarded by a little boy who flapped the flies away with a green bough. Then past the door of the Mosque, where a (no doubt painful) preacher was holding forth to a congregation all dressed in white and seated on the ground. No coughing drowned his saw, no shuffling of chairs disturbed his eloquence,

the listeners sat as solid as limpets on a rock, as his
voice rose and fell in measured cadences, reminding
one of the long rollers in a calm, just off the line.
The door of the mosque was a poor specimen of the
bronze-plated work adorned with pious sentences,
which can be seen to such perfection in the mosque
at Cordoba; the knocker of the familiar round Arab
pattern, which the Moors have left in half the houses
throughout Southern Spain. Next, through a narrow
passage, where a few Jews and tribesmen sat whilst
waiting for an audience, passing beneath a horse-
shoe arch, and up on a dark and almost perpendicular
staircase, we emerged into a lofty ante-room where
several men sat on the floor preparing saffron, which
covered half the room with a dense carpet of bright
purple blossom, whilst in a corner lay a clean white
sheepskin with a mass of orange saffron fibres all
gathered in a heap. At one end of the room a narrow
doorway, where two men with long guns in their
hands kept watch, and people going out and in continually, some emerging crestfallen, and others radiant, as in the times when kings, even in Europe, gave
personal audience, and their subjects spoke with them
face to face.

Here we waited almost half-an-hour, no doubt on
purpose to impress us with the amount of business
which the Caid had to transact. For myself, I was
not sorry, as I had full leisure to observe all that was
going on. Though all the people in the room and
the two guards must have known who we were, no
one showed curiosity, and one man talked to me, pretending to comprehend all that I said as if he wished
to put me at my ease. We slipped our shoes off at
an intimation from our guide and entered the
" Presence Chamber," a narrow room with an " arte-

sonado"* ceiling in the Hispano-Moorish style, but
vilely daubed in Rickett's blue and dingy red, and
with cheap common gilding making it look tawdry
and like the ceiling of an old-fashioned music-hall.

In a recess within the wall two boys were sitting
doing nothing in rather an aggressive way. To my
eye they looked rather androgynous, but not more so
than many young men one sees in Piccadilly on a
fine afternoon, and who would tolerate even a suspicion about the noble Shillah race! † The room was
carpeted with fine, almost white, matting, over which
here and there were thrown black and white rugs
from Sus, all worked in curious geometric patterns,
and woven from the softest of wool mingled with
goats' hair, and with long fringes at the edge.

Upon a dark red saddle-cloth ‡ and using an angle
of the wall to lean against, his wounded leg stretched
out before him on a sheepskin, and with cushions at
his back, his Excellency sat. Luckily Arab manners
(and in these matters Berbers follow the Arab lead)
prescribe no " Kiddush," or, most infallibly, situated

* Ceilings divided into an infinity of little squares, and with pendant
knobs here and there, and much inlaid work and gilding, are called
"artesonado" in Spain, and I know no word in English by which to
render it.

† "Shillah race," see books on Morocco, written sometimes by those
whom Disraeli described as "flat-nosed Franks," and who, no doubt
humiliated by having met in the Arabs a finer type than their own, turned
to the Berbers with the relief that the earthen tea-pot must find when
taken away from the drawing-room companionship of "powder blue"
china, and put back again on the kitchen dresser.

‡ These saddle-cloths, called in Morocco "libdah," are carried by
respectable Moors when going to the Mosques to pray; Talebs and men
of letters (who ride mules) generally have one loose upon their saddles, to
sit upon when they dismount. Men of the sword disdain them and use
them only underneath their saddles, where they place seven of them, of
several colours, blue, red, and yellow, and add an eighth, when on a journey,
of white wool and separate from the others (which are all sewed together),
so that it may be removed and washed.

as we were, we should have been obliged to make
it, with what grace we could. So we advanced,
were formally presented by the Chamberlain,
shook hands, and after being greeted quietly but
courteously, and after Lutaif had answered quite
in the style of Faredi, sat down upon a rug and
leaned against the wall, tucking our feet well underneath our clothes to show our breeding, and remained
silently waiting to hear what the Caid had to say.

Mohammed-el-Hosein and Swani advanced, lifted
the Caid's "selham," kissed it, and then retreating
sat down, so to speak, below the salt, whilst in the
doorway the two sentinels stood as unmoved as if
they saw a Christian every day. Two or three elders
sat round the room as solid as "josses" in a temple,
two "talebs," besides our friend the "Taleb of the
Atlas," were writing letters, and the Chamberlain
stood at attention till the Caid waved him to take a
seat.

No doubt his Excellency took mental notes of us,
and certainly I looked him over carefully, thinking
that in a personal discussion upon horseback, out on
the Maidan, he would prove a very awkward foe.

Just about forty years of age, thick-set, and dark
complexioned, close black beard trimmed to a double
point, rather small eyes, like those of all his race, he
gave no indication of the cruelty for which he was
renowned; not noble in appearance as are many of
the Sheikhs of Arab blood, but still looking as one
accustomed to command; hands strong and muscular,
voice rather harsh but low, and trained in the best
school of Arab manners, so as to be hardly audible.
Just for a moment, and no more, I got a glimpse of the
inside man as I caught his eye fixed on me, savage yet
fish-like, but in an instant a sort of film seemed to pass

over it, not that he dropped his gaze, but seemed deliberately to veil it, as if he had reserved it for a more fitting opportunity. By race and language he was a Berber, but speaking Arabic tolerably fluently, and adapting all his habits and dress to those in fashion amongst Arab Sheikhs. His clothes white and of the finest wool, and clean as is a sheet of paper before a writer marks it black with lies. The "talebs" never stopped opening and writing letters, now and then handing one to the Caid who glanced it over and said " Guaha " (good), and gave it back to have the seal affixed with one of the three large silver seals which stood upon a little table about six inches high. The sealing-wax was European, and kept in a box of common cardboard, which had been mended in several places with little silver bands to keep the sides together, as we should mend a lacquered box from Persia or Japan. Behind the Caid, to mark his seat, upon the wall were painted three " ajimeces,"* roughly designed in blue and red and green in the worst taste. For furniture, in addition to the matting and the rugs and leather-covered cushions, the cover cut into intricate geometric patterns, the room contained a small trunk-shaped box (perhaps entirely stuffed with gold, Allah hu-alem), a Belgian single-barrelled nickel-plated breech-loading gun hung on a nail, and the before-named double-barrelled English gun (from the Haymarket of the mysterious Londres or Windres, in the isle of Mists), and a large pair of double field glasses; some bags of hide, two porous water bottles, a bundle of reed pens, and two or three pieces of bread, the staff of life, which fills so large a place in Moorish

---

* An " Ajimez " is one of the little long-shaped horse-shoe windows, so frequently seen in Moorish buildings; often in the sides of towers, as in those of the Giralda at Seville.

thoughts and life, and which an Arab of the old school breaks, but never touches with a knife. Two negro boys with dirty handkerchiefs, and boughs of walnut, stood on the right and left-hand of the Caid, and flapped away the flies.

Oh, what a falling off from, when, in Medina el Azahra, the great palace outside Cordoba, the Greek ambassador beheld the Caliph's court, the wonders of the great gold basin filled with a sea of quicksilver, and the slave boys, beautiful as angels, who fanned their lord with jewelled fans made of the feathers of the wondrous bird from Hind, which on its spread-out tail carries a hundred eyes. But in Kintafi, even the Caid himself held in his hand a branch torn from a bush, and flapped occasionally with his own august hand, when the myriads of flies became impertinent.

People were going in and out perpetually, like bees into a hive, or politicians pretending they have important business in the House of Commons. ˙Some brought petitions, others begged for mules, horses, a gun, or anything which came into their minds, and generally the Caid gave something, for Moors all pique themselves upon their generosity.

But besides suppliants, Jews and various artificers were hanging about the ante-room. A silversmith advanced¦ to show a half-completed silver-sheathed and hafted dagger, engraved with pious sentences, as "God is our sufficiency and our best bulwark here on earth," and running in and out between the texts a pattern of a rope with one of the strands left out, which pattern also ran round the cornice of the room we sat in, and round the door, as it runs round the doors in the Alhambra and the Alcazar, and in thousands of houses built by the Moors, and standing still, in Spain. The dagger and the sheath were handed to

me for my inspection, and on my saying that they
were beautifulty worked, the Caid said keep them, but
I declined, not having anything of equal value to give
in return, and being almost certain if I sent a present
from Mogador, that it would never reach its owner's
hands. So we gravely put the dagger backwards and
forwards with many courteous waves, "It is yours,
take it I pray, although unworthy your acceptance";
and I "The dagger is in worthy hands, let it remain
with one who had the good taste to order such fine
work, and has the hands to use the weapon when
there is need." A pretty little comedy, my share of
which I conducted through Lutaif, not wishing to
fall into barbarities of speech and make myself
ridiculous before so many well-spoken men.

Slave boys, in clothes perhaps worth eighteen pence,
served coffee, rather an unusual thing in visiting a
Moor, for all drink tea. The tray was copper, beautifully chased, and adorned with sentences from the
Koran, the service varied, and consisting of a common
wine glass, one champagne glass of the old-fashioned
narrow pattern, three cheap French cups, and a most
beautifully engraved old Spanish glass goblet out of
which his Excellency drank. The coffee-pot looked
like a piece of "Empire," the coffee most excellent,
and brought most probably by some pilgrim from
Arabia, and used only on great occasions such as the
present was.

The talk ran chiefly upon our journey, why had we
come, why dressed like Moors, where were we going,
and why we had no letter from the Sultan; and, above
all, why had we not called at his house in passing as was
usual for all Moors (of our assumed condition) to do
when on the road? I answered that we were going to
Tarudant, that we were dressed as Moors because the

people were not accustomed to see Christians, and might have insulted us ; and that we did not call upon him knowing he had so many visitors, and not wishing to intrude.   As to a Sultan's letter, that was unnecessary, for I knew well if I had one he would find some good reason to stop us, under the pretext that the roads we should encounter would be unsafe.   Moreover, that I had travelled much in Morocco, and did not like to have a Sultan's letter, for if I had one, no one would let me pay for food, and that I could not bear to be a burden on the poor tribesmen amongst whom I passed.

My object in visiting Tarudant seemed to him incomprehensible, as it was merely curiosity, and for a moment it crossed my mind, shall I make up some reason, such as a vow to make a pilgrimage, a wish to see if there were mines in the vicinity, or something which should seem sufficient in his eyes ?   But in a minute was glad I had not done so, for he asked, did I know the English adventurers who, a few months ago, had tried to land upon the coast of Sus.   As at that time I did not, I answered that they were personally unknown to me, but that I totally disapproved what they had done, especially because our Government had warned no British subject to try to come to terms with the Sus chiefs, and that the Sultan had expressed a wish that nothing of that nature should be done.   I added that personally I reverenced all governments, especially my own, having been once a member of the great council of our Empire, which, I took care to state, with all the patriotism I could command, was, on "reliable" authority, said to be the largest and finest in the world.   He answered "Guaha, that is so.   Allah himself appointed governments, placed the sword of justice in their hands, and

it was for them to say what should be done and see
their wishes were respected." To this I gave assent,
and he inquired was I still of the council, and, when
I answered no, asked if I had quarrelled with the
Viziers, or done anything unpleasing to them, or was
I only tired of public life. Finding our parliamentary
system too intricate to explain, I said I was tired of
the cares of state, and he replied, " Yes, they are
heavy, and I myself have never wished to go to
Court." As I knew well if he ever ventured there
his life was not worth a rotten egg, I applauded
his resolve, spoke of the pleasures of a country life,
and, as all hitherto had passed through the good
offices of Lutaif, thought that my chance had come,
and mustering up my Arabic told him he should
be content with what God gave him, for as he was, he
was a Sultan in himself. He smiled, whether at the
compliment or my bad Arabic, I do not know, and
beckoned to Mohammed-el-Hosein to come and speak
with him.

Mohammed-el-Hosein advanced, kissed his " Selham," and in an instant became a gentleman and
conversed on equal terms. What they conversed
about I do not know, as all their talk passed in the
noble Shillah tongue, but I conclude the Caid was
satisfied with what Mohammed said, for, signing to
the slave who poured the coffee out (a knave who had
a heavy silver earring in his ear, from which depended a cross-shaped ornament with Solomon's Seal
engraved upon it) he told him to give Mohammed
coffee; he did so, in a white egg-cup, which, as it
stood behind the coffee-pot, I had not previously
observed. " Do you in Europe travel about all
through the different countries without letters from
your Queen ? " " No," I rejoined, " we take a letter

signed by our Grand Vizier, and show it, if asked for, at the frontiers of the various States." "Of course you have one?" he immediately replied. I answered "Yes;" and just remembered I had left it behind me in the hotel in Mogador, but luckily he did not ask to see it, or I should have had to show him a letter which I had with a large seal upon it, which probably would have answered just as well.

I pressed him to allow us to go into Tarudant, but he became mysterious, said the roads were bad, the people dangerous, and that to save our lives he had acted in the way that he had done.

Nothing so disagreeable as to have your life saved in your own despite. Fancy the feelings of a would-be suicide when some intruding fellow, like a great Newfoundland dog, jumps in and pulls him out, and then on landing asks him for his thanks!

After the coffee, talk ran a good deal upon various things, polygamy and monogamy, always an interesting subject to all Orientals, who, being primitive in tastes and habits, set much account on primary passions (or affections) and think more of such matters than we do, talking quite openly and without periphrasis on things we do, but never talk about, or if we do, lower our breath in talking. Strange and incomprehensible to a logician, that a man should say, I am hungry, thirsty, tired, and think there is something wrong, indelicate, or indifferent, in mentioning the kindred passions, presumably implanted in his body by the same All-wise Creator who endowed him with the capacity to feel thirst, hunger, or fatigue. The Caid was of opinion that polygamy was natural to mankind, and asked me if the English did not really think so in their hearts. It is most difficult, without having been duly elected, to speak for a whole nation, so I replied that many acted as if they thought polygamy was right, but that I ventured to opine that "advanced thinkers" in general inclined to polyandry, and that seemed to be the opinion which, in the future, would prevail. This he thought clearly wrong, but I explained that "advanced thinkers" were inclined to hold that women could do no wrong, and that all infamy of every nature had its root in man.

The prisoners in the Riff* next were enlarged upon, and the Caid asked if they had been released, and what I thought about the whole affair. Thinking the opportunity favourable to air my Arabic again, I said laboriously that I had heard there were some prisoners in the Riff, and added that there were prisoners also in the Atlas, but no doubt the Sultan would soon order their release

His Excellency's wounded leg was, on the whole, the subject which gave most scope fc~ talk. Neither his Arabic nor mine was fluent enough to explain, or understand quite fully, what had taken place. More coffee having been ordered, the Chamberlain entered into an explanation which Lutaif explained when I (as happened now and then) became bewildered in the current of his speech. About two months ago the unlawfully begotten people in the Sus, egged on by certain British traders,† had rebelled against their

---

* At that time, October, 1897, several Spanish, Greek, and Italian sailors were detained by the Riff Tribes, having been captured when their vessels were becalmed near the shores of that province. European diplomacy having, as usual, failed, a Jew from Tangier with the aid of the French Consul in Tangier arranged for their liberation, and they arrived in Tangier on the same day that I arrived from the Atlas. The populace, chiefly Spaniards from Malaga, who had " had trouble" (knife thrusts given and received), welcomed us with acclamation, that is, they stared at us and shouted.

† The Globe Venture Syndicate, I imagine.

Lord. The chief offenders were sons of Jews (Oulad
el Jahud), who had withdrawn themselves into a fortified position three or four days' journey from Thelata-
el-Jacoub. The Caid was ordered to co-operate with
the troops in Sus and bring the rebels back to allegiance, or destroy them all. Most probably the Caid
had no objectien to an expedition out of his territory,
though in point of fact his own allegiance to the
Sultan did not much trouble him. However, mounted
on the white horse, which I saw wounded and drinking
in the river, and leading on his men, the Caid had
advanced against the revolted tribesmen, who were
strongly posted amongst rocks protected with an out-
work of " Zaribas "* made of prickly bushes, from
behind which they fired upon the Caid's forces who
had no shelter, and soon suffered heavy loss. The
saddles emptying on every side, the Caid was left
almost alone with about twenty men, amongst whom
was I who speak (the Chamberlain remarked in passing,
but without any self-consciousness), his horse received
a bullet in the chest, another in the head, but still the
Caid advanced, keeping his horse's head as much as
possible between him and the fire. At last another
bullet struck the horse close to the nose, and he
wheeling, the Caid received a bullet in the left leg and
fell! "Then," said the Chamberlain, "I rode close
up to him, and the bullets tore up the grass on every
side, when our men rallying brought us off, I and four
others carrying the Caid under a heavy fire, and the
white wounded horse walking beside us, till we reached
our camp."

During the tale the Caid sat imperturbable as a
"joss" cut out of soapstone, but punctuating all his
henchmen said with an occasional "Guaha," or

* Corrals, or enclosures.

some pious ejaculation fit for a man of quality to use.

In the camp they placed the wounded Caid upon a mule, and fighting for the first two days almost incessantly, upon the evening of the sixth day they brought him home, two slaves having supported him on either side stretched on the mule, too weak to sit upright, and with four more helping the wounded horse, which the Caid on no account would leave to be the prize of Kaffirs such as those who dwelt in Sus.

My opinion of all concerned rose not a little on listening to the history and on learning that the Caid had hesitated not an instant to sacrifice his life, and those of all his followers, to save his favourite horse. And all the time the tale was going on I thought where had I heard all this before, for every incident seemed to me in some strange way familiar. At last I recollected that Garcilasso de la Vega (Inca) in his "Comentarios Reales del Peru," when he relates the civil wars between the followers of the Pizarros and the forces of the Viceroy, tells how Gonzalo de Silvestre, after the battle of Huarina, found himself alone upon a horse wounded twice in the head, and in the chest, and that he gave himself up for lost, thinking his horse would fall, when "feeling him a little with the bridle, the horse threw up his head, and, snorting, blew blood through his nostrils and seemed relieved, then went on galloping, and presently I passed one of our partizans retreating, badly wounded, on a mule, not able to sit upright for his hurt, and by him walked an Indian woman, with her hand upon the wound to stop the blood "* Gonzalo de Silvestre and the wounded man and horse, all got off with their lives,

* "Garcilasso de la Vega, Comentarios Reales del Peru," Fifth Book, Part II, Chap. 21.

no doubt the same tripartite deity assisting them, who in his indivisible aspect came to the assistance of the Chamberlain and of the Caid.

"Could I then undertake to examine the leg and perhaps extract the ball?" was put to me through the medium of the Chamberlain. For a moment I hesitated, thinking that if the ball was near the skin I would hazard it, and so earn the eternal gratitude of the Caid and be sent on to Tarudant with honour and with an escort of the Caid's followers to guard me on the way. One look dispelled my hopes, for the wound was high up in the thigh, close to the femoral artery and had almost healed, although the patient said it gave him pain, and stopped him from getting on his horse, though when once mounted he could make a shift to ride. Reluctantly I had to say I was not able to undertake so serious a case, and the Caid's face fell, so I advised him to send for an English doctor who I knew was staying in Morocco city for his health, and who would have been glad to see so strange a place, and put the patient upon his legs again. If he has done so by this time I do not know, or even if the Caid made up his mind to send for him; but the chance for a doctor was unique, and therefore has, most probably, been missed.

Governors of provinces in Morocco, and throughout the East, are rather shy of going to the Capital, even in such a case as this; for once there the Sultan often takes the opportunity of making them disgorge some of the money which they have plundered in their government. On the first rumour that the Governor is in disgrace, the tribe rebels, blocades the castle, burns it down if possible, and some neighbouring Sheikh sends to the Sultan and offers a large sum to be made Governor in the disgraced man's place.

Even if things do not go quite so far as that, a journey in Morocco has its inconveniences, for generally the wives take the chance of the husband's absence to dig up his money and send it to their friends. This happened to the Caid of Kintafi when wounded in the Sus, and he, on his return finding his money gone, divorced two of his wives, and treated all the others to some discipline, which the Chamberlain assured me had restored peace and order to his Excellency's house.

Our interview having lasted almost two hours, we rose to take our leave. I thanked the Caid for his continued hospitality, assured him that I should not easily forget Kintafi, promised to send him a doctor if he wished, and quite forgot I was a prisoner. He on his part transmitted his good wishes through the medium of his henchman and Lutaif, and said he hoped we would not leave Kintafi for a few days more, as he was anxious to speak to us again. This was not quite the ending of the interview I had expected, for it amounted to an order we should not leave the place, so in conveying to him my best thanks for all his hospitality, I told him that I would let him known the latest news about the prisoners in the Riff on my return to Mogador, and in the meantime hoped Allah would guide him in all he did, and that he would continue to dispense his hospitality to all who passed, because, as Sidna Mohammed himself has said, "that hospitality, even when unasked for, blesses both the host and guest."

Lutaif, who had the pleasure of translating this farewell, did not much like his task, but faced it manfully, and so amidst a shower of compliments we took our leave, and left the presence of our illustrious host for good. Still an experience not to have been

missed, and differing extremely from the ordinary
visit paid by the travelling European to a Moorish
Caid on equal terms, that is, when dressed in European clothes, furnished with letters from the Sultan
and the Ambassador of the traveller's country, when
one drinks tea, exchanges compliments, and learns
as little of the real go on of an Oriental house, as
does a man born rich learn the real workings of the
people's minds with whom he lives his life.

An Eastern potentate of the Arabian Nights, with
all the culture of the Arabs of the Middle Ages absent,
but as he was, the arbiter of life and death in a wide
district. A gentleman in manners, courteous to those
whom he had all the power to treat with rudeness
or severity; a horseman, and a fighter; a tyrant
naturally, as any man would be if placed in his position, but no more tyrannical in disposition than is
some new elected County Councillor, who wishes to
make all men chaste and sober, because he himself
is impotent and enjoys a never to be satiated thirst
for ginger beer. Half independent of the Sultan,
leading his own troops, dispensing justice, as he
thought he saw it, in his own courtyard, and to me
interesting in special as a sort of after type of those
great Arab Emirs who sprang from the sands of
Africa and of Arabia, shook Europe, flourished in
Spain, built the Alhambra and Alcazar, gave us the
Arab horse and the curb bit, and kept alive the
remains of Greek philosophy in Cordoba and in
Toledo, when all the rest of Europe grovelled in
darkness; then by degrees fell into decadence, and
sank again into the sands of Africa, to still keep alive
the patriarchal system, the oldest and perhaps the
best conception of a simple life mankind has yet
found out. Allah Ackbar; lost in a wilderness of

broadcloth, I still praise God that such a man exists, if only to contrast him in my mind with the self-advertising anthropoids who make one fancy, if the Darwinian theory still holds good, that the God after whose image the first man was made had surely been an ape. Through passages and courtyards we reached the open space on which our tent was pitched, escorted by a guard of men well armed with guns and daggers, which appendages made them none the less loth to take a tip on coming to the tent than if they had been so many gamekeepers, who take their unearned money after a grouse drive, or a hot corner in the coverts, with an air of doing you a service, and whose contempt for you is only equalled by your disgust both at yourself and them.

But over everyone a change had come, for we had stood before the face of the great man with honour, and those who scarcely in the morning returned our salutations, gravely saluted us and condescended to enquire after our welfare and our health.

Swani and Mohammed-el-Hosein were radiant, more especially because the Caid had sent a sheep, which they had already slain and given to a "master" (maalem) to roast *en barbecue*. Although I personally was disappointed that we had not been able either to get an answer from the Caid as to our return still less to get permission to go on, still I was glad to have seen him, placed as I was, and wondered if an English Duke in the Georgian times would have treated an Arab wandering in England, and giving out he was an English clergyman, as well as the wild, semi-independent Berber Sheikh treated the wandering Englishman who assumed to pass, not merely as a clergyman, but as a saint.

Four men appeared bearing the sheep on a huge

wooden dish, smoking and peppered so as to start us sneezing ; and when the "Maalem" had torn it into convenient portions with his hands, we all fell to, Lutaif and I with the appetite that civilisation gives for such a meal, and the rest like wolves, or men remembering the Hispano-Moorish proverb to the effect that meat and appetite go not always together, though both are sent by God.

CHAPTER X.

EARLY next day the effects of our audience began to manifest themselves. The sick, the halt, the lame, and impotent, all besieged the tent, having been kept away apparently by the uncertainty of the Caid's attitude towards the Nazarenes. But as all Europeans are supposed not only to know something of medicine and to carry drugs about with them on all occasions, the afflicted fairly besieged me, and I dispensed my medicines with a freedom quite unrestrained by fear of consequences, and not restrained as doctors are in "policed" countries, where every now and then the public fall into a panic when a case of human vivisection, carried out (upon the poor) in the pure joy of scientific life, leaks from inside the precincts of some hospital. Gratitude, which dies with knowledge, but flourishes luxuriantly as long as the medicine man is a being quite apart, working his wonders unrestrained by scientific bounds, showed itself in several ways. But, as per usual, most pathetically in inverse proportion to the riches of the patient, for several who should have recompensed my skill (or zeal) according to the goodness of their clothes, slunk off, as people do at home after street acrobats have been performing; and when the little boy who has risked his life upon a pyramid of father, big brother, and several uncles, straining in his baggy cotton tights (which give him the appearance of a cab horse shaken in the legs), is just about to come round holding out his tambourine. So I dispensed my stock, which I had brought to spread my fame and smooth my path in Tarudant, quite cheerfully; ophthalmia, tetanus, sciatica, elephantiasis, ulcers, and twisted limbs, with rheumatism, deafness, and "El Burd," I alleviated by the faith of those who took my drugs. The more extraordinary and complicated were the instructions which I gave, the better pleased the patient was, and sometimes came back twice or three times to ask if the quinine or seidlitz powder was to be taken on every fifth or ninth recurring day. One poor "Bezonian," for whom I had prescribed something or other, came in the evening, and lugging out from underneath his cloak a dirty pocket-handkerchief, produced a handful of greasy copper coin, worth, perhaps, one penny halfpenny in all, and with excuses for his poverty in Shillah, which came to me through Arabic, entreated me to pay myself for my prescription. I answered as nobly as I could, "the credit is Allah's," and the poor man advanced and kissed me on the shoulder, and went out, perhaps to tell to-day of the great Christian doctor who would take no fee. Others brought eggs and bread, and these I took, as it would have been an insult to them to refuse, and besides that, I fancy the mere idea of having paid, made my hell broths appear more efficacious to the simple folk. But who, even in England, that does not believe that the two guineas which he pays to see some great specialist* in Harley Street does not advance his case, and were it five I fancy the greater part of

* A philosopher has remarked that liar, damned liar, and skilled witness stand in a progressive ratio, and for all I know "specialists" may hold much the same position in the world of medicine.

patients would leave the doctor's mansion cured, or else omit to go, and all is one.

My most popular receipt for coughs may yet achieve the popularity which is reserved for faith healing amongst the Christian world. Take four Beecham's Pills, and bruise them in a mortar with an ounce of cloves and two of Argan oil, a piece of rancid butter, and a cup of "magia" (spirit made from dates); rub well upon the chest, anoint the feet, and take a spoonful of the same liquid in tepid water, now and then, continuing our light and nourishing couscuso and shisha,* and please Allah the cough will disappear.

Tired of dispensing, I strolled out to the olive grove, sat down, began to smoke, and watched two men seated close by dressed in white robes, and evidently of the richer sort. One read a letter to his friend, with explanations upon every line, and with apparently some trouble to himself, for every now and then he drew a character in the sand with his forefinger, and compared it with the doubtful character in the document he read. In the same fashion I have seen grave, reserved, grey-bearded men in South America sit entertained for hours in "painting"* horses' marks upon the sand, and reasoning wisely upon every one of them. The man who listened said not a word, but looked entranced with admiration at the deep knowledge of his friend. I take it, reading and writing should not be abused, or it may chance with them to fare even as it has fared with sweet religion, which first a mystery concealed in a

* Shisha is a kind of thin porridge not unlike the skilly of our Christian prisons.

† "Painting a mark from the Spanish expression 'pintar una marca.' In the same way in Western Texas 'Pinto,' a piebald horse, became 'paint,' cabresto,' a halter, 'cabress,' and so on, in all conscience and tender heart."

learned tongue, and thus respected and believed without inquiry, then became understandable by its trans-
lation to the vulgar speech, lost credit, and to-day
has fallen into a fashion, and changes in complexion,
form, and authenticity, as quickly as a bonnet brought
from Paris in the spring falls into dowdiness and
becomes ridiculous almost before the owner is aware.

We marvelled greatly that we had not been able to
discover what were the Caid's intentions in regard
to us, and, casting up the time, found we had passed
nine days already in the place. Curious, in prison, or
in a ship, or stuck alone in some wild hut on prairie,
or on Pampa, to remark how long the time seems for
the first few days, and then begins to race, so that
before one is aware a month is past which at the first
looked like eternity to face. And stranger still, how
in a week or so, the newspapers and books, the so-
called intellectual conversation, news of the outside
world, the theatres, churches, politics, and the things
which by their aggregated littleness, taken together,
seem important, fall out of one's life. The condition
of one's horse, the weather, crops, the storm, or coming
revolution, all take their places and become as important as were the unimportant great events, which
a short time ago, served up distorted in an evening
paper, wiled away our time.

Thus life at Kintafi after a little became quite
natural to us, and at least as cheerful for a continuance as life in Parliament, in Paris, London, or any
other of the dreary hives of pleasure or of thought.
We rose at daylight, drank green tea and smoked,
went down to bathe, came back and breakfasted,
looked at the horses led to water, listened to the
muezzin call to prayers, walked in the olive grove or
watched the negroes in the corn field ; engaged in

conversation with some of the strange types, we read el Faredi, speculated on how long the "rekass" would tarry on the road from the Sultan's camp, and wondered at the perpetual procession of people always arriving at the castle to beg for something, a horse, a mule, a gun, some money, or in some way or other to participate in the Caid's Baraka* Had I but been allowed to ride about and explore the country, I should have been content to stay a month. However there was no order, and all those who are not strong enough to disobey have to stick strictly to an order in the East.

As an example of how orders are obeyed, one day during my sojourn at Kintafi, Lutaif and I had wandered about a mile following the Wad el N'fiss and crossing it once or twice to save the bends. As we were walking we had to take our slippers off and cross barefooted, picking our way over the pebbles in the fierce stream, which made it difficult to walk. On our return, just at a ford where the current ran particularly swift, we met two mounted men, followers of the Caid, whom we knew well, and one of whom I had prescribed for in my character of medicine man. Thinking the chance a good one, I asked the man to let me ride across, knowing his feet were hard as leather, and intending to have given him a trifle for lending me the horse. The man excused himself with many apologies, and said he had been sent to exercise the horse, and had no order to let any one ride on it, and dare not upon any pretext let me get upon

---

* Baraka literally means a blessing. It is also used in thanks, as " Baraka Lowfik," The blessing of God be on you. And not infrequently as a sort of general term for goodness or generosity. Arabs rarely say Baraka Lowfik in thanking a Christian, but use the less religious phrase " Kettir heirac." Neither do they (in Morocco) ever salute a Christian with Salam Aleikoum (peace be with you), as peace is only for Believers.

its back. He had no reason to be uncivil, and was no doubt in terror of what the Caid might do had the news come to him that he had gone an atom beyond his strict command.

Easterns of any nation are good company to be thrown with on an occasion such as the one in which I found myself. Lutaif had a never failing fund of stories about things he had seen and heard, and told them with the absolute lack of self-consciousness which alone makes a story pleasant, and which distinguishes an Eastern story-teller from the Western, who in his story always has an eye on the effect of what he tells.

At present in the Lebanon it seems there is an exodus of all the educated young men towards America ; and in New York there is a Syrian quarter where they speak Arabic, carry on small industries, and, curiously enough, are known to the natives as "the Arabians," a designation which must sound most strangely to a Syrian's ear. One of these Syrian young men, but in this instance quite uneducated, and speaking only a rough Arabic *patois*, started to try and reach America, where the streets are paved with gold. Having shipped as a deck hand on board a steamer at Beirout, he reached New York. There he was put ashore, and failed to get employment ; wandered about the streets ; was taken to the Turkish consul, and by him shipped to Marseilles as a vagrant who was unable to support himself in the free land where every man is better than his neighbour if he has more money in his purse. Dropped ashore at Marseilles, he got aboard an Italian steamer going to the River Plate, was found and flogged, then fastened to the mast for six or seven hours, and when the vessel touched at Malaga, shoved ashore, after receiving several

hearty kicks.   There, almost starving, and ignorant
of Spanish, he set out to tramp to Gibraltar, almost
sixty miles away.   But most unluckily he reckoned
without the *odium theologicum ;* for happening to wear
a Turkish fez, and Spain just at that time was engaged
in the squabble at Alhucemas, in the Riff, the country
people were in a fervour of religious rage against the
Moors. New York, Marseilles, the Italian steamer,
all were as nothing to what he had to suffer in his
tramp in the land specially the Blessed Virgin's*
own. No one would have him in the villages, and
when he asked for bread they met in the fashion of
the Holy Scriptures, with a stone.   The children
hooted him, the shepherds minding their sheep slung
stones at him, and after three days' journey, in a
most miserable plight, he reached Gibraltar where
he met a Moor, who gave him a bag to carry to a
certain place.   The bag turned out to contain cigars
which the Moor wished to smuggle on board a ship.
Up comes a policeman, beats him a little with a short
club (as he explained), and takes him off before a
magistrate.   There not a soul spoke Arabic, and he
was remanded to the cells, where, as he said, he was
quite comfortable and better off than in that cursed
"town called Spain."   At last an interpreter arrived
and the poor man found himself free, but starving,
and in despair crossed to Tangier, and there on my
return I found him saving up coppers to pay his
passage once more to New York.

Back in our tent the staring recommences, as for
some reason many of the wilder tribesmen are, so to
speak, in town to-day. They sat outside the tent
like sparrows on a telegraph, and looked at us as if
we were the strangest sight they ever had beheld.

* Andalusia is known to Spaniards as La tierra de Maria Santisima.

Even the stolid glare of a hostile (or stupid) audience at a public meeting was nothing to their gaze. At times I thought had we but brought a monkey and an organ our fortunes had been made, and we should have to buy a camel to carry off the avalanche of copper coin.

And still no sign of the rekass; and so the 28th and 29th slipped past, leaving us still a-thinking, still cavilling, and wondering how much longer we should have to stay.

Almost the most interesting, and certainly the most pathetic, of my patients, arrived during the 29th. A long, thin, famine-stricken man dressed in rags begged me for medicine for a " sad heart," and certainly he had good cause for sadness, though I fancy that the peseta * which I gave him may have done him at least as much good as the last of my quinine. It appeared that the late Sultan, Mulai el Hassan, had destroyed his house, taken his property, and driven him to exile. Quite naturally the present Sultan had too much filial respect for his late father to undo any action, just or unjust, that he thought fit to do. Therefore my patient, whose "sad heart" had stood out for three whole years, was still a suppliant, and his present errand was to try and interest El Kintafi in his case. For six long months he had been in the place trying his luck without success. Sometimes the Caid would promise him his help, and then again tell him to come when he had thought the matter over and resolved what was the best to do. Meantime the man slept in the mosque by night, by day stood at the gate, and when the Caid rode out clung to his

* The recent war having reminded the public that a country called Spain exists, I feel that I am not obliged to explain how little English money a peseta is worth at the present rate of exchange.

stirrup and implored his aid. He said, "I see him every six or seven days, but there is no hope but in God." Still he was cheerful, and had his rags well washed ; and was as resigned and dignified as I am certain that no Christian, out of fiction, could possibly have been. "God the great Helper"; but then how slow but merciful in this case, if only by the faith he had implanted to endure his own neglect. And so the sad-hearted man of sorrows made his notch upon my life, as the old Persian and the "Oudad" had done, and still perhaps waits for the Caid on mornings when his Excellency rides out to hunt or hawk with a long train of followers, issuing from the horse-shoe arch, with negroes holding greyhounds in the leash, horsemen perched high on their red saddles, the sun falling upon long silver-mounted guns, haiks waving in the air, whilst from the ramparts of the castle comes the shrill note of joy the women raise when, in Morocco, men go out to hunt, to war, to play the powder ;* or when, at weddings, the bride, stuffed in a gilded cage upon a mule, is taken home.

An aged Israelite with a long train of mules came from the Sus that morning. He wore a sort of compromise between Oriental and European clothes, which gave him an incredibly abject look, the elastic-sided boots and ivory-handled cane contrasting most ill-favouredly with his long gaberdine ; and his ten-carat watch-chain, with a malachite locket hanging

---

* The Powder Play (Lab-el-Barod), is known in Algeria as the Fantasia. Both in that country and in Morocco it is the imitation of an Arab tribal battle. The horsemen rush forward and fire their guns in parties or singly, stand up in the saddle, fire under their horses' necks, and over their tails, throw their guns in the air and catch them, and perform all the evolutions which their ancestors performed with javelin and spear. This exercise prevailed in Spain till the middle of the last century under the name of the " Juego de Cañas." It is still played in the East with reeds.

from it, rendering the effect of his maroon cloth caftan mean and civilised. He told me that his chief business was to lend money to the Caids, and that his mules were packed with silver dollars, being the interest on the capital lent to various governors in Sus. He expressed no fear of any attack upon his caravan; and when I quoted the saying that " if the caravan is attacked the poor man has nothing to fear," returned, "nor has the Jew, who is indispensable to the great ones of the earth." Nevertheless he bore about him several old bullet wounds, and carried underneath his gaberdine a first-rate Smith and Wesson pistol, which he said he would not care to be obliged to use. I put him down as one who, given the opportunity, would shoot an unbeliever like a dog, having generally observed that readiness to shoot goes in an inverse ratio with readiness to talk, and that the man who always has a pistol in his hand might just as often, for all purpose of defence, carry a meerschaum pipe. The way he travelled was curious, for, in the Sus amongst the Berber tribes, he had to take a tribesman, to whom he paid a certain sum, to see him safely through the tribe, who, in his turn, delivered him, on leaving his territory, to another man, and so on right through the country which he had to pass. This system is recognised throughout the Atlas range, and generally wherever the Berber tribes inhabit, and is known as el Mzareg, that is, the protection of the lance, for anciently the protecting tribesman bore a lance, but, nowadays, usually is satisfied with the stout cudgel which all hillmen use. Baruch, the Hebrew with the ivory crutch-handled stick, informed me that, in the Sus, nearly every Jewish family was obliged to have his corresponding Mzareg, who protected and also fleeced them; and that, in consequence, most of those

"Pedlars of the ghetto," in spite of all their industry, were poor. A curious down-trodden race the Atlas Jews, ostensibly the slaves of every one, and in reality their masters; for owing to the incapacity for commerce in the Berbers, every affair where money changes hands has to be brought about by the assistance of some quick-witted Jew. And so, just as in Europe, though without being in other respects superior to the races amongst whom they live, the Atlas Jews control the warlike Berbers as easily and as completely as their brethren control all those with whom they come in contact on a business footing throughout the world. Baruch had his home in Mequinez, and was not from Toledo, but an Oriental Jew, his people, as he said, having come into Morocco after the great dispersion, and he himself being of the tribe of Benjamin; though, when I asked him how he knew, he said it was a tradition in his family, and that the ancients never spoke untruth. Into this matter I forbore to enter, and generally gave an assent, quoting the Toledan-Jewish proverb, "That if Moses died, Adonai still survived,"* which he at once knew in its Arabic form, and asked me, as Israelites in the East will often do if you appear to know a little of their lore, "if I, too, was of the chosen race?" This worthy Baruch, in appearance like a head cut out of walnut wood, set round with fleecy wool, asked me, when passing Mequinez, to remember I had my house there, and said that I should find him, Baruch ben Baruch, as a father and a friend. Unfortunately, since then I have not passed Mequinez; but, if I do so, hope to eat my "adafina" in my father's house.

These promises and resolutions one makes in passing through the world to return to some place which

* "Si Moshé murio, Adonai quedo."

has struck our fancy, to see some friend who lives
ten thousand miles away, are like the apple blos-
soms blown across a lawn by a May wind; for are not
dead flower-leaves and broken promises but the illusions of a possibility which might have turned out
bitter in the fruit. And so, our medicine done, our
stock of patience almost exhausted, another day went
past, leaving us no other resource to pass the time but
to lounge up and down the Maidan, and when evening
came welcome the sunset on the spacious amphitheatre of hills.

As the sun sank, the ochre-coloured earth began
to glow, each stunted hill bush stood out and became
magnified, the rose and purple streaks of light shifted
and ran into each other, then faded into violet and
pale salmon-colour haze and falling on the snow-
capped hills lighted them up, making them rever-
berate the light upon the rose-red walls and yellow
towers, so that the castle seemed to burn, and the
muezzin upon his tower appeared to call the faithful
to their prayers from a red stalk of flame.

CHAPTER XI.

EARLY upon the morning of the 30th we were astir, and heard a report that a rekass had been seen entering the castle-gates the night before. Still, everything went on as usual at Thelata-el-Jacoub, men came and went, tall Arabs and squat Shillah; our animals all stood dejected and half-starved; a little pup having made friends with my Amsmizi horse, who played with him in a perfunctory way. The prisoners on the flat roof sprawled in the sun, passing the Peace of God, on terms of absolute equality with other men, who paused and gravely gave them back their salutation; birds drank and bathed in the little mill-stream under the oleander bushes; butterflies, marbled and black-veined whites, argus, fritillaries, and others quite unknown to me floated along in the still air, or hung suspended over the petals of a flower, and the brown earth of the " Maidan " gave back the heat like a reflector.

And still no tidings of our long looked for orders to be gone. All our companions in adversity, the Persian, the man with the "sad heart," the tribesmen in the tent which had been pitched close to our own; even the three Sheikhs from Sus at last had gone, having, after their long delay, settled their business, and assured me of their friendship should I visit Sus; their minds made up never again to venture inside the

lion's den. Our tents alone, like mushrooms, dotted
the Maidan, and over all the valley the late autumn
sun shed a deep calm, making the hills stand out as
if cut out of cardboard in the middle distance of a
theatre.

The enormous mud-built castle, with its flat roofs
and flat-topped flanking towers, took a prehistoric air,
and for the first time I imagined I was looking at some
old Carthaginian building; for its architecture resem-
bled nothing I had ever seen, being as unlike an Arab
Kasbah as to a feudal castle in the north, with somehow a suggestion of a teocalli, such as Bernal Diaz,
or Cortes, described in Mexico; or as if related in
some curious way to the great buildings in Palenque,
temples at Apam, or the more ancient dwellings of
the Aztec race upon the Rio Gila. Sheep walked
behind their shepherds, who played on reed pipes as
in the times of Hesiod; goats went to pasturage, the
kids skipping and playing with the ragged boys,
whilst from the distance came the wild sound of the
Moorish "Ghaita," which, like the bagpipes, is ever
most alluring heard from afar; from the hills floated
the scent of thyme, germander, gum cistus, and the
aromatic undergrowth of this last outpost of the
European flora, jutting into the sands of Africa. The
river prattled on its stony bed, and on its bank the
horses of the Caid went down to drink, and listlessly
I strolled to look at them, thinking, perhaps, that I
should have to wait until the autumn rains had made
the mountain paths impassable, and that the Caid
would be obliged to send me back against his will
through the mysterious passes of the south.

And as I looked, drinking in the strange semi-
Arcadian, semi-feudalistic scene, the Chamberlain,
attended by his guards, crossed the Maidan, came to

my tent, and, sitting down, informed me that it was the pleasure of the Caid that we should start. I asked had the "rekass" arrived from the Sultan, but the Chamberlain would give no definite reply, until I told him that our men had seen the messenger arrive. What were the exact terms of the Sultan's message I did not learn, but they could not have been extremely pleasant either for me or for the Caid, for in Morocco the Sultan never likes to be put in the position of risking complications with Europeans who might appeal to their home government, and usually casts all the onus both of action and of failure on his Caids.

Now was the time to make a last despairing effort to go on to Tarudant; therefore, I tried the Chamberlain in every way I could think of, but without success. Though I had not by this time half the money with me, I offered him a hundred dollars, to which he answered as before, "What is the use to me of a hundred or a thousand dollars without my head?" I shifted ground, and said I could not think of leaving without a personal interview with the Caid to thank him for his hospitality. But here again the faithful Chamberlain was ready with a message, "that it pained his Excellency not to receive me, but his wound had broken out afresh, and that he sent many salams and wished me a prosperous journey back to the coast." So as a last resource I asked the Chamberlain "What if I get on horseback, and ride straight on to Sus?" only to be met with a grave question if I thought I had the best horse in the valley, and if, supposing any tribesman was to fire by accident, if I thought my clothes were stout enough to turn a ball.

Seeing there was no chance, I made a virtue of necessity and ordered my tent to be taken down, and all got ready for the road.

The Chamberlain behaved with infinite tact, allowing no one to come near us, either to steal or ask for
money, and took his "gratification" with an air of
having earned it by laborious work; then shook my
hand, and said he hoped some day to meet me, and
that I was to think he had only acted as he had by
the orders of his chief. He then shook hands, first
with Lutaif, then with Mohammed-el-Hosein and
Swani, and took his leave, leaving us all alone on the
Maidan, in a broiling sun, with nothing to eat, and
ten or twelve hours of the hardest mountain roads to
pass before it was possible to procure food for our
animals or for ourselves. How all the others felt I
do not know, but for myself, when I reflected on my
journey lost, my twelve days of detention, and how
near I had been to reaching Tarudant being stopped
but by the merest chance, I felt inclined to laugh.
Knowing that almost all the houses were in ruins on
the way, and that the only place where it was
possible to buy barley for the mules was at a little
castle called Taquaydirt-el-Bur, which belonged to
the Caid, and the Sheikh of which was known as a
fanatical and disagreeable man, I sent Lutaif to the
castle for the last time to get a letter from the Caid
to his lieutenant on the road. Quite evidently they
were determined we should go, for in about half-an-
hour Lutaif returned with the letter and a negress
carrying some bread and couscousou, on which we
made a hearty breakfast, knowing that we should get
nothing more till night.

When one has little to pack, arrangements for a
journey are soon despatched, and we had nothing but
our tent and a few rugs; no food, no barley for the
mules, and the precious stock of medicines, which
was to have made my name in Tarudant, was long

run out. The men all worked like schoolboys packing to go home, especially Mohammed-el-Hosein,
who had never thought to leave the place alive, or at
the least to lose his mules, and be well beaten for his
pains. His spirits rose enormously, and he assured
me he was ready even now to try the road by
Agadhir. Swani sang Spanish and English sailors'
songs, not to be quoted until the " woman movement" either makes women accustomed to the tone
of much of sailors' conversation, or else refines our
mariners and makes their talk more fit for ears polite,
or hypocritical. Ali was like a man in a dream, and
felt his mule all over to see if it had suffered by the
long exposure to heat and rain, with barely any food.
It winced, and kicked at him to show its love, and to
assure him that its spirit was not injured by its
fast.

So all being ready, and not a soul about, I
mounted, took the black Amsmizi horse by the head
and felt his mouth, touched him with the spur, and
let him run across the empty Maidan, turned him
and made him rear, and plunging down the steep
path to the beach, just met the horses of the Caid
for the last time, being led out to drink. The
wounded cream colour, now almost quite recovered,
stood up and gave a long defiant neigh, and as we
rode under the castle walls upon the stony bed of the
N'fiss, the figure of the Chamberlain appeared, and
waved to us in a friendly fashion, so that my last
impression of the place was his grave figure, silent
and robed in white, and the fierce stallion neighing
on the beach.

About a mile, following the river's bed, the trail
leads through a scrub of oleanders, rises and enters
a fantastic path worn in the limestone rock, cut here

and there into pyramids and pinnacles by time, by traffic, and by winter rains, and looking something like the "seracs" formed in the ice upon the edge of certain glaciers. We followed it about a quarter-of-a mile, and turning, saw the castle of the Thelata-el-Jacoub for the last time.

But as I checked my horse, who, now his little spurt of spirit over, felt the twelve days' lack of food, and hung his head, I gazed upon the monstrous, mud-built, yellowish-red pile, marked once again the olive grove upon the edge of the Maidan, just caught the mosque tower with its green metallic tiles, the corn-fields, and the wild narrow valley stretching to the snow-capped hills, the river like a steel wire winding in and out between its steep high banks, and in my heart thanked fortune which, no doubt for some wise (though hidden) purpose of its own, had kept me prisoner for twelve well-filled days in such a place. Lutaif, in spite of all his piety, as he took his last look at the valley of Kintafi, I fancy muttered something which sounded like an imprecation on Mohammed and his faith, but yet confessed that even in the Lebanon there was no valley wilder or more beautiful than that of the N'fiss. Mohammed-el-Hosein felt at his beard as if to assure himself it still grew on his chin, and without stint cursed Caid and castle, tribe, place, and all the dwellers in it to the fourth and fifth generation of the sons of mothers who never yet said No. Swani was of opinion that of all men he had seen the noble Shillah were the most like Djins, and beat even the "Jaui,"* who, as all men knew, are sprung from monkeys, in ill-favouredness of face and wickedness of heart.

* Jaui is the word used in Arabic to designate Malays, Chinese, and the Eastern Mohammedans in general.

Our feelings thus relieved, we set ourselves to drive our half-starved beasts over the mountain roads. The miles seemed mortal, and the scenery, though wonderful enough, chiefly remarkable for the unending hills, the frequent elbows made by the N'fiss, now deeper and much fiercer than when we came, owing to the recent rains, which forced us to cross repeatedly and get wet every time; for the snow, which now lay thickly on the higher hills, and though the sun was hot, still made the wind as cold as winter, and our clothes like paper on our backs. And as we spurred along calling, when a mule stumbled upon a narrow path above the river, upon Sidi bel Abbas, the saint of wayfarers, we racked our brains to discover how we had been found out. The sun, the winds, the want of food, the rain and dust of the road, had by this time rendered us almost as dark as Moors, and we were certain that we looked the character, for all the passers-by saluted us with "Peace," and never turned their heads to look at us, taking us evidently for travellers from the Sus. My own idea was that the man we had taken from Amsmiz had passed the word along the road. The others thought, some one thing, some another, and so we talked away, till at the last Mohammed-el-Hosein resolved the matter, saying that Allah had not wished us to succeed. Once more we crossed the rugged "couloir," where I had seen the miserable donkey fallen on the road surrounded by his wretched owners, or compeers. Again we stopped to rest the animals under the oleander bushes by the stream; but this time all dejected, hungry, and without refreshment, but a pipe of kief, which Ali brought triumphantly out of a dirty bag, and which we smoked by turns, sitting like Indians at a council, waiting for the word.

Just about sundown we came to Taquaydirt-el-
Bur, to find it full ; a sort of festival in process in the
mosque; mules, horses, donkeys, and armed men per-
vading all the place ; a whistling north wind blowing
from the snow; nothing to eat, and to be kept at least
an hour sitting upon our beasts, whilst the Sheikh
read the letter we delivered from the Caid. At last
a filthy negro came and called us in; and riding
through the dark and tortuous passage to the inner
court, my horse fell twice, once on a donkey and
again upon a mule : and the confusion, struggling,
kicking, cursing, and plunging in the dark, made me
despair of getting through without a broken bone.
When we emerged the inner court was full, men
slept beside the donkeys, upon their pack-saddles ;
and on the plaster benches running round the
wall beside them were their guns, their daggers,
quarter staffs ; and underneath their heads their
money, valuables, corn for their horses, or anything
they chanced to value most. Luckily none of them
knew that we were Christians, but thought most
likely we were guests the Sheikh considered worthy
of his care, for no one looked at us, and we were glad
to pack into a room above an oil-press, smelling
abominably of oil, filthy, and with an opening in the
roof through which we saw the stars. Upon the
doors and shutters were some most curious concen-
tric patterns cut deep in the wood. They were not
Arab nor like any European work, nor yet were made
by Jews, but they reminded me, as the Kasbah at
Kintafi had done, of the strange temples of Palenque,
the patterns on the Aztec Calendar, and the Sacri-
ficial Stone built into a side wall of the great church
at Mexico. Miserably we sat squatted before a pan
of charcoal trying to dry our clothes, and after some

hours waiting, a man appeared with a dish of eggs fried in high smelling Argan oil, which we despatched at once, and tried to sleep ; but between cold and the assaults of every kind of insect, found it impossible, tired with the journey and hungry as we were. All through the night a sort of " tenebræ " seemed to be going on in the neighbouring mosque; "ghaitas" were played, and every now and then a man broke out into a long high chant, the congregation answering him at stated intervals. Long before day I roused our people up, saddled, and then we picked our way through the courtyard where the travellers were still buried in sleep, and got upon the road just as the stars were paling, and a whistling wind blowing from off the snow, which chilled us to the bones. Moham-med-el-Hosein and Swani were afraid the Caid might change his mind and send men after us to bring us back ; so we pushed on as fast as we could go for about four hours, until the half-starved beasts began to tire, then walked a spell, and finally sat down to rest (this time without even a pipe of kief), and let the beasts try to pick up some grass.

Until that moment, so hurried had been our journey, I had not determined where to go ; and after consultation, it being manifest we could not reach Morocco City by nightfall with our jaded beasts, and as I was not anxious to camp in the mountains another night without a chance of food, I determined to push on to Tamasluoght, the Sherif of which, Mulai el Haj, I knew and to whom I had sent a letter from Kintafi, asking him to agitate for our release. From where we were, the Zowia of Tamasluoght was distant at least eight hours' march, and if we wanted to arrive with light the time was short enough. So we pushed on ; stumbling along the mountain paths, dismounting now

and then to lead our animals; all silent and occasionally a little cross. The road branched to the east, and
separated from the Amsmiz path close to the place
where we had seen a salt mine on our journey towards
the Sus. Here for the first time we entered a real
cedar forest; the trees not high, rarely exceeding
thirty feet in height, but thick and growing closely so
as in places to exclude the light. The trail led in and
out between the trunks, and at times narrowed to
about two feet in breadth, and went sheer down for
seven or eight hundred feet. Unmindful of the proverb
that "he who passes a bridge on horseback looks
death in the face,"* we passed without dismounting
till Lutaif's saddle slipping, almost precipitated him
down the precipice. Dimly, and at an immense depth
below, we saw the salt mine, looking like a glacier,
and shining white as snow; the mode of working
being to dig innumerable pits, from which the water
ran into a sort of reservoir, where the salt lay heaped.
Miserable donkeys crawled along the mountain paths,
all grossly overladen; and men passed stripped half-
naked, but perspiring even in the chilly air, bent like
Swiss porters carrying tourists' boxes, under great
loads of salt.

At last we began to leave the mountains, and emerged
on to a broad and fertile plateau, much like Castille,
and growing the same crops of wheat, chick peas and
vetches, with the resemblance increased by the mud-
built houses, looking so like the hills that now and
then we came upon a village almost before we could
be sure if the brown heaps were irregularities of the
ground, or houses, so exactly did the colours blend.
In one of the small hamlets we bought bread and fed
our horses, and pushed on again, till about four

* "Quien a caballo pasa la puente, tiene la muerte ante la frente."

o'clock, after winding up an interminable staircase of rock, all of a sudden the plain of Morocco burst upon us; the great city in the distance, and the Kutubich standing like a lighthouse of Islam, to guide the wanderer home. From thence the descent was rapid; and in another hour, we found ourselves in a different climate, and again came to a country where it had not rained for months; burnt up and dry, with all the water-courses turned to brown holes, and a dull shimmering in the still air broken but by the grasshoppers' shrill note. The next three hours were mortal, and about sundown our animals reeled through the olive groves, which for a mile or more surrounded the Zowia of Tamasluoght. We passed some water wheels, and drank at the first of them; passed underneath the curious apparatus like a switchback, supported on brick towers at intervals of a hundred feet, by means of which water is taken to the Sherif's house; rode through some sandy lanes, with houses here and there; came to the gateway, and were met by Mulai el Haj in person, who said he had not thought we should have got out of Kintafi on such easy terms.

No one could be more absolutely unlike our late lamented host than Mulai el Haj, an Arab of the Arabs, descended from the Prophet, courtly and fair in presence, with the dignity that rank (in the East) confers on its possessor. A man of peace in fact, a semi-sacred character, and a sort of cross between the Pope and a feudal baron of old time; rich, influential, and occupying in the south the position held in the north by the Sherifs of Wazan. When at last our diplomats became aware that the French had secured a footing in Wazan, and by their railway to Ain Sefra a point of descent on Fez and on Morocco City, it

occurred to them to secure Mulai-el-Haj, as a set-off to
the all-prevailing influence of the French throughout
the north. So they induced our government to extend British protection to the Sherif of Tamasluoght;
but the protection has been so grudgingly extended
as to be hardly of avail.

Into the ethics of the European occupation of Morocco
I do not propose to go; but if at any time that occupation should occur, as it is certain that Europe would
not see us in Tangier, and as the French have thoroughly
secured the north, and as the Germans will no doubt
bid for some towns upon the coast, it might perhaps
be still advisable to seize the south, and so control
the Sus, secure Morocco City, and thus keep a way
open for the Saharan trade, and opening Agadhir, or
some port on the Wad Nun, check French advance
from St. Louis, Senegal, and Dakar, and their posses-
sions in the south. For myself I need hardly say I
should prefer to see Morocco as it is, bad government
and all, thinking but little as I do of the apotheosis
of the "bowler" hat, and holding as an article of faith
that national government is best for every land, from
Ireland to the "vexed Bermoothes," and from thence
to Timbuctoo.

If we are thieves in Europe, as China plainly shows,
why in the name of fortune should England lag behind?
Have we not plundered and robbed for centuries, and
why now refrain, when we so plainly see that thieving
is in our blood, as witness the pious efforts of our
descendants in the States to steal an island for the love
of God? When we arrived at Tamasluoght, nothing
was further from my mind than politics, the advance
of empires, ethics of conquest, Hinterlands, and things
of that sort, on which the opinion of the first fool in
the street is just as valuable as that of the politician

fool, who stumbles out his halting speech to his be-
mused electors, who elect him for his likeness to themselves in density of head.

Mulai-el-Haj ushered us into a sort of kiosque, built
in the style of the Alhambra, with a small court in
front, in which grew cypresses and oranges, and would
hear no word of anything before he had seated us on
a comfortable divan in the recess of a window in his
guest-chamber, which opened on a little garden where
a fountain played, the water splashing on a marble
basin, and the scent of flowers rising up to the room.
After the Arab fashion he never left us for a moment;*
and whilst a repast was being got ready, set tea before
us, and then coffee, and, to pass by the interval, fresh
bread and butter in a cracked, though lordly dish.
All was perfectly appointed in Arab style, the china
French, the basin in which we washed our hands of
brass most beautifully worked, and a black (uncomely)
slave girl with heavy silver anklets handed round
the cups. In her confusion at the sight of Christians,
instead of handing us a napkin she handed something
which looked like the trimming of her drawers,
and being rebuked in Shillah, retired in tears, and
another equally ill-favoured damsel took her place.
Her name I think was "Johar," and the Sherif explained with gravity that negresses were as immodest
as the hens; and that the slave had better have kept
the trimming of her drawers to veil her face, though,
as he said, what with the tattoo marks and negro
features, it contained little to tempt the eyes of a
believing man. To this I gave a qualified assent, and

---

*This fashion is still kept up amongst old-fashioned and provincial
Spaniards, who, on the rare occasions on which they admit a stranger to
their houses, never leave him till bedtime. It is called "to accompany the
guest" (acompañar el huesped), and to omit it would be the height of
ill-breeding.

through the medium of Lutaif guided the conversation on to more general grounds, on which a man,
used from his youth, as Europeans are, to think all
women angels in disguise, might safely join.

The Sherif, having gone to the mosque for a brief
interval, I walked into the courtyard to see my horse,
whom I found almost done up, too tired to eat; the
mules nearly exhausted, one of them lying down, and
the men sitting beside them, too tired even to light a
fire. Lutaif, who was not much accustomed to such
trots, and who moreover had ridden a tired mule for
most part of the day, had nearly fallen asleep during
the tea and coffee and the long talk with the Sherif,
but now was rested, and strolled with me about the
place.

The house was built in the usual Moorish style; with
crenelated walls, flanking towers, and dome-shaped
roofs. It had innumerable courts, a mosque, a
women's wing, a granary, store houses, baths, and
everything in the first style of modern Arab taste. All
round the houses stood cypresses, many of great age
and height; over the mosque two or three palm-trees
waved, and oranges and olives extended for some
acres upon every side. There was a garden in the
Eastern taste, where water trickled in a thousand
little rills; canes fluttered, rustling like feathers in
the air; jasmine and honeysuckle climbed up the
" azofaifa " trees, sweet limes and lemons with
pomegranates were dotted here and there; some
periwinkles, but larger and paler than those grown
in Europe, grew in the grass here; and there stood
geranium bushes, straggling and run to seed; and
over all the air of decadence, mixed with content,
which makes to me, an Eastern garden that of all
others where I think a truly slothful and religious

man should find heart-ease, and reading in some book of things beyond the power of intellect, leave them without solution, and sit still giving thanks for gardens as a true Christian should.

Just as with us, to whom the feudal castle and the red brick Queen Anne or Jacobean "mansion" have been as snares, leading our architects to pander to our lack of taste, or in order to excuse their own plentiful want of all invention to befoul the land with stuccoed castles adorned with useless machicolations and pepper-boxes from which no sentinel could see; with arrow slits from which to shoot at nothing; with cannons in stone projecting from the futile battlements, the whole brought "up to date" with windows of plate glass, the enchanting edifice itself being all neatly planted round with stiff Norwegian spruce; so, here, the Alhambra and Alcazar have ensnared the modern Moors. Each petty Sheikh or Caid of some small tribe, when he sets out to build his house, in another fashion, follows precisely the same strange line of conduct. The wholesome conservatism of the Arab race admits no change in outward forms of architecture, and their architects still please the eye with solid work and long expanse of walls unbroken up with frippery, with attempt at useless ornament. Inside, however, all is horror, mere desolation, and a symphony in Reckett's Blue, of crude red and yellow ochre. The windows are set with stomach-aching glass, worse than the stuff which came from Munich in the sixties, fit only to fill the windows of an "Ebenezer," "Little Bethel," or other place where the Lord God is ordered once a week to send his rain, fine weather, change the seasons, or abrogate his laws, to please the preachers, who honour him, apparently, as

we should honour a physician, for the uses we may
have of him. And curiously enough, as if in fact
taste was an accidental thing, as I often think it is—
for if not, why should an Arab or an Indian prefer a
European blanket to his own beautiful patterns ?—outside the awful red and green and yellow window there
was a grating of wrought iron, delicate and intricately
worked as it had been a frozen spider's web, with dew-
drops on it all congealed by frost. The inside of
the house was decorated in a sort of pseudo-Persian
style, with double doors all gilt, and with a little
horseshoe opening in the middle of them through
which to pass, and on each side a formal tree like
those one sees so often on the inside binding of a Persian book. In fact, a modern replica of the Alhambra done without art, the gildings and the columns
common, heavy and overcharged, and nothing really
good except the gratings of the woodwork, and the
tiles which, made to-day in Fez, seem to have but
little deteriorated in glaze and colour from those left
by the Moors in Spain.

Prayers over, the Sherif came back to keep us
company, and sat till midnight talking of all sorts of
things.

He appeared to think that we had great luck in
not having been sent as prisoners to the Sultan's
camp, for if we had been sent, we might have remained for weeks journeying about with the army
before we were released. I was not sure if on the
whole I was glad to have missed the experience, but
as it would have been impossible to explain my
reasons, I held my peace. Mulai-el-Haj, being an
English protected subject, felt or assumed to feel
great interest in English things. He asked most
ceremoniously after our Grand Vizier (Lord Salisbury),

was curious about the Queen, talked of the rising of the Afridis, and hoped that God would give the victory to our armies, a consummation which in his heart of hearts he could not really have wished, for no Mohammedan ever desires that Kaffirs shall triumph over "those of the faith." His questions answered with great detail, he launched into a disquisition on the present state of things in Morocco under the Viziership of Ab-Ahmed, "for the young Sultan rules but by his hand."

What he communicated, may or may not have been his real opinion, for Arabs are apt to say that which they think will please their hearers; but situated as he was, that is, being a rich, powerful (and tolerably selfish) man, it may be that his words really conveyed his thoughts. "I have known tyrannies by Allah, and the late Sultan, Mulai-el-Hassan (may God have pardoned him), was not a lamb. His father was something sterner, and their viziers, were apt, as viziers always are, to fill their purses at the expense of powerful men. But since I first became a man, never a state of things so bad as now. Ab Ahmed passes all measure, grinds the faces of the poor, maintains the Sultan in a state of tutelege, taking his wives if so it pleases him, and sending them to his own house; he also sends the public money into France and puts it in their cursed banks, so that if the time for vengeance comes, he can escape and live upon it." Then looking round the room and moving up his cushions close to mine and laying one hand on my arm, he asked "Do you catch all I say?" for poor Lutaif had almost dropped asleep. I understood him as he spoke slow and plainly, and he began. "Has England quite forgotten us, or does she sleep? Time was when she was not wont to wait long when a country lay open as does Morocco to her

power." I thought he understood our policy and
what has made us so beloved by everyone, but nod-
ded, and he went on. "I can insure the southern
chiefs of all the tribes. I, Mulai-el-Haj, who speak,
but who through the intrigues of Ab Ahmed dare not
leave his house ; twice have they fired at me walking
in my own garden ; once when on my horse almost a
mile outside, and even now I know that men are
waiting for me did I go out. But still I can insure
the southern chiefs from here to Tazeroualt, westward to Tuats, to Tafilet, and through the Atlas ;
the dwellers in the plain around the City of
Morocco, all either send emissaries or visit me by
night. I tell you, even the wildest of those who
think a Christian is not a human being, are so hard
pressed, that if the English came they would meet
them on the road and pour out milk.* God instituted
government, as he made moon and sun, set one by
day to shine, the other to guide wanderers by night,
and as he set the stars in the blue heavens, so he set
Caids and Governors, Sheikhs, Mokadems, Cadis, and
all the hierarchy of rulers, each in his place to rule
mankind. The tail can never be so honourable as is
the head, and whilst men still exist they must be
ruled, but justly ruled, and this Ab Ahmed knows no
justice in his heart." Passion, O' me, I thought, he
is no socialist, nor for that matter is the poorest Arab,
all thinking that authority came straight from God.
Then he continued, "For two years I have never
dared to go to Morocco City, though but three hours
away. My houses there are ruined. Ab Ahmed has
taken one of them, and the other stands open a prey
to wind and rain, with all the woodwork torn away

---

* To pour out a libation of milk on the road is a sign of welcome in
Morocco.

and burnt. Your 'Bashador' two years ago advised me to make friends if possible with the Vizier. Therefore I bought a female slave, not to go empty handed, for I knew well that those in office always expect a present from all those they see. Three hundred dollars did I pay for the girl, not that she was a houri whom the sheep would lift their heads to look at if she walked across a field, but passable, and fitting to present to a man who like Ab Ahmed filled the office of Vizier.

And so I went to see my enemy. Why he should be my enemy I do not know, except that I am rich and am known to favour England, which he detests; but as it is, may Allah put his mercy some day into the hearts of flint. The girl I placed upon a mule, and taking with me twenty or thirty well-armed men rode to Morocco City. Arrived before his door, I had to wait two hours, I a Sherif, to wait two hours to please the mulatto dog; and then the slave, who led me to him, brought me through many passages and left me standing outside a half-opened door, whilst he went in. Long did I stand there, and being angry at the indignities that I was passing through, forbore to listen till at last I heard Ab' Ahmed say to his slave, 'where is the man?' The negro answered, 'he is come,' and then Ab Ahmed angrily replied, 'did you not take him where I told you' (i.e. to be killed), and the slave excused himself, saying: 'I thought you wanted him in here.' After a moment I heard Ab' Ahmed say: 'I told you plainly to take him to be killed, but God has spared him, let him come in." And then the slave threw the door open, and I advanced, was kindly welcomed, sat and drank tea, thinking each cup was poisoned, but made no sign, knowing that Allah, who had spared my life a moment previously, could turn the poison into sugar, if he willed it so.

We sat and talked, and then I gave the slave girl to him, and she was led away into his house. I took my leave, and he with courteous words urged on me return and visit him; but who that once escapes from the lion's den places his head again under his paw? God has indeed been gracious to me, praise his name, The One." As he stopped speaking I thought, indeed, who that would pity a snake-charmer, who is bitten by a snake, or any one, who cometh near wild beasts, but did not say so, but confined myself to praises of his prudence and of the special providence which had saved his life.

I next enquired if he had got my letter from Kintafi, saying jocularly that I had looked for him to come to my assistance waving a Union Jack. To my surprise he denied all knowledge of the letter, and said he had only heard of my captivity by accident. On going to Morocco City, the day after, I found a special messenger had been sent off to him bearing the letter; but after all blessed are they who expect little, they shall be satisfied.

At mid-night, and when Lutaif had long subsided into slumber on the divan, leaving me to puzzle out the worthy gentleman's discourse as best I could, he took his leave after urging me warmly to bear his compliments to our Grand Vizier. I pitilessly woke up Lutaif and had a consultation with him, what we should do, it being quite impossible for the animals to return to Mogador without some rest, and equally impossible to remain at Tamasluoght, where the Sherif would let us pay for nothing, either for ourselves or for our beasts. Morocco City was but three hours off, and as I expected letters there, we arranged to stop two or three days and feed our animals, and then push on across the plains for Mogador. Next morning saw us in the saddle by ten o'clock; and after a courteous exchange of compliments with the Sherif, and renewed entreaties on his part to put his view of the state of affairs in Morocco before the Grand Vizier on my return, we took our leave.

Thus for the second time I passed a night at Tamasluoght, having once, four years before, been there with Mr. Harris* on the occasion when the Sherif was agitating for British protection; and as I saw him standing before his door and bidding us good-bye, a courteous, prosperous, saintly Moorish gentleman, it came back to my mind that I had said to Mr. Harris that his protection, as far as English interests were concerned, was thrown away.

If we protect at all, except from pure philanthropy, we should protect lean, sunburnt sheikhs, who pass their lives on horseback, and at whose call spears and long guns rise from the desert like frozen reeds stick through the ice in ponds in winter time; and if that sort is not available, why those of the same kidney as the man in whose house I slept next night, Abu Beckr el Ghanjaui, prince of all Moorish intriguers and diplomatists; one who will stick to any cause through thick and thin if it is worth his while, and who, I fancy, if he chose to speak all that he knows of British policy in Morocco, could made some diplomatic folk get up and howl, or send them snorting like Indian ponies through the Foreign Office.

* Walter B. Harris, author of " Tafilet," and many works on Morocco, and one of the few Europeans who really knows the country and the Moors.

CHAPTER XII.

ONCE through the olive groves of Tamasluoght, the city of Yusuf-ibn-Tachfin* lay glistening on the plain, almost hull down on the horizon. Above the forests of tall date palms which fringe the town, the tall mosque towers rose, the Kutubich and the minaret of Sidi Bel Abbas high above the rest. From the green gardens of the Aguedal the enormous stone-built pile of the Sultan's palace, all ornamented with fine marbles brought from Italy and Spain, towered like a desert-built Gibraltar over the level plain. Across the sea-like surface of the steppe long trains of camels, mules, and men on foot crawled, looking like streams of ants converging on a giant ant-hill, whilst in the distance the huge wall-like Atlas towering up, walled the flat country in as the volcanoes seem to cut off Mexico from the world outside. The situation of Morocco city much resembles that of Mexico, which has a pseudo-Oriental look, the flat-roofed houses and the palm trees completing the effect.

A hot three hours, kicking our tired beasts along,

---

* Morocco city was founded by Yusuf-ibn-Tachfin in 1072, on the site of the ancient Martok, built by the ancient Africans, and near where some say the Romans had a city with the strange name of Bocanum Homerum, sounding like nothing Roman and perhaps an attempt of the Romans to write some Berber word. Yusuf-ibn-Tachfin was the first prince of the Almoravides who invaded Spain and overthrew the forces of Alfonso VI. of Castille at the great battle of Alarcos, and reigned over Southern Spain and Africa until the Almohades broke their power.

brought us outside the city walls, and passing underneath the gate, which zig-zags like an old Scotch
bridge, we emerged into the sandy lanes running
between orange gardens, which form a kind of suburb
of the town, and where the Soudanese blacks, the men
from Draa and the Wad Nun, do mostly congregate.
No one would ever think, from the aspects of the lanes
unpaved and broken into holes by winter rains,
that he was actually inside a city which is supposed
to cover almost as much ground as Paris. Still,
it took almost three-quarters of an hour to ride
from the outside walls to the centre of the town. We
passed through narrow lanes where camels jammed
us almost tò the wall ; along the foot-paths beggars
sat and showed their sores ; dogs, yellow, ulcerous
and wild as jackals, skulked between our horses' legs,
until at last we came out on an open space under the
tower of the Kutubieh, in which square a sort of
market was in progress, and a ring of interested
spectators sat, crouched, and stood, intent upon a
story-teller's tale. I sat a moment listening on my
horse, and heard enough to learn the story was after
the style of the Arabian nights, but quite unbowdler-
ised and suitable for Oriental taste.

A certain prince admired a beauteous dame, but an
old Sultan (always the wicked baronet of Eastern
tales) desired her for his harem, and engaged a certain
witch, of whom there were great store throughout his
territory, to cast a spell upon the prince, so that the
lady should fall into a dislike of him. He, on his part,
resorted to a wizard who stirred the ladies of the
Sultan's harem up to play strange pranks and turn
the palace upside down, let young men in o'nights,
stay out themselves too late, and generally comport
themselves in a discreditable way. A faithful slave at

last made all things right, and after a most realistic
love scene the prince and princess were married and
lived happy ever after; or, as the story-teller, a sad
moralising wag remarked, until the prince should take
another wife. Humanity, when crushed together in
the heat, either in London ball-rooms or in " plazas "
in Morocco city, sends up a perfume which makes one
regret that the cynical contriver of the world endowed
us with a nose ; so that I waited but a little and rode
on, turning to take a good look at the great mosque
and tower as I went. Outside the mosque, the name
of which in Arabic means " Mosque of the Books,"
from the word " Kitab," a book, is not imposing.
What it is inside I believe no Christian knows.
Had I that moment, dressed as I was, sunburned
and dirty, got off and entered it, I might have seen,
but the thought did not cross my mind, and afterwards, when known for a European, it might have
cost my life. The tower springs straight from the
sandy square as the Giralda rises from the level of
the street in Seville. One man built both, so runs tradition, and certainly the Kutubieh tower to-day reminds
one greatly of the description of the Giralda when
San Fernando drove out the Moorish king of Seville,
and planted the banner with the Castles of Castille,
above the town. The same gilt globes, of which the
Spanish speak, are on the Moorish tower, and the
same little cupola, which the Christians took away in
Seville, replacing it by a renaissance " fleche," upon
which stands the towering figure cast by Bartolomé
Morel. The tower, almost three hundred feet in
height, is built of dark-red stone, with the alternating
raised and sunk patterns (called in Spanish "Ajara-
cas"), cut deeply or standing boldly out from the
solid masonry. At one time tile work filled most of

the patterns, or was embroidered round the edges of the windows, but neglect and time have made most of it drop away. Still, just below the parapet runs a broad band, which from the square appears to be full four feet broad, of the most wonderful black and green iridescent tiles I ever saw. When Fabir, who, tradition says, built it for the Sultan El Mansur, and it stood glorious, adorned with tiles like those which still remain, the gilding fresh upon the great brass balls, even the mosque at Cordoba itself could not have been more glorious, and El Mansur could not have easily foreseen that on his lonely tomb under the palm trees, beside the river at Rabat, that goats would play. Allah, Jehovah, all the Gods are alike unmindful of their worshippers, who made and gave them fame; what more may the great builders of the Crystal Palace and the gasometers at Battersea expect, when they have had their day? Medina, Mellah, Kaiserieh, Sidi Bel Abbas, the tomb of Mulai Abdul Azis, all have been described so many times and by such serious and painstaking writers, who have apparently measured, re-measured, and calculated the cubic capacity of every building in Morocco city, that it would have been a work of supererogation on my part to have laid a measuring tape once more on any of them.

Morocco city struck me, and has always done so, for I have been there twice, as the best example of a purely African city I have seen. Fez has the mixture of Spanish blood in its inhabitants which the expulsed from Malaga, Granada, and from all the "Andalos," brought and disseminated. In the high houses, which make the streets like sewers to walk in, you hear men play the lute, and women sing the Malagueña Caña and the Rondeña as in mountain towns in Spain. Quite half the population have fair hair, some pale

blue eyes, and their fanaticism is born of ancient per-
secution by the fanatic Christians of Spain.   In every
house, in every mosque, in almost every saint's tomb
is fine tile work, stone and wood carving, the eaves
especially being often as richly decorated as they
had been Venetian and not African.   The streets are
thronged, men move quickly through them and the
whole place is redolent of aristocracy, of a great religious class, in fact has all the air of what in Europe
we call a capital.

Morocco city is purely African, negroes abound ; the
streets are never full, even in the " kaiserieh," you
can make your way about.   With the exception of the
Kutabieh Tower, and some fine fountains, notably
that with the inscription " Drink and admire " (Shrab-
u-Schuf) inscribed upon it, and the fine gate of the
Kasbah of the best period of Moorish work, there is
no architecture.   Sand, sand, and more sand in
almost every street, in the vast open spaces, in the
long winding narrow lanes, outside the walls up to
the city gates ; sand in your hair, your clothes, the
coats of animals.   Streets, streets, and still more
streets of houses in decay.   Yellow adobe walls,
dazzling white roofs and dense metallic semi-tropical
vegetation shrouding the heaps of yellowish decaying
masonry.   No noise, the footfalls of the mules and
camels falling into the sand as rain falls into the sea,
with a soft swishing sound.

The people African, men from the Draa, the Sus,
the Sahara, Wad Nun and the mysterious sandy
steppes below Cape Bojador.   Arabs quite in the
minority, and the fine types and full grey beards of
aged Sheikhs one sees so frequently in Fez exchanged
for the spare Saharowi type, or the shaved lip and
cheeks and pointed chin tufts of the Berber race.

For music tom-tom and gimbry, the Moorish flute, ear-piercing and encouraging to horses, who when they hear its shriek step proudly, arching their necks and moving sideways down the streets as if they liked the sound. The songs quite African, the interval so strange, and the rhythm so unlike that of all European music as at first hearing to be almost unintelligible, but which at last grow on one until one likes them and endeavours to repeat their tunes. Hardly an aristocratic family in the place, and few Sherifs, the richer of the population being traders with the Sahara.

A city of vast distances, wearisome perspectives, great desolate squares, of gardens miles in length, a place in which you want a mule to ride about, for to attempt to labour through the sand on foot would be a purgatory. And yet a place which grows upon you, the sound of water ever in your ears, the narrow streets arched over all with grape vines ; mouth of the Sahara, city of Yusuf-ibn-Tachfin, town circled in with mountains, plain girt, sun beaten, wind swept, ruinous, wearisome, and mournful in the sad sunlight which enshrouds its mouldering walls.

Fez and Rabat, Safrou, Salee and Mogador with Tetuan, Larache, Dar-el-Baida and the rest may have more trade, more art, more beauty, population, importance, industry, rank, faith, architecture, or what you will, but none of them enter into your soul as does this heap of ruins, this sandheap, desert town, metropolis of the fantastic world which stretches from its walls across the mountains through the oases of the Sahara ; and which for aught I know may some day have its railway station, public houses, Salvation Army Barracks, and its people have their eyes opened, as were those of Adam and Eve, and veil their nakedness in mackintoshes. Through streets

and open spaces, past mosque doors, with glimpses
of the worshippers at prayers seated upon the floor,
or lounging in the inner courts, through streets
arched in with vines, the trellis work so low that upon
horseback one had to bend one's head in passing,
and at the side door of the missionary's house (Dar-
Ebikouros) I got off, and, sending up a boy, was met
by Mr. Nairn, who for a moment did not recognise
me in the Moorish clothes. There, as upon my first
visit to Morocco city, I received a hospitable and
courteous welcome. Long we sat talking of our
captivity. I learned about the hurried visit of the
" Oudad " with letters, his departure without a word,
and found that no one had expected us so soon. Mr.
Nairn, who spoke both Arabic and Shillah well, had
passed on one occasion close to Kintafi, but not
having been near the castle, was not recognised, but
like myself had been unable to push on to Tarudant.
This in a measure consoled me for my failure, as Mr.
Nairn had lived long in the country, spoke the language well, and with his dark complexion and black
hair, dressed in the Moorish clothes, must have looked
exactly like a Berber mountaineer. After a welcome
and most necessary bath I left his hospitable house
and rode to Sid Abu Beckr's, almost the only man
in Morocco city from whom it is possible for a
European to get a house. And, as I rode, I mused
upon the mystery of faith, and marvelled to see the
honest single-hearted missionary still with the cross
upon his shoulders, ploughing the stony vineyard of
the Moorish heart, quite as contentedly and just as
hopefully as four years ago. Yet, not a ray of hope,
without a convert or a chance of making one, and
yet contented, and hoping for the time when he
should see the fruit of all his work. Crowds thronged

his courtyard in the morning to get medicines, and I fancy as he dispensed his drugs, in the goodness of his heart he tried to do all that was in his power to lead his patients to what he thought the truth. Women in numbers came, not for the medicines, so much as for the bottles, which they valued highly to keep oil for cooking in, throwing the medicine carefully away, but cherishing the flask and bearing it about them always, slung in a little case. Bottles may yet save souls when preaching fails, for women who receive them may so work upon their husband's hearts, that by degrees, from the errors of Mohammed and the mere two ounce phial, they rise to the imperial pint and Christianity; and so societies at home should send more bottles out, artfully coloured and with the necks fashioned to hold a string, so that if bibles prove of no effect, bottles may yet prevail.

Not that I mean to undervalue missionaries, they have their uses, but in a different way from that in which perchance they think themselves. What they can do is to set forth, in countries like Morocco, that they are not mere merchants trying to deceive all those with whom they deal; and in Morocco city Mr. Nairn and his wife, and the young men and women of his household, have the respect of all the Moors for the pureness of their life, and their untiring kindness to the poor; and the more educated of the Moors see that they are like their own religious sects, that is, their minds are fixed, not upon gain, but prayer, and, in the East, madness and holiness are held akin, and both, as being sent from heaven, are respected.

In a few hundred yards I left all holiness behind, and getting off at Abu Beckr's door, found that astute and clever politician seated as usual at the receipt of

custom, counting some money which he had just
received, a pistol by his side and a large iron box
wide open by him in which to store the gold.

Sid Abu Beckr el Ghanjaui is known from the Atlas
to the Riff, and from the Sahara to Mogador, feared
and disliked, and yet respected, for the Moor above
all other things respects success. Not that, by any
means, he thinks the less of those who fail. Success
and failure are both sent by God, they were ordained
(Mektub), and the mere man is but the instrument of
Allah's will. For the last thirty years Sid Abu Beckr
has been the British agent in Morocco, during that
time he has made many enemies, as any man of ability
placed in his position could not fail to do. Of obscure
origin and deeply tinged with negro blood, he is, perhaps, to-day the richest and the ablest man in the
whole country. Few men in any land have been the
victims of more calumnies, but, on the other hand,
few men have had more friends. To some, a slave
dealer, a traitor, spy, and perjured sycophant; to
others, a true friend of England, a man who has suffered much for his devotion to her cause. To me, a
clever, scheming politician, who has known the right
way in which to play upon the weaknesses of a long
series of ambassadors. A friend to England without
doubt, as "thrasher" is to sword-fish when they
attack a whale. A true "faux maigre," thinnish yet
flabby man, scant bearded like a eunuch, reedy voiced,
and in complexion atrabilious; his shoulders bent,
eyes with spots upon the yellowish whites, and pupils
like a cat's; slight nervous hands, persuasive manners,
and, in fact, one who impresses you at first sight as a
keen intellect confined in a mean envelope, but yet
not despicable; the fact, perhaps, of having set his
reputation and his life so frequently on the success of

an intrigue, having given the dignity of carriage which those who risk their lives habitually so often bear.

Not what is called an educated Moor, still less of the Moorish upper classes by his birth, he yet to-day has as much power in Morocco as any man outside the circle of the court. He says he speaks no English, though I think he understands it, but he takes care to conceal such knowledge of it as he may have, so that in speaking to him, those who speak no Arabic, speaking through an interpreter, may give him ample time for the consideration of every word he says. Not for a moment off his guard or disconcerted, for the story goes that once, during an ambassadorial visit, a slave dealer came with some merchandise, and that, in answer to the query of the ambassador, if those were slaves? Beckr replied they were, but, as he was an English subject, when they entered through his doors they became free at once.

For some reason, not perfectly explained, the Non-conformist conscience, some years ago, was greatly exercised about the man. All that was infamous was put down to his charge. He was a slave-dealer, a brothel-keeper, I think a murderer, and, of course, an adulterer, that being the crime the " Conscience Bearers" detested most, being shut out from all participation by the exigencies of their life. All went on merrily as things are apt to go in England when the accused is a good long way off : questions were asked in Parliament as to why England countenanced such a man as Abu Beckr in a position of confidence. Ministers answered what was put into their heads, having no faintest inkling presumably of who poor Beckr was, or what the whole storm in a teapot was about. Like other bullies the " Noncom. conscience " is a coward if fairly met and

treated roughly, and as there was after all no money
in the matter, the questioners eventually tailed off.
Then Abu Beckr brought an action in the court in
Gibraltar, and explained how it was he had been
charged with the commission of so many crimes.   It
turned out that being a Moor he certainly had slaves,
and even bought and sold them as we do horses, but
as such was the everyday custom of the land, and he,
when he took British protection, had not become a
Wesleyan Methodist, where was the harm.   As to
the second charge, he had, of course, four wives, and
no doubt many women in his house, but, as he pertinently said, that his religion allowed him, and as
far as he knew yet, he had not changed his faith.   So
he triumphantly floored his antagonists, got damages,
received eventually a silver tea service from the
British Government, and retired to his home to laugh
at every one concerned.

No people in the world so stolid on the outside, and
so acute in mind, in questions of diplomacy as are the
English.   The only question really damaging which
the primed questioners might have put in Parliament,
they took good care never to mention.   Had they but
asked about the policy of certain of our ambassadors
in Morocco, and who advised it, and how negotiations
were carried out, they might have made a point.   But
when we have a good thing we always make it common by our iteration ; and though morality and
asparagus are both good things, it does not do to eat
the one or talk about the other till they grow loathe-
some to the private palate and the public mind.   A
public man ought to be moral, or he will most certainly some day be caught ; but, after all, as a public
man, the public is surely more concerned with the
morality of his public than his private acts ?   And it

is possible that the most socially virtuous of County Councillors may yet, in his public dealings, be a liar and a thief.

Abu Beckr, though he knew I had arrived in town, most likely took me for a Moor from Fez, between whom and the people of Morocco city little love is lost, for somewhat roughly he asked me what I wanted, and did not offer me a seat. I listened to him for a moment, and watched his cunning diplomatic smile, as he looked at me from the corner of his eyes to find out who I was. Then I said in English, "Good morning, Sidi Beckr"; and he laughed and said he had known me all the time, but wanted to see what kind of Arabic I spoke. As he had only seen me once before some years ago, and dressed in European clothes, I only smiled, and said my Arabic was worse than ever, and that I wanted him to lend me some house in which to rest my servants and myself.

A man was brought to accompany us to an empty house hard by; he bore a monstrous key, and after leading us through several narrow streets, stopped at a brand new house, and throwing the door wide open said it was fit for any king, and that he generally received five dollars upon Abu Beckr's account for opening the door. I told him instantly that I should mention to his master what he said, then took the key out of his hand, gave him a dollar, and asked Lutaif to tell him to what place the Koran condemns all those who palter with the truth. The usual scrubbing and swilling out took place, which always has to be undertaken before it is possible to occupy an empty Moorish house. Once swilled and dried, we installed our scanty property, sent out for food, put up our horses in a fondak not far off, and fell asleep.

Upon awakening we found the dinner beside us, and a negro squatting, and patiently watching till we should awake.

During the interval, Swani and Mohammed-el-Hosein had both gone to the bath, and then I fancy, after the fashion of all sailors and muleteers after a voyage or trip, gone on the spree, for in the morning they appeared like Mr. Henley's "rakehell cat," looking a little draggled and the worse for wear, and swearing that they had not touched a drop of drink. The patient Ali never stirred away, being, as he said, rather afraid to venture out alone amongst the people in the crowded streets. After a journey in Morocco the men always ask for new shoes, so to show my disgust at the immoral conduct of the others, I took Ali out and made him happy with a pair of evil smelling yellow leather shoes, adding a pair of gorgeously embroidered orange-coloured slippers for his House.

A dirty little negro boy came to inform us that Sidi Abu Beckr expected us to dine that afternoon at two o'clock, the fashionable hour in the Sherifian capital.

During the interval I walked about the streets, pleased that the Moorish clothes relieved me from the attentions to which I had been subjected on my former visit to the place. Through the interminable streets I strolled, past ruined fountains and the doors of mosques half opened, from whose interiors came a sound of prayer, as from the beehive comes the murmured prayer of bees. Long trains of camels pressed me into corners to escape their snake-like heads, and suddenly, and without consciousness of how I got there, I found myself in a remembered spot. A little alley paved with cobble-stones and bordered on each side with open shops, in which sat squatted white figures working hand looms which filled the alley with their clack. At the end an archway with a wooden gate hanging ajar. I entered it with a strange feeling of possession, and found everything familiar; the tank, with edges of red stucco work, the "Azofaifa"* trees, the bordering hedge of myrtle, the white datura, the curiously cut semi-Italian flower beds, in which grew marjoram and thyme, the open baldachino at the end, under whose leaky roof a friend and I had spread our rugs and spent ten happy days four years ago, smoking, lounging about, and talking endlessly of nothing, as only friends can talk, was all unchanged. What are four years of inattention beside the perennial decay of all things Eastern; the winter rain and summer sun had scarcely put an extra stain or two upon the plaster work, the door was made to last for ages, and the trees had but become a little more luxuriant; so, sitting down, I smoked and fell a-musing on the time when in Morocco all would be changed, and places like the Riad† el Hamri, where I then sat, exist no more. Railways (praise Him who giveth wisdom to mankind) would puff and snort, men hurry to and fro, tramways and bicycles make life full and more glorious; women unveiled would sell themselves after the Christian way for drink and gold ; men lie drunk on holidays to show their freedom from debasing superstition ; all would be changed, and the scent of camel's dung give place to that of coal dust; and perhaps Allah, after regarding with complacency the work of man, would rest contented as he did in Eden when his first two Frankensteins had forced his hand.

* Azofaifa is the jujube tree (*Zizyphus jujuba*). The Spanish Word azofaifa is derived from the Arabic zofaif.

† Riad means a garden. In Andalucia it is still used under the form of Arriate.

Sid Abu Beckr met us in the courtyard of his
house, dressed in light green robe, spotless white
haik,* new yellow slippers, and a large rosary in his
hand, although the oldest citizen of Marakesh had
never seen him pray. Leading me courteously by
the hand into an upper chamber looking upon a courtyard, and decorated in the purest modern Alham-
braesque, he seated me, Lutaif, and then himself, on
cushions, and we eat solidly for a full hour, until the
welcome sight of tea, served in small gold cups, an-
nounced our sufferings were at an end.

Nothing would get out of his head at first that I
was not an agent of the Globe Venture Syndicate, or
had a mission from the British Government to try and
establish some sort of undertaking with the chiefs of
Sus.   His apprehensions set at rest, or at the least so
he pretended, he, too, began to give his views upon
the state of current politics. All that the Sherif of
Tamasluoght had said he quite corroborated, but with
the difference, that what he said was the opinion of a
quick-witted, clever man, and therefore, to my mind,
to some extent brought less conviction than the mere
wanderings of the artless " saint."

Most Arabs of the richer class are quite incapable
of seeing anything but from a personal standpoint,
and thus it is that, bit by bit, their national power has
fallen into decay.   In Spain, Damascus, Tunis, and
the Morocco of to-day chiefs have arisen, and their
sole idea has been to push their individual fortunes.
Except the Emir Abd-el-Kader, none have had even
a glimpse of trying to restore the Arab power.

So Abu Beckr regaled us with stories of Ab Ahmed's villainy, his own position and personal in-

* The haik is supposed to be the Roman Toga, and it is certainly very
like it.

security, and assured me that the end was near, and
that if England still stood hesitating, France would
step in, and lastly, getting for a moment out of his
egotism, said, " What avails it that I am so rich when
my favourite son died of small-pox only three weeks
ago, and I have no one to whom to leave my wealth ?"
Then he got up and said he had never showed his
wealth to anyone (which was untrue), but as he found
me so sympathetic to his views (I not having said a
word), he would show me all his treasures and his
house.   Accordingly, we followed him into an interior
court, on one side of which a door with about twenty
padlocks stood.

Sidi Abu Beckr having assured himself that no one
but ourselves was looking on, began to clash and
bang amongst the locks and bars, piling the padlocks
on the ground, unloosening chains, and making as
much noise as a battle of armour-plated knights must
have produced in the never-to-be-forgotten days of
chivalry, when, in their mail, the scrofulous cham-
pions tapped on one another's shields.   At last the
door swung open and disclosed a room packed full of
boxes, silver dessert services, china of all sorts,
lamps, clocks, and every kind of miscellaneous wealth
collected in the long course of an honourable career
by strict attention to all economic laws.   Boxes were
there of iron, painted in colours, made in Holland
and in Spain, standing beside hide cases, teak chests,
and old portmanteaux, Saratoga trunks and safes,
cash boxes, sea chests, and packing cases, and all
apparently stuffed to the very lids.   With pardonable
pride, and with a flush stealing upon his parchment
cheek, he did obeisance to his gods.   " This is all
silver Spanish dollars, this Sultan Hassan's coins,
this packing case is jewellery.   I had it all in pledge.

This, silver in the bar, and these hide bags are gold dust, but the king of all," and here he touched an antiquated safe, "is el d'hab (gold), chiefly in sovereigns. Yes, I know the waste of interest, but do not think you see half of my wealth; the bulk of it is safely placed in England—consols, I think they call it—safe, but small returns, and smaller since the accursed Goschen lowered the rate. This that you see I keep beside me, partly from caprice, for el d'hab has always been my passion, passing the love of women, horses, or of anything that God has made to ease the life of man." And as he spoke he patted the safe with his slippered feet, and looked as if he knew a special providence watched over him, but knowing did not truckle to the power, but rather took it, as a tribute to himself and his ability, as being well assured that providence is always with the strong. As I looked at him, proud of his wealth, his cunning and his good fortune, it seemed as if our nation, with its power, its wealth, and its insensibility, was fitly represented by the worthy man, who, from a camel driver's state, by the sheer force of industry and thrift, had made his fortune.

Blessed are those who rise, to them the world is pleasant and well ordered, all things are right, and virtue is rewarded, (in themselves); thrice blessed are the pachydermatous of heart, the deaf of soul, the invertebrate, insensible, the unimaginative; nothing can injure, nothing wound them; nature's injustice, man's ineptitude, fortunes' black joking, leaves them as untouched as a blind cart-horse, who, in struggling up a hill, sets his sharp caulkered foot upon a mouse. But as mankind, in strangeness and variety of mind, is quite incomprehensible, Sidi Abu Beckr had but hardly locked the door upon his hoards than he set to bewail his sonless state. "Allah has given me children (so he said) sons, grown to men's estate, but all unprofitable, idle and profligate, and of those who spend their time in folly, all but one, a boy to whom I hoped to leave my wealth. All that you see was to be his, the silver, gold, this house, my lands, investments in your country, all I have, and as I thought that Abu Beckr had not lived in vain, the pestilence fell on my house and left me poorer than when I was a camel driver; but it was written; God the most merciful, the compassionate, the inscrutable, He alone giveth life, and sends his death to men. Come let me show you where my blessing died."

Lutaif who, since the word smallpox had first been mentioned, had held his handkerchief up to his nose, now for the first time in the journey almost broke into revolt. Pulling my "selham," he whispered "let us go, the infectious microbes stand on no ceremony," and, in fact, wished to retreat at once. Not from superior bravery, but because I knew if there was mischief, it was already done, I laughed at all his fears, told him to trust providence, as a good man should do, and that for microbes, probably by this time a new school of scientific men said they were non existent, and put down all diseases to some other cause. Seeing he got no sympathy from me and perhaps after prayer (prayers, idle prayers) he followed, and Abu Beekr conducted us to a room and opened wide the door. Within, piled up upon the floor were heaps of rugs, and evidently no window had been open for a month. "Here (he said) died my son, and nothing has been touched since he was buried, upon this very rug he breathed his last." And as he spoke, he lifted up a carpet from the Sahara, woven in blue and red, and moved it to and fro so

that the microbes, if there were any, must have had
fair play to do their work.   Lutaif turned pale, and
once more pleaded to be off, but Abu Beekr was in-
exorable and putting down the rug, led us again
through a long pessage and opening yet another door,
said, "here the mother died, and nothing has been
altered since her death."   At last Lutaif grew desperate and seeing there was no escape began to grow
at ease and followed us through countless passages,
peeping into rooms, in each of which some member of
the family had died.

On our return to the alcove, where tea awaited us,
we passed a figure swathed in white which turned
aside to let us pass, its face against the wall.   Abu
Beekr took it by the hand and introduced it as the
mother of the dead boy's mother, and a hand wrapped
in a corner of a veil stole out, and for a moment just
touched mine, but all the time the eyes were fixed upon
the ground, after the style of Arab manners, which
ordains that a woman must not look a strange man
in the face.   Something was mumbled, in the nature
of a complimentary phrase nnd then the sheeted
figure slipped mysteriously away, but no doubt tnrned
to look at the strange animals through some grating
in the wall.

Lutaif explained that the honour done us was remarkable, and that no doubt Abu Beckr had stopped
her to show how free from prejudice he was.   The
visit ended with more tea and a long talk, in which
again I was assured the end was near, and that the
Grand Vizier had made the life of every one intoler-
able, ruined the land, rendered the Sultan despicable
and that all educated men longed for the advent of
some European power.   Having heard the same tale
from the Sherif of Tamasluoght, and as I knew both

he and Abu Beckr were rich men and above all things
feared attacks upon their wealth, I mentally resolved
to talk the matter over with some Arab of the old
school and hear his views.

Standing before the door, we found a soldier with a
lantern waiting to see us home, and bid farewell to
Abu Beckr, watching him stand beneath the archway
of his house in his green robe and white burnouse,
looking a figure out of the pages of the " Arabian
Nights," but with a scheming brain and subtle mind,
able to hold his own with trained diplomatists and to
defeat them with the natural craft implanted in him
by a wise providence which arms the weak with lies,
makes the strong brutal, and is apparently content
to watch the struggle after the fashion of an English
tourist gloating upon a Spanish bull fight on a fine
Sunday afternoon.

After a two days' stay, with horses and mules well
fed, I left the city, passed through the battlemented
gates, and saw the walls, the gardens, palm trees,
towers, and last of all the Kutubieh sink out of sight,
then set my face westward to cross the hundred and
thirty miles of stony plain which stretches almost to
Mogador. After the first day's ride, our animals
showed signs of giving out, the starving at Thelata-
el-Jacoub having reduced them so much in condition
that the two days' rest had done but little good.
Those who have ridden tired horses, through stony
wastes heated to boiling point by the sun's rays, and
without chance of finding water on the road, can estimate the pleasure of our ride. On the third day, just
about noon, and after toiling painfully at a slow walk
through interminable fields of stone, we reached the
Zowia of Sidi-el-Mokhtar where a portion of the
tribe Ulad-el-Bousbaa (the sons of Lions) were estab-

lished, the other portions of the tribe being respectively in Algeria and in the Sahara.

Nothing could possibly have been more desert-like
than the surroundings of this desert tribe. On every
side stones, stones, and still more stones. For vegetation thorny Zizyphus, hard wiry grass, stunted
euphor biaceæ, with colocynths growing here and
there between the stones; a palm-tree at the well, and
a gnarled sandarac tree, looking as if it had never
known a shower, and with the leaves as hard as pine
needles, stood like a sentinel defying thirst. The
Zowia itself seemed even more Eastern than most
buildings of its kind, the walls merely baked mud, the
towers but hardly overtopping them, and all the
animals of a superior class to those raised by the
ordinary Moors. The tribe ranks high for fighting
qualities, as riders, shots, and swordsmen, and though
small, can hold its own against all comers. The
women, taller and thinner than the women of the
Moors, were dressed in blue, after the desert fashion,
and in procession walked to the well, with each one
carrying an amphora upon her head.

The Sheikh, a Saharan Sherif, by name Mulai
Othmar, was the best specimen of a high-caste Arab
I had ever seen. Tall and broad-shouldered, lean and
tanned by the sun to a fine tinge of old mahogany,
grave and reserved but courteous; he asked us to dismount, put corn before our beasts, and sent a dish
of couscous for ourselves, sat and conversed, drank
tea, but would not smoke, saying to smoke was
shameful, but all the same not able to forbear to ask
if tobacco was as strong as kief. Strength being the
first object to an Arab, he not unnaturally believed
that as our powder far exceeded theirs, so did tobacco
far exceed their kief in strength, and seemed a little

disappointed when I told him kief was stronger far than any cigarette.

During the two hot hours of noon, whilst the south wind blew like a wind out of a furnace, we squatted underneath the Zowia wall, shifting about to dodge the sun, as it moved westwards, and the Sherif stayed talking with us, as befits a man of blood. Though simply dressed in clean white clothes, he looked a prince, and all our men saluted him with ten times more respect than they had used towards either Abu Beckr, or the Sherif of Tamasluoght. Much he imparted of the Sahara, its lore, traditions, told of the " wind drinkers,"* who, in the ostrich hunts, carry their masters a hundred miles a day. Much did he tell us of the Tuaregs, who, being Berbers, are at constant feud with all the Arab tribes. In the Sahara was no money, but a good mare was bought for forty camels or two hundred sheep ; guns came from Dakar, or St. Louis Senegal, and were called either " Francis," or else " Mocatta," though he could give no explantion of the latter term. Beyond San Louis was situate the mysterious Ben Joul,† to which place he said the " Inglis " came, a nation at eternal enmity with the " Francis," fair in complexion, and addicted to strong drink, but pleasant to deal with, and in business having but a single word.

Morocco seemed to him too green and overgrown with vegetation, so that a man grew dazzled when he looked at it ; he thought no landscape half so fine as a long stretch of sand, flat and depressionless as is the sea, and with a stunted sandarac here and there, a

---

* " Wind drinkers," Shrab-er-Reh in Arabic, is the term applied in the Sahara to the best breed of horses.

† Geographers seem to have overlooked Ben Joul, perhaps without due cause.

few rare "suddra" bushes, and in the distance, an
oasis, green as an emerald, with its wells, its melon
fields, and clustering date palms, with their roots in
water,† and feathery branches in the fire of the sun.
No friend of French or English intervention the Sherif
Mulai Othmar, but a believer in the regeneration of
the Moors, by a new intermixture of the desert blood
which in times past has often been the salvation of
the Arab race.   From what he said the ancient Arab
manners must have been preserved in all their purity
in the Sahara, and, but for the introduction of villainous
saltpetre, differ but little in essentials from a thousand
years ago.

The low black tents of camels' hair, the wandering
life, the little Arab saddles, used to-day in Syria and
in Arabia, and differing widely from the high-peaked
saddle of Morocco, the finer breed of horses, and, above
all, the pure speech of the Koreish not mixed with
Spanish and with Berber words as is the Arabic of
the Morocco Moors, all show the great tenacity with
which the desert tribes have clung to usages and to
traditions hallowed by custom and by time.   Finding
the Sherif spoke such good Arabic, Lutaif and I
agreed to refer to his decision a question of literary
interest which had engrossed us for the past few days.
A controversy at the time was raging in Morocco
amongst the men of letters, as to whether the word
"Mektub" (It is Written) might not be spelt "Mektab."

Much had been written, as is usual in such cases, on
either side, old friends had quarrelled, and each side
looked upon the other as people of no culture and outside the pale of decent men.   My preference was for

† A palm tree is is said by the Arabs to grow with its roots in water and
its head in fire.

" Mektub," but Lutaif, who had the prejudice which knowledge of a language sometimes induces, was in favour of " Mektab." The Sherif considered carefully, and gave his dictum that either could be said, although he added, those who say " Mektab " show want of education. So we were left in the position of the grammarian, whose last words were, " l'un et l'autre se disent."

Thus, in a week, I had met three Arabs all representative of their several classes, and, as usual, liked the man best who had been least influenced by European ways. Mulai Othmar disdained the idea of European protection, saying it was fit for Jews and slaves but not for men, and that, for his part, sooner than ask for protection from any European power, he would return into the desert and follow a nomadic life. I took my leave of him with a feeling of real regret, such as one feels occasionally for those one sees but for an instant, but whose features never leave one's mind. If there are, in the Sahara, many such as he, there is regeneration yet for the Arab race, so that they resolutely refuse all dealings with Europeans; reject our bibles, guns, powder, and shoddy cottons, our political intrigues, and strive to live after the rules their Prophet left them in his holy book. If they forsake them, as in some measure the inhabitants of Morocco certainly have done, slavery, sure and certain, is their lot; and in the time to come our rule, or that of the French or Germans, will transform them into the semblance of the abject creatures who once were free as swallows, and who to-day lounge round the frontier towns in North America calling themselves Utes, Blackfeet, Apaches, or what not, ghosts of their former selves, sodden with whisky, blotched with the filthy ailments we have introduced, and living contradictions of the morality and the religion under which we live.

By noon next day we had almost dropped the Atlas out of sight; the enormous wall of rocks rising straight from the plain had vanished; the tall snow-peaks above the chain alone remained in sight, and they appeared to hang suspended in the air, without a base. The vegetation changed, and once again the ground grew sandy, and the white * broom just bursting into flower covered it here and there in patches, as with an air of snow new fallen and congealed upon the branches of the plants. And yet again we passed a range of foothills, rocky and steep, from the top of which, like a blue vapoury haze, we saw the sea; and as we led our jaded animals down the abrupt descent, a Berber shepherd standing on a knoll was playing on his pipe. He stopped occasionally and burst into a strange, wild song, quavering and fitful, the rhythm interrupted curiously, so as to be almost incomprehensible to ears accustomed to street organs, pianos, bands, sackbut, harp, psaltery, and all kinds of music which we have fashioned and take delight in according to our kind, but which I take it would be as void of meaning to a Berber as is our life. I checked my horse, and sitting sideways for an instant, tried to catch the rhythm, but failed, perhaps because my ears were echoing still with the roar of cabs, whir of machinery, and the sweet stroke of hammers falling upon iron or brass, or merely because a thousand years of cant welled up between me and the autochthonous brown wool-clad figure standing on the rock. But though I could not catch that which I aimed at, I still had pleasure in his song for, as he sang, the noise of trains and omnibuses faded away;

* Called Retam by the Arabs, and Retama by the Spaniards.

the smoky towns grew fainter ; the rush, the hurry, and the incredible nothingness of modern life sank out of sight ; and in its place I saw again the valley of the N'fiss, the giant Kasbah with its four truncated towers, the Caid, his wounded horse, the Persian, and the strange entrancing half-feudal, half-Arcadian life, which to have seen but for a fortnight consoled me for my failure, and will remain with me a constant vision, seen in the mind, of course, as ghosts are seen, but ever fresh.

Next day about eleven o'clock, driving our horses through the Argan scrub, in front of us, tired, torn dirty, and on foot, we reached the Palm-Tree House.

APPENDIX A.

I.

"SOME OBSERVATIONS ON THE SHILLAH LANGUAGE."

THE Shillah tongue, that is, the speech of the southern branch of the great Berber family, since 1799, when Venture de Paradis made his vocabulary, has greatly interested students of philology. Its great antiquity is undoubted, the term Amazirgh by which the Shillah designate themselves, occurring in the pages of several classical writers under the form of Mazyes, Mazisci, and Mazyes. Though akin to the dialect spoken in the Riff mountains, and that of the Kabyles of Algeria, and possessing considerable affinity to the Tamashek spoken by the Tuaregs, it yet has considerable dialectic differences from all of them, though they have been usually held to be of one stock. The chief peculiarity that strikes a stranger is the formation of the feminine in nouns which is marked by the addition of a T at the beginning and the end of the word, As Amazirgh (noble), which becomes Tamazirght, when used for the speech of the Shillah people. Tarudant and Tafilet are merely Arabic words turned into Shilllah by the addition of the two T's, and rendered feminine to agree with the Arabic word Medina, a city.

The Shillah proper inhabit the whole range of the southern Atlas, the province of Sus, with that of the Ha-ha, and extend southward to the oasis of Tafilet, though there Arab and Shillah (Berber) tribes live close beside each other.

Place-names to which the word Ait (*i.e.*, Ben or Mac) is prefixed, as Ait-Usi, Ait-Atta, Ait-M'tuga, etc., indicate that the district is inhabited by a Berber tribe.

I subjoin a short list of words, written down whilst detained in Kintafi, but without pretending to their absolute correctness, as my knowledge of Arabic (our means of communication) is very slight, and nothing is more difficult than to get uneducated men to repeat words, familar, and therefore easy to themselves, several times over, so that a stranger may catch them. In order to show the entire dissimilarity of the two languages, I give the Arabic as well as the English equivalents.

Tamazirght.	Arabic.	English.
Athghroum	Hobz	Bread
Aman	El ma	Water
Araras	T'rek	Road
Agmar	Aoud	Horse
Asardoun	Baralla	Mule
Ariyal	Hamar	Ass
Adrar	Gibel	Mountain
Anri	Bir	Well
Asif	Wad	River
Ergaz	Rajel	Man
Tamaghrat	M'raa	Woman
Afruch	Oueld	Son
Tafrucht	Bind	Daughter
Arroumi	Nazrani	Christian
Tagartilt	Hazira	Mat
Tifluth	Bab	Door
Imaguru	Sareuk	Robber
Whyh	Eiwah	Yes
Oho	Lawah	No

The language is, to my ear, not so guttural, but more nasal than the Arabic of Morocco. I think that a stranger, ignorant of both languages, would acquire Shillah more easily than Arabic. Like the Romany, or Calo, spoken in Spain, Shillah has been greatly corrupted by an admixture of the dominant tongue, so much so that the native verbs are largely lost, and their use supplemented by verbs taken from Arabic.

In writing, the Shillah use the Arab* character, and as far

* The Tuaregs in writing Tamashek use a character of their own, but this is unknown to the Shillah.

as is known, only one book, known as *El Maziri*, a compendium of the observances and ceremonies of the Mohammedan religion, has been written in the Shillah tongue.

The language abounds in the nasal gh, which may be rendered by an extremely nasal r, but which, like the Arabic h (Ha), is almost impossible to be learnt, except from someone acquainted with the proper pronunciation, as no written directions explain the peculiar sound.

Many treatises on Shillah, Kayble, and Tamashek, and their differences and affinity, have appeared at different times, chiefly in French. Perhaps the best is that of the Marquis de Rochemonteiz, "Essai sur les rapports grammaticaux entre l'Egyptien et le Berbere," Paris, 1876. Leo Africanus also asserts the affinity of the two tongues.

APPENDIX B.

THE author addressed the two following letters to the *Daily Chronicle* and the *Saturday Review* when detained at Kintafi. The freedom which he now enjoys having brought with it a form of mind more fitting to an ideal captive, he now doubts whether he would not have done better to have addressed his two letters to the *Record* and the *Rock*. Nevertheless he publishes his letters, hoping that an intelligent, and no doubt idealistic public will discern in them that resignation, trust in a higher power (as Turkey), hope, charity, or whatever is proper, that in such circumstances ought to have been found in such letters.

"THELATA EL JACOUB, KINTAFI,
"ATLAS MOUNTAINS,
"*22nd October*, 1897.

"The Editor, *Daily Chronicle*, London.

"SIR—It appears that like St. Paul I am destined to be in prison oft. Whilst endeavouring to cross the Atlas into the almost unknown province of Sus, I was arrested by the Governor of this province on October 19th, and have been detained here on various pretexts ever since. To-night one of our followers is to gird up his loins, tighten his turban, take his staff in his hand, pull up the heels of his shoes, testify to the existence of the one God, and strike across the hills to place this "copy" in the hands of the British Vice-Consul at Mogador, about two hundred miles away.

"Though we are civilly treated, our position is the reverse of pleasant. We are allowed to walk about, but we cannot go far from our tent, and we have no idea why we are detained. I spare you any remarks on the flora and fauna of the district, for Inshallah, I propose to inflict them on a harmless and much book-ridden public. I merely state briefly that this house, an immense castle built of mud, is situated in an amphitheatre of hills, all capped with snow, and that a brawling river, the Wad N'fiss, runs past our tent; goats wander in the hills, tended by boys wild as their ancestors, whom Jugurtha led against the Romans. Horses and mules are driven down to drink by negro slaves, prisoners clank past in chains, knots of retainers armed with six-foot guns stroll about carelessly, pretending to guard the place; it is, in fact, Arcadia grafted on feudalism or feudalism steeped in Arcadia. The call to prayers rises five times a day; Allah looks down, and we sit smoking cigarettes, waiting for you to turn your mighty lever on our behalf.

" For my companion in adversity I have a Syrian Christian, who acts as my interpreter, and who writes this for reasons known to you. Should Britain fail us, we hope that that great prince, the Sultan Abdul Hamid (God hath given him the victory), will send his fleet to our assistance, for, as we know, each of his Christian subjects is as a portion of his heart.

" Things look a little serious, as we are quite uncertain how long the Governor may keep us here. Therefore, I hope that this may go into your best edition, and be the means of making the Foreign Office act at once on our behalf, if we are not released.

" Yours faithfully,

" R. B. CUNNINGHAME GRAHAM.

" P.S.—Pray assure the public that we shall steadfastly refuse to abjure our faith."

Having thus done all in my power to invoke the protection of the Nonconformist Conscience (powerful amongst the noble Shillah race) for myself, and that of his Sultan for Lutaif, I recollected a business engagement, and wrote the following letter to excuse myself for non-completion of contract. I have ever held contracts as the most sacred of all the affairs of life.

" Thelata el Jacoub, Kintafi,
"Atlas Mountains,
" 22nd October, 1897.

" The Editor, Saturday Review.

" Sir—It will, I fear, be impossible for me to review the work called the Canon. about which I spoke to you. I hope, therefore, that you will place it in competent hands, for it is a well-written and curious book. You know that, as a general rule, I am reluctant to undertake reviewing, but in this case I should have been glad to make an exception to my usual practice.

" Before reviewing a book, I like to place a copy of it upon my table, and, after looking carefully at the outside of it, peruse the preface, glance at the title page, read the last paragraph, and then fall to work. On this occasion, title and last paragraph, even the preface (which I understand is worthy of consideration), are beyond my reach. Not to be prolix, I may explain that for the last four days I have been a prisoner in the Atlas Mountain, at the above address, and that there seems no speedy prospect of my release. For details see the Daily Chronicle, to which I have addressed a letter, with one to our Ambassador at Tangier, which will, I hope, arrive some day for when night falls our messenger is to endeavour to cross the hills to Mogador, our nearest post-town, some two hundred miles away, and to inform the Consul of our case.

" I am, Sir, yours faithfully,
" R. B. Cunninghame Graham."

APPENDIX C.

THE following article appeared in the *Saturday Review*, and may serve to show one of the elements of difficulty against which I had to contend. Quite naturally, the country people thought that I was a filibuster.

THE VOYAGE OF THE "TOURMALINE."

I.

The southern province of Morocco—that which extends from Agadhir-Ighir to the Wad Nun—is called the Sus. Hanno is said to mention it in his famed "Periplus." The Romans knew it vaguely. Suetonius may or may not refer to it when he speaks of a rich province below the Atlas; but his work is lost, and what remains comes down to us through Pliny, who himself laments the Romans took so little trouble to explore the coast. Polybius wrote of it; but what Polybius knew about the Sus is left so vague, that renowned, grave, arm-chair geographers have almost come to blows about it, as men of literature have done as to the whereabouts of "Popering-in-the Place."

But Pliny certainly saw the lost writings of King Juba, and in them he met the word Asana. This Asana is conjectured (again by wise and reverend men) to have been "perhaps" Akassa, the Berber name of the Wad Nun. So that the ancients do not help us much to any knowledge of the Sus. Marmol and Leo Africanus talk of the province, but neither of them saw it, though Leo penetrated to Tamaglast, a village near Marakesh, supposed by some to be the hamlet now called Fruga. Thus little was known about the province, although travellers from Europe, as Arab writers tell us, visited the capital Tarudant, coming by Agadhir, during the sixteenth and seventeenth centuries, for purposes of trade.

All sorts of legends thus sprang up about the place : demons inhabited it ; a mountain spoke ; magicians not a few lived near the Wad Nun ; La Caba, the daughter of Count Julian, who brought the infidel to Spain, was buried in Tarudant, as the legend says ; and everything throughout North Africa, strange and miraculous, occurred in Sus. Rich mines were there—gold, silver, and " diamont," iron, tin, and antimony, with manganese and copper; the people were the most honest wildest, wisest, and most ferocious in the world ; great ruined castles, known to the natives as " Kasbah el Rumi," were dotted here and there, though who the " Romans " were no one could tell, but probably they filled the place of the " Moros," who, as is well known, built all houses, towers, and buildings, of whatever nature, which exceed a hundred years in age throughout all Spain.

Coming to more modern times, in 1791, the Sultan sent to the Governor of Gibraltar for a doctor to cure his son, at that time governor in the province of the Sus. An Army surgeon called Lemprière was chosen, and, disembarking at Agadhir, journeyed to Tarudant. As far as anything is known, he is the first European who entered Tarudant since the sixteenth century, when it is certain that merchants from Holland used to journey to the annual fair. He crossed the Atlas from Bibouan to Imintanout (by the same pass, in fact, which I attempted in last October), and arrived in safety at Mogador. He gives us little or no information about the Sus, but vaguely speaks of mines, says that the country about Tarudant was fertile and well cultivated, and describes the pass he crossed as skirting along tremendous precipices, which, to my certain knowledge, is not the case.

After him comes Jackson, who published his account of the Empire of Morocco in 1809. Ball, in his appendix to Hooker's " Morocco and the Great Atlas," refers to Jackson's book as

being the most copious ever written about the Sus.   Certainly
he had special advantages, for he passed sixteen years in
Mogador, and Agadhir (now closed to trade), spoke Arabic
and Shillah, but all he says does not amount to much.   The
map he made Ball considers inferior to that of Chenier, published a hundred years before his time.   And so of Admiral
Washington, Gerhard Rohlfs, Gatell, and Oskar Lenz.   They
all say little, for the good reason little is known.   Although
the last three travellers passed through the land, they went
disguised, in terror of their lives, and are believed to have
known little or no Arabic.   So that it comes to this, all that
we know with certainty is that a province called the Sus exists,
that it stretches from close to Agadhir to the Wad Nun, a
distance of some two hundred miles, with a varying breadth
of about seventy at the north, where it is bounded by the Atlas
mountains, the Wad Sus, and the province of the Ha-ha to a
hundred or more at the extreme south, as no one knows how
far the boundaries of the province stretch up the waters of the
river Nun.

Round about Agadhir the country has been visited, and is
reported to be very like the provinces of Shiadma and the
Ha-ha, which bound it to the north, that is, it is in general
configuration, flat and sandy, with stretches here and there of
reddish argillaceous soil, but both soils greatly grown over
with thorny bushes, and here and there well cultivated.
Politically the province owns the Sultan of Morocco's sway,
but his authority extended lately but to Tarudant, the district
called Taseroualt, in which is situated the Zowia of Si Hamed
O'Musa, now represented by Sidi Haschem, and to the great
Arab tribe of the Howara who occupy the country between
Fonti and Tarudant.   Up to the banks of the Wad Nun, where
there are Arab tribes again (but wild and independent of the
Sultan), most of the inhabitants of the country are of the Berber
race.   This race, the original inhabitants of the country before
the Arab conquest, has never been entirely conquered, and
between them and the Arab conquerors a strong enmity
exists.

The chief trade of the province has always been with

Mogador since the port of Agadhir was closed by the great-grandfather of the present Sultan. It consists of wool and camels' hair, goat-skins and hides, bees' wax, a little gold dust, ostrich feathers, gum-arabic, cattle and sheep, almonds, and all the products of the Sahara, for most of the trade from the western portion of that district comes to Mogador. In return, they take Manchester goods, powder, tea, sugar, cheap German cutlery, and all the wonders which human nature has to suffer to produce, and enrich the manufacturers of Leeds, Manchester, Birmingham, Liège, Roubaix, and the like in turning out. So thus the situation briefly stood.

A province, large and wealthy, the mouth of trade with the Sahara, supposed to contain rich mines, though on this head nothing is known with certainty, except that a little copper is worked near Tarudant, but the natives say gold, silver, iron, and magnetic ironstone exists ; fertile in climate, thickly populated and ill affected to its ruler; fanatical and largely swayed by a sort of general "Witanagemot" known as the "Council of the Forty," and yet the population bound to get all supplies of European goods through the one port of Mogador.

Many and various have been the attempts to open trade direct. Pirates and filibusters, and traders with a moral sense of what was due to civilisation and to themselves, had all attempted many times to supply the poor heathen with their European trash, but never with success. Sometimes they landed, were taken prisoners, and a "diplomatic question" was superinduced until they were released. At other times they disappeared on landing and were never heard of, but still reports poured in to Mogador of the great riches of the Sus. These riches to my mind are non-existent, for I have known hundreds of Susi traders, merchants, camel-drivers, tribesmen, "saints" and acrobats, from Taseroualt, but never saw a Susi who was rich.

In generel, I found them tall, thin, dark-coloured men, very intelligent, fanatical, great travellers, petty traders, now and then ostrich hunters, and sometimes slave-dealers, but all were poor, although when asked they always talked about gold-mines, the riches of their land, and showed an evident desire that the various ports along the coast should be left open for European trade.

Then came the death, about four years ago, of the late Sultan Mulai el Hassan (may God have pardoned him!), and the disturbances consequent on the accession of a minor to the throne. The Susis without doubt thought the time suitable for movement, and no doubt hoped to be independent, and to buy powder, tea, and sugar and cotton goods without the trouble of coming up to Mogador. Rebellions more or less partial, took place throughout the province, and were subdued.

About two years ago, in Mogador, appeared one Captain Geyling, a Jewish Austrian subject, who, by some means or another, got into communication with certain discontented chiefs, whom he induced to sign a treaty with him to open up a port, start trade with the interior, work the mines, and generally to allow the country to be brought under the humanising influence of European trade. This done, he straight repaired to London, and tried to form a company, but found out, like Lydgate did before him, that "lacking money he mighte never speede."

Then a hiatus, which perhaps some of the gentlemen who planked their money down may like to fill up for the benefit of those who take an interest in unofficial efforts to extend the shadow of our flag.

We next find Captain Geyling back in Morocco, dressed in a single-breasted black frock-coat and fez, and turned in the interval into a pseudo-Turk under the title of Abdul Kerim Bey. Here history says, as the advance agent of the Globe Venture Syndicate he travelled like a prince, taking as many tents as would befit a travelling managerie, plate and more plate, servants and horses, mules, guns, presents for the Caids, and impelled by a consuming thirst, to get concessions for his paymasters. With him as military advisor, attaché, or what not, went Major Spilsbury, and why he let himself be towed about the place by Geyling only he can tell.

All the requirements for a filibuster, which Jameson lacked so plentifully, Splisbury had in great perfection; active determined, quiet and temperate, a linguist, leader of men, and one of those willing to risk his life ten times a day for any syndicate, upon most reasonable terms. Always about to make a fortune with schemes innumerable, in which if you embarked you still stayed poor, or became poorer, but with this difference from the schemes of most men of his class, that he himself was never richer by a penny, by any one of them. Geyling had said he knew the Sultan well, and as that potentate was somewhere in the south, Geyling proceeded north and waited upon the Sherif of Wazan, the spiritual head of all things in Morocco. There he seems not to have had much luck, and then went east to Fez, back to the coast, and after two or three months' perambulation up and down the land, went to Morocco city, where he ought to have gone first. There neither Sultan nor Vizier would see him, and with his tail between his legs, he returned to Mogador, and in a little inn kept by a Jew, quarrelled with Spilsbury, who, if reports be true, threatened to beat him with a stirrup leather, and the companionship broke up. Geyling Kerim went homewards to Vienna, Novi Bazaar, or for all I know joined his repatriated co-religionists in their new colony in Palestine. But Spilsbury, being apparently determined to play things out "on a lone hand," remained in Mogador, and then embarked upon a series of adventures, especially extraordinary when I remember that he speaks no Arabic.

How, wherefore, in what manner, or by what means, he came across him I do not know, but he fell in with an acquaintance of my own, one Mr. Ratto, born in Mogador, and speaking Arabic, and Shillah, French, English, Spanish and apparently all other tongues with equal ease. What actually they did, only themselves are in a position to record, but I suppose that, taking advantage of the unsettled state of things, the Sultan's absence punishing refractory tribes, and the desire which every Arab chief has of getting arms to make himself quite independent of all mankind, they must have entered into negotiations with some of the chiefs of the wild tribes in Sus. Spilsbury seems to have satisfied the Syndicate in London that they could trade direct with Sus, receive concessions from the chiefs, land and construct a factory, and in time make ourselves sole masters of the place. No doubt they reasoned: if we are once established, when troubles come, England must for her honour protect her subjects, and in protecting them, protect their interests, and they know that England once committed to interference in any country (said to be rich), must of necessity remain to restore order, introduce good government. and generally to further the cause of progress and mortality, which is specially her aim in every country peopled by an interior race. What treaty Spilsbury took home is matter of conjecture, but not unlikely he got signatures from chiefs, who signed, thinking if all went well they would gain, and if things turned out badly they could say they had been deceived, and signed a document that they had not understood. One name is certain was appended to the deed, that of M'barek-ou-Ahmed, who is now securely chained in some pestilential prison in Fez or Mequinez. Be all that as it may, Spilsbury was shortly back again in Mogador, trying to hire a vessel to convey himself, a Jew interpreter, and several samples of his goods down to Akssis, a port between Wad Nun and Agadhir. But by this time the Sultan had got wind of the affair, and sent his emissaries into the Sus to bribe the chiefs into allegiance, and what is more he had communicated with the English Ambassador in Tangier, who having sent the news to London, the expedition and its aim was laid before the Foreign Office. Presently an official notice appeared declaring that the British Government viewed with concern the meditated attempt to open trade with a part of the Emperor of Morocco's territory against his will, and if any person went for such a purpose, he must go at his own risk. Spilsbury probably cared nothing for the protection or the displeasure of either Government, so he pushed on his preparations just as if nothing had occurred worth mentioning.

The ukase of the British Government had made it difficult to operate from Mogador, but Spilsbury, nothing dismayed, engaged a Jew interpreter, and all alone, or at the most with two or three companions, sailed for the Canaries, hired or bought a schooner, and after a passage of an abnormal length, contending all the time with contrary winds, sailed to Akssis, landed, and started to palaver with the chiefs who were expecting him, with several thousand men encamped upon the shore, having been warned most probably by Mr. Ratto to hold themselves in readiness against his coming.

Nothing more different than the inception of the Jameson affair and that so boldly planned by Spilsbury. Both "gentlemen adventurers, or if you like, both "advance agents" of the British Empire. One "flagwagging" and backed up by all the "fruits secs" of the British army, champagne and sandwiches laid on at every twenty miles upon the road ; the other almost alone upon a coast not visited twice in a century by Europeans, and in the hands of men who kill a man with as few compunctions as a settler up in North Queensland flogs a "black" to death. If he had goods to sell I know not, if he had samples of trade powder and trade guns, that is to me unknown, but anyhow, by the assistance of his interpreter, he entered into a council with certain of the chiefs, as the Sherif of Taseroualt, the aforenamed M'barek-ou-Ahmed, and others whom it is better not to name, and was about to sign a treaty with them, to open trade direct, put up a factory, work the mines, and generally prepare the way before the faces of the Globe Venture Syndicate.

But for an accident Spilsbury might have been Emperor of Agadhir, the Lord Protector of the Sus, or Rajah of Tamagrut, but fate or the Sultan of Morocco had otherwise disposed.

Most of the chiefs of Sus were at Akssis with many of their followers, but one Sheikh with about fifty horseman had kept aloof during the progress of the negotiations, either because he had not been considered big enough to square, or as some think because he was secretly acting under orders from the Moorish Court.

Just as the chiefs were about to sign, and each one had agreed how many rifles he was to receive on Spilsbury's return with a well-laden ship, the Sheikh mounted his horse, marshalled his followers and plunged into the middle of the crowd, yelling and firing several shots, exclaiming " Out with the Christians; I will not be a party to any dealings with our hereditary foes." Thinking they were attacked in force, the followers of the other chiefs returned the fire, all was confusion, and Spilsbury, to save his life, had to retreat precipitately on board his ship, and to complete the scene, the smoke of a steamboat was seen coming down the coast, Now, as no vessels between Agadhir and the Wad Nun come near the coast, which is one of the most deserted in the world, Spilsbury knew at once it must be a vessel of the Moorish Government upon the search for him. Luckily night was near, and a fair wind sprang up which took him to the Canaries, from whence he shipped aboard a steamer and returned to England to plan another trip.

What actually he did in England during the next six months I do not know, but in November I met him at a London club, the proud possessor of the steam yacht "Tourmaline," carrying a quick-firing gun, an assorted cargo of goods fit for the Morocco trade, and some nine thousand rifles with which he intended to arm his friends, the followers of Sidi Haschem, and the other Sheikhs of Sus. The vessel lay at Greenhithe, and was to sail next morning for Antwerp to take the rifles in; yet Spilsbury sat smoking quietly without a trace of "Union Jackism," no word of "moral purpose," not a suggestion of being, as Dr. Jameson seemed to think he was, a sort of John of Leyden going to set a people free. Simply an ordinary club man, talking of what he was about to do, as he had talked of fishing in Loch Tay. A well-dressed, quiet-mannered filibuster, not bellowing that he would make the Arabic language popular in Hell, after the "fighting Bob Tammany" style, but quite aware that he was venturing his life, and perilling for ever such reputation as he had. As a law-abiding citizen, I tried to show him all the error of his ways, spoke of the wickedness of all he was about to do, and watched him get into a cab with mingled feelings of disgust at the peddling syndicate which, for its miserable five per cent., was about to bring the name of England into contempt, and admiration for the man who was going quietly to risk his life in such a wretched cause.

How he sailed, reached Akssis, landed some rifles, was interrupted in his dealings by the arrival on the one hand of

the Sultan's troops under Caid el Giluli, and on the other by
the advent of the Moorish Government's armed transport, "El
Hassani"; how he exchanged shots with her, rescued his boat,
but failed to save his four companions who remained captives;
and how he with the yacht "Tourmaline" is still detained, or
was up to the other day, under surveillance in Gibraltar, is
well known to all. But what befel his four companions and
the unfortunate M'barek-ou-Ahmed, his intermediary, has never
been made public in this country yet. So, to make matters
plain, I quote the letter of a French Algerian gentleman settled
in Mogador :—

"Vous me demandez des nouvelles de The Globe Venture
Cie, c'est bien une aventure que les bondholders Anglais ne
goberont pas facilement. Vous savez que le commandant en
chef, Major Spilsbury, est arrivé à Akssis entre Agadhir et
Wad Nun, et là il a débarqué 500 fusils, 100 caisses cartouches,
4 balles cotonnades, 25 caisses thé, &c.

"Le Major a eu le bon esprit de rester à bord, mais a fait
débarquer un jeune Anglais, le second du bord, un allemand
comptable, un Juif interprète, et un marin portugais. Voilà
un bouillabaisse ! Enfin ils se sont établi sous trois tentes sur
la plage, avec le Sheikh avec qui le Major avait fait connais-
sance chez M. Pepe Ratto, et huit ou dix Arabes de l'endroit.
Après deux jours la frégate 'El Hassani' de sa Majesté
Chérifienne est arriveé, en même temps le Caid El Giluli arrive
par terre avec 500 cavaliers, entoure les tentes et toute la
boutique est prise. Il y a eu quelque coups de fusils, deux
hommes du Major (Arabes) sont blessés, la Tourmaline
s'éloigna vers Lanzarote, les quatre Européens et le Juif sont
pris, aussi que le chef Arabe (M'barek-ou-Ahmed) avec vingt
de ses amis, et l'aventure est fini.

"Les Arabes ont été conduit au Sultan qui les a envoyé
avec chaines se pourrir dans les prisons de Fez, et les quatre
Européens sont depuis près de trois mois dans la maison du
Caid el Giluli à Ha-Ha, à savourer la Shisha (vous en con-
naissez le gout oh Sheikh Mohamed el Fasi), en attendant les
ordres de Sidna. . . . . Le pauvre Sheikh, M'barek-ou-Ahmed,
n'avait aucune influence sur les tribus, et il ne marcha que sur

la promesse que les 'fregatas Inglise' viendront débarquer des soldats anglais, le pays sera pris, on fera du Sheikh un Caid, et cela accompagné de cent dollars, 20 livres de thé, et un sac de sucre, et le pauvre Sheikh a eu l'eau (et le thé) à la bouche.

"Un soldat qui avait conduit les prisonniers au Sultan, a dit, que sur la route, le pauvre Sheikh disait tout le temps, 'Oh, le Nazrani m'a trompé, ce sont des trompeurs les chrétiens, il m'avait promis que des frégates et des soldats anglais avec des canons débarqueront, et aux premier coup de fusil, son bateau s'est sauvé ; par Dieu, ce chrétien doit être un Juif ! mais c'était écrit, Allah Ackbar.'"

R. CUNNINGHAME GRAHAM.

THE END.

Books of Related Interest in Century Classics

A Vanished Arcadia
Being some account of the Jesuits in Paraguay
1607–1767
R.B. Cunninghame Graham
Introduction by Philip Healy

A sad tale of calumny and intrigue lies behind the Jesuits' expulsion from South America following their tireless defence of the Indians, which provided the scenario for Roland Joffe's film, *The Mission.*

Lords of the Atlas
Gavin Maxwell

An excellent introduction for any visitor to Morocco, *Lords of the Atlas* is a history of the country from 1893 to 1956. In the author's own words, a 'hundred years ago very few contemporary Europeans had ever visited Morocco... Fewer still had ever penetrated into the savage territories of the High Atlas or into the palm oases of the Pre-Sahara beyond them. The country, despite its geographical position as a neighbour to Europe, remained as unknown as Tibet, xenophobe and mysterious, guarding splendours, and horrors that the wildest Traveller's tales could not exaggerate...'

In Morocco
Edith Wharton

In 1917 this prolific American novelist decided to visit Morocco, began collecting material for a guide book and produced a personal memoir as well as an evocative portrait of the country.

Leisure of an Egyptian Official
Edward Cecil
Introduction by Lord Hardinge of Penshurst
A highly amusing description of a day in the life of Lord
Edward Cecil, said to be the wittiest man in England,
who spent 18 years attached to the Egyptian Civil
Service in Cairo before and during World War I.

A Year Amongst the Persians
Edward Granville Browne
Introduction by Denis MacEoin
Edward Browne was one of the most distinguished
scholars of Islamic languages at Cambridge, which was
doubtless instrumental in enabling him to write probably the most revealing book ever written about Iran
and its people. It was based upon a year spent there,
between 1887–8, and introduces the reader to things that
are perennial about the country.

Pilgrimage to Nejd
Lady Anne Blunt
Introduction by Dervla Murphy
Lady Blunt was an exceptional woman - fluent in
Arabic, knowledgeable about Arabic history and litera-
ture, resourceful and courageous. She and her husband,
Wilfred Scawen Blunt, crossed 100 miles of central
Arabian desert in 1878, attired in Bedouin cloaks and
turbans and riding camels. They were remarkable for
travelling rough, without the usual retinue or para-
phernalia, and in the range of subjects which interested
them.

The Owl's Watchsong
J.A. Cuddon
Written by an author who has lived and worked in

Istanbul, this is a captivating study of the city set against the background of the past, from its sultans and harems to its bazaars and mosques.

Visits to Monasteries in the Levant
Robert Curzon

Curzon's account of his wanderings in Egypt, Abyssinia, the Holy Land and Albania in search of medieval manuscripts in the 1830s stands alongside Kinglake's *Eothen* as one of the enduring classics of Near Eastern travel writing. His unfailing eye for colourful detail and anecdote will delight the modern reader as much as his courage and cheerfulness in the face of discomfort and danger.

Eothen
A.W. Kinglake

Described by John Julius Norwich as 'one of the most wholly enjoyable travel books ever written', *Eothen* is based on Kinglake's journeys to Constantinople, Cyprus, Palestine, Egypt and the Lebanon in the 1830s, and the experiences were recorded, and embellished, with an irrepressible sense of humour. Jonathan Raban regards it as the most formative influence on modern British travel writing.

Revolt in the Desert
T.E. Lawrence
Introduction by Raleigh Trevelyan

An immediate bestseller when published in 1927, this is a succinct account of the events described at prodigious length in *Seven Pillars of Wisdom*. The Arab Revolt, its consequences for the war and politics after it, and Lawrence's role remain one of the most intriguing stories of the period.

Sultan in Oman
James Morris

Reviewed in the *New Statesman* as 'a minor literary masterpiece', James Morris's book describes an expedition mounted by the Sultan of Muscat to secure sovereignty over the mountain territory of Oman. It provides a remarkable account of a truly medieval Islamic State before its rapid adjustment to the modern world.

The Empty Quarter
St John Philby

Harry St John Philby was one of the most respected of British desert explorers, and was chief of the British political mission to Arabia in 1917-18. After years of exploration in the area, he achieved in 1932 his dream of crossing the Rub'al Khali, the 'Empty Quarter', which is the most savage and impenetrable desert in southern Arabia. His unique account covers all he saw, and his descriptions of the obscure and now 'civilized' desert tribes are of particular value.

Alexander's Path
From Caria to Cilicia
Freya Stark

A vivid description of the southern coastline and mountains of Turkey, tracing the route taken by Alexander the Great twenty-two centures earlier. It exemplifies Freya Stark's sensitivity to the present and knowledge of the past.

Beyond Euphrates
Autobiography 1928-1933
Freya Stark

The sequel to *Traveller's Prelude* this is Freya Stark's

description of her first independent journeys to the East – to Baghdad and Tehran, Jordan and Syria, the wilds of Luristan and the shores of the Caspian.